My Best
for the
Master

Readings
from the
New International Version
to Prepare Your Heart
for Sunday

David C. Cook Publishing Co.
Elgin, Illinois   Weston, Ontario

LifeJourney Books is an imprint of
David C. Cook Publishing Co.
Elgin, Illinois and Weston, Ontario

Scripture taken from The Holy Bible: NEW INTERNATIONAL VERSION.
Copyright © 1973, 1978, 1984 by the International Bible Society. Used by
permission of Zondervan Bible Publishers.

Lessons and/or Readings based on International Sunday School Lessons. The
International Bible Lessons for Christian Teaching. Copyright © 1983 by the
Committee on the Uniform Series.

Cover by Cathy Colten

first Printing, 1987
92 91 90 89 88 87 5 4 3 2 1
Printed in the United States of America

Library of Congress Cataloging-in-Publication Data
Bible. English. New International. Selections 1987
    My Best for the Master/ (Compiled by) Edythe Draper.
    ISBN 1-5555-13912-4
    1. Devotional calendars. I. Draper, Edythe. II. Title.
BS390.D732 1987
242' .2--dc19   87-20303

Let your light shine

You are the light of the world. A city on a hill cannot be hidden. Neither do people light a lamp and put it under a bowl.

Instead they put it on its stand, and it gives light to everyone in the house. In the same way, let your light shine before men, that they may see your good deeds and praise your Father in heaven.

Live a life worthy of the Lord...please him in every way: bearing fruit in every good work, growing in the knowledge of God, being strengthened with all power according to his glorious might so that you may have great endurance and patience, and joyfully giving thanks to the Father, who has qualified you to share in the inheritance of the saints in the kingdom of light.

Preach the Word; be prepared in season and out of season; correct, rebuke and encourage--with great patience and careful instruction.

Be strong and courageous, and do the work. Do not be afraid or discouraged, for the Lord God, my God, is with you. He will not fail you or forsake you until all the work for the service of the temple of the Lord is finished.

Matthew 5:16. Matthew 5:14-16. Colossians 1:10-12. 2 Timothy 4:2. 1 Chronicles 28:20.

You are the salt of the earth

Salt is good, but if it loses its saltiness, how can you make it salty again? Have salt in yourselves, and be at peace with each other.

Set an example for the believers in speech, in life, in love, in faith and in purity.

In everything set them an example by doing what is good. In your teaching show integrity, seriousness and soundness of speech that cannot be condemned.

Live as free men, but do not use your freedom as a cover-up for evil; live as servants of God. Show proper respect to everyone: Love the brotherhood of believers, fear God, honor the king. Live in harmony with one another; be sympathetic, love as brothers, be compassionate and humble.

Fight the good fight, holding on to faith and a good conscience. Some have rejected these and so have shipwrecked their faith. Among you there must not be even a hint of sexual immorality, or of any kind of impurity, or of greed, because these are improper for God's holy people.

Whatever is true, whatever is noble, whatever is right, whatever is pure, whatever is lovely, whatever is admirable–if anything is excellent or praiseworthy––think about such things.

Matthew 5:13. Mark 9:50. 1 Timothy 4:12. Titus 2:7, 8. 1 Peter 2:16, 17. 1 Peter 3:8. 1 Timothy 1:18, 19. Ephesians 5:3. Philippians 4:8.

Blessed are those who hunger and thirst for righteousness, for they will be filled

O God, you are my God, earnestly I seek you; my soul thirsts for you, my body longs for you, in a dry and weary land where there is no water. I spread out my hands to you; my soul thirsts for you like a parched land.

My soul will be satisfied as with the richest of foods; with singing lips my mouth will praise you. For he satisfies the thirsty and fills the hungry with good things.

The Lord will guide you always; he will satisfy your needs in a sun-scorched land and will strengthen your frame. You will be like a well-watered garden, like a spring whose waters never fail.

"My people will be filled with my bounty," declares the Lord.

Matthew 5:6. Psalm 63:1. Psalm 143:6. Psalm 63:5. Psalm 107:9. Isaiah 58:11. Jeremiah 31:14.

Go and be reconciled to your brother

I tell you that anyone who is angry with his brother will be subject to judgment. When you stand praying, if you hold anything against anyone, forgive him, so that your Father in heaven may forgive you your sins. If he sins against you seven times in a day, and seven times comes back to you and says, "I repent," forgive him.

Get rid of all bitterness, rage and anger, brawling and slander, along with every form of malice. Be kind and compassionate to one another, forgiving each other, just as in Christ God forgave you.

A new command I give you: Love one another. As I have loved you, so you must love one another. All men will know that you are my disciples if you love one another.

Love covers over all wrongs. Love ... is not rude, it is not self-seeking, it is not easily angered, it keeps no record of wrongs. Love is the fulfillment of the law.

Matthew 5:24, 22. Mark 11:25. Luke 17:4. Ephesians 4:31, 32. John 13:34, 35. Proverbs 10:12. 1 Corinthians 13:5. Romans 13:10.

Settle matters quickly with your adversary

Starting a quarrel is like breaching a dam; so drop the matter before a dispute breaks out.

If someone wants to sue you and take your tunic, let him have your cloak as well. If any of you has a dispute with another, dare he take it before the ungodly for judgment instead of before the saints? Do you not know that the saints will judge the world? And if you are to judge the world, are you not competent to judge trivial cases? Do you not know that we will judge angels? How much more the things of this life!

The very fact that you have lawsuits among you means you have been completely defeated already. Why not rather be wronged? Why not rather be cheated?

The Lord's servant must not quarrel; instead, he must be kind to everyone, able to teach, not resentful.

Who is wise and understanding among you? Let him show it by his good life, by deeds done in the humility that comes from wisdom.

It is to a man's honor to avoid strife.

Matthew 5:25. Proverbs 17:14. Matthew 5:40. 1 Corinthians 6:1-3, 7. 2 Timothy 2:24. James 3:13. Proverbs 20:3.

You have heard that it was said, "Eye for eye, and tooth for tooth." But I tell you, Do not resist an evil person

If someone strikes you on the right cheek, turn to him the other also. Do not say, "I'll pay you back for this wrong!" Wait for the Lord, and he will deliver you.

Do not repay anyone evil for evil. Be careful to do what is right in the eyes of everybody. If it is possible, as far as it depends on you, live at peace with everyone.

Let us fix our eyes on Jesus, the author and perfecter of our faith, who for the joy set before him endured the cross, scorning its shame, and sat down at the right hand of the throne of God. Consider him who endured such opposition from sinful men, so that you will not grow weary and lose heart.

Endure hardship as discipline; God is treating you as sons. God disciplines us for our good that we may share in his holiness. No discipline seems pleasant at the time, but painful. Later on, however, it produces a harvest of righteousness and peace for those who have been trained by it.

You need to persevere so that when you have done the will of God, you will receive what he has promised.

Matthew 5:39. Proverbs 20:22. Romans 12:17, 18. Hebrews 12:2, 3, 7, 10, 11. Hebrews 10:36.

If someone forces you to go one mile, go with him two miles

Who is going to harm you if you are eager to do good? It is better, if it is God's will, to suffer for doing good than for doing evil. Whoever tries to keep his life will lose it, and whoever loses his life will preserve it.

Give to the one who asks you, and do not turn away from the one who wants to borrow from you. The man with two tunics should share with him who has none, and the one who has food should do the same.

Do to others as you would have them do to you. And if you do good to those who are good to you, what credit is that to you? Even "sinners" lend to "sinners," expecting to be repaid in full. But love your enemies, do good to them, and lend to them without expecting to get anything back. Then your reward will be great, and you will be sons of the Most High, because he is kind to the ungrateful and wicked.

For you know the grace of our Lord Jesus Christ, that though he was rich, yet for your sakes he became poor, so that you through his poverty might become rich.

Matthew 5:41. 1 Peter 3:13, 17. Luke 17:33. Matthew 5:42. Luke 3:11. Luke 6:31, 33-35. 2 Corinthians 8:9.

Love your enemies

While they were stoning him, Stephen prayed, "Lord Jesus, receive my spirit." Then he fell on his knees and cried out, "Lord, do not hold this sin against them." When he had said this, he fell asleep.

Love your enemies, do good to those who hate you, bless those who curse you, pray for those who mistreat you. If you love those who love you, what reward will you get? If you greet only your brothers, what are you doing more than others?

If you come across your enemy's ox or donkey wandering off, be sure to take it back to him. If you see the donkey of someone who hates you fallen down under its load, do not leave it there; be sure you help him with it.

If your enemy is hungry, give him food to eat; if he is thirsty, give him water to drink. In doing this, you will heap burning coals on his head, and the Lord will reward you.

Do not gloat when your enemy falls; when he stumbles, do not let your heart rejoice, or the Lord will see and disapprove and turn his wrath away from him. Jesus said, "Father, forgive them, for they do not know what they are doing."

Matthew 5:44. Acts 7:59, 60. Luke 6:27, 28. Matthew 5:46, 47. Exodus 23:4, 5. Proverbs 25:21, 22. Proverbs 24:17, 18. Luke 23:34.

It is better, if it is God's will, to suffer for doing good than for doing evil

For Christ died for sins once for all, the righteous for the unrighteous, to bring you to God.

Therefore, since Christ suffered in his body, arm yourselves also with the same attitude, because he who has suffered in his body is done with sin. As a result, he does not live the rest of his earthly life for evil human desires, but rather for the will of God. If you should suffer for what is right, you are blessed. But how is it to your credit if you receive a beating for doing wrong and endure it? But if you suffer for doing good and you endure it, this is commendable before God.

As an example of patience in the face of suffering, take the prophets who spoke in the name of the Lord. Moses ... chose to be mistreated along with the people of God rather than to enjoy the pleasures of sin for a short time. The apostles left the Sanhedrin, rejoicing because they had been counted worthy of suffering disgrace for the Name.

God ... after you have suffered a little while, will himself restore you and make you strong, firm and steadfast.

---

1 Peter 3:17, 18. 1 Peter 4:1, 2. 1 Peter 3:14.1 Peter 2:20. James 5:10. Hebrews 11:24, 25. Acts 5:4. 1 Peter 5:10.

Be perfect, therefore, as your heavenly Father is perfect

It was he who gave some to be apostles, some to be prophets, some to be evangelists, and some to be pastors and teachers, to prepare God's people for works of service, so that the body of Christ may be built up until we all reach unity in the faith and in the knowledge of the Son of God and become mature, attaining to the whole measure of the fullness of Christ.

Then we will no longer be infants, tossed back and forth by the waves, and blown here and there by every wind of teaching and by the cunning and craftiness of men in their deceitful scheming. Instead, speaking the truth in love, we will in all things grow up into him who is the Head, that is, Christ. From him the whole body, joined and held together by every supporting ligament, grows and builds itself up in love, as each part does its work. Live in harmony with one another; be sympathetic, love as brothers, be compassionate and humble. Do not repay evil with evil or insult with insult, but with blessing, because to this you were called so that you may inherit a blessing. For, "Whoever would love life and see good days must keep his tongue from evil and his lips from evil and do good; he must seek peace and pursue it. For the eyes of the Lord are on the righteous and his ears are attentive to their prayer, but the face of the Lord is against those who do evil."

Over all these virtues put on love, which binds them all together in perfect unity.

Matthew 5:48. Ephesians 4:11-16. 1 Peter 3:8-12. Colossians 3:14.

In everything, do to others
what you would have them do to you

All men will know that you are my disciples if you love one another. Love does no harm to its neighbor.

Keep on loving each other as brothers. Do not forget to entertain strangers, for by so doing some people have entertained angels without knowing it. Remember those in prison as if you were their fellow prisoners, and those who are mistreated as if you yourselves were suffering.

Religion that God our Father accepts as pure and faultless is this: to look after orphans and widows in their distress and to keep oneself from being polluted by the world.

We who are strong ought to bear with the failings of the weak and not to please ourselves. Each of us should please his neighbor for his good, to build him up. And do not forget to do good and to share with others, for with such sacrifices God is pleased. If you really keep the royal law found in Scripture, "Love your neighbor as yourself," you are doing right.

May the Lord make your love increase and overflow for each other and for everyone else.

Matthew 7:12. John 13:35. Romans 13:10. Hebrews 13:1-3. James 1:27.
Romans 15:1, 2. Hebrews 13:16. James 2:8. 1 Thessalonians 3:12.

Do not judge, or you too will be judged

For in the same way you judge others, you will be judged, and with the measure you use, it will be measured to you.

You, therefore, have no excuse, you who pass judgment on someone else, for at whatever point you judge the other, you are condemning yourself, because you who pass judgment do the same things. There will be trouble and distress for every human being who does evil ... but glory, honor and peace for everyone who does good: first for the Jew, then for the Gentile. For God does not show favoritism. Therefore let us stop passing judgment on one another. Instead, make up your mind not to put any stumbling block or obstacle in your brother's way.

Judge nothing before the appointed time; wait till the Lord comes. He will bring to light what is hidden in darkness and will expose the motives of men's hearts. There is only one Lawgiver and Judge, the one who is able to save and destroy. But you--who are you to judge your neighbor?

He has showed you, O man, what is good. And what does the Lord require of you? To act justly and to love mercy and to walk humbly with your God. Be merciful, just as your Father is merciful.

Matthew 7:1, 2. Romans 2:1, 9-11. Romans 14:13. 1 Corinthians 4:5. James 4:12. Micah 6:8. Luke 6:36.

Do not slander one another

Why do you look at the speck of sawdust in your brother's eye and pay no attention to the plank in your own eye? How can you say to your brother, "Let me take the speck out of your eye," when all the time there is a plank in your own eye? You hypocrite, first take the plank out of your own eye, and then you will see clearly to remove the speck from your brother's eye.

If you keep on biting and devouring each other, watch out or you will be destroyed by each other. Anyone who speaks against his brother or judges him speaks against the law and judges it. When you judge the law, you are not keeping it, but sitting in judgment on it.

With the tongue we praise our Lord and Father, and with it we curse men, who have been made in God's likeness. Out of the same mouth come praise and cursing. My brothers, this should not be. Can both fresh water and salt water flow from the same spring? My brothers, can a fig tree bear olives, or a grapevine bear figs? Neither can a salt spring produce fresh water.

Come near to God and he will come near to you. Wash your hands, you sinners, and purify your hearts, you double-minded. Blessed are the pure in heart, for they will see God. The lips of the righteous know what is fitting. The tongue of the wise brings healing.

James 4:11. Matthew 7:3-5. Galatians 5:15. James 3:9-12. James 4:8. Matthew 5:8. Proverbs 10:32. Proverbs 12:18.

Ask and it will be given to you.
For everyone who asks receives

Do not be anxious about anything, but in everything, by prayer and petition, with thanksgiving, present your requests to God. Pray in the Spirit on all occasions with all kinds of prayers and requests. With this in mind, be alert and always keep on praying for all the saints.

If you remain in me and my words remain in you, ask whatever you wish, and it will be given you. This is to my Father's glory, that you bear much fruit, showing yourselves to be my disciples.

If any of you lacks wisdom, he should ask God, who gives generously to all without finding fault, and it will be given to him. This is what the Lord says, he who made the earth, the Lord who formed it and established it--the Lord is his name: Call to me and I will answer you and tell you great and unsearchable things you do not know.

Now to him who is able to do immeasurably more than all we ask or imagine, according to his power that is at work within us, to him be glory in the church and in Christ Jesus throughout all generations, for ever and ever! Amen.

Matthew 7:7, 8. Philippians 4:6. Ephesians 6:18. John 15:7, 8. James 1:5. Jeremiah 33:2, 3. Ephesians 3:20.

Seek and you will find

Seek the Lord while he may be found; call on him while he is near. Devote yourselves to prayer, being watchful and thankful.

Acknowledge the God of your father, and serve him with wholehearted devotion and with a willing mind, for the Lord searches every heart and understands every motive behind the thoughts. If you seek him, he will be found by you.

This is what the Lord says ... "Seek me and live; do not seek Bethel, do not go to Gilgal, do not journey to Beersheba. For Gilgal will surely go into exile, and Bethel will be reduced to nothing. Seek the Lord and live."

The Lord is good to those whose hope is in him, to the one who seeks him; it is good to wait quietly for the salvation of the Lord.

Look to the Lord and his strength; seek his face always.   Your face, Lord, I will seek.

Matthew 7:7. Isaiah 55:6. Colossians 4:2. 1 Chronicles 28:9. Amos 5:4-6. Lamentations 3:25. 1 Chronicles 16:11. Psalm 17:8.

Knock and the door will be opened to you

In him [Christ] and through faith in him we may approach God with freedom and confidence. Let us then approach the throne of grace with confidence, so that we may receive mercy and find grace to help us in our time of need. Let us draw near to God with a sincere heart in full assurance of faith, having our hearts sprinkled to cleanse us from a guilty conscience and having our bodies washed with pure water. Let us hold unswervingly to the hope we profess, for he who promised is faithful.

And without faith it is impossible to please God, because anyone who comes to him must believe that he exists and that he rewards those who earnestly seek him. Come near to God and he will come near to you. Humble yourselves before the Lord, and he will lift you up.

The Lord is near to all who call on him, to all who call on him in truth. He fulfills the desires of those who fear him; he hears their cry and saves them.

Matthew 7:7. Ephesians 3:11. Hebrews 4:16. Hebrews 10:22, 23. Hebrews 11:6. James 4:8, 10. Psalm 145:18, 19.

How great is your goodness

Which of you, if his son asks for bread, will give him a stone? Or if he asks for a fish, will give him a snake? If you, then, though you are evil, know how to give good gifts to your children, how much more will your Father in heaven give good gifts to those who ask him!

You care for the land and water it; you enrich it abundantly.The streams of God are filled with water to provide the people with grain, for so you have ordained it. You drench its furrows and level its ridges; you soften it with showers and bless its crops. You crown the year with your bounty, and your carts overflow with abundance. The grasslands of the desert overflow; the hills are clothed with gladness. The meadows are covered with flocks and the valleys are mantled with grain; they shout for joy and sing.

Give thanks to the Lord, for he is good; his love endures forever. Let them give thanks to the Lord for his unfailing love and his wonderful deeds for men, for he satisfies the thirsty and fills the hungry with good things.

Know that the Lord is God. It is he who made us, and we are his; we are his people, the sheep of his pasture.

Psalm 31:19. Matthew 7:9-11. Psalm 65:9-13. Psalm 107:1, 8, 9. Psalm 100:3-5.

Jesus went through all the towns and villages teaching in their synagogues

They found him in the temple courts, sitting among the teachers, listening to them and asking them questions. Everyone who heard him was amazed at his understanding and his answers.

"No one ever spoke the way this man does," the guards declared. The Jews were amazed and asked, "How did this man get such learning without having studied?"

Each day Jesus was teaching at the temple ... and all the people came early in the morning to hear him.

Jesus replied, "If anyone loves me, he will obey my teaching." These words you hear are not my own; they belong to the Father who sent me. Heaven and earth will pass away but my words will never pass away. The words I have spoken to you are spirit and they are life.

Lord, to whom shall we go? You have the words of eternal life.

Matthew 9:35. Luke 2:46, 47. John 7:46, 15. Luke 21:37, 38. John 14:23. John 14:24. Mark 13:31. John 6:63, 68.

Jesus went through all the towns and villages preaching the good news of the kingdom

So many gathered that there was no room left, not even outside the door, and he preached the word to them.

So many people were coming and going that they did not even have a chance to eat.

On the Sabbath day he went into the synagogue, as was his custom. And he stood up to read. The scroll of the prophet Isaiah was handed to him. Unrolling it, he found the place where it is written: "The Spirit of the Lord is on me, because he has anointed me to preach good news to the poor. He has sent me to proclaim freedom for the prisoners and recovery of sight for the blind, to release the oppressed, to proclaim the year of the Lord's favor."

Then he rolled up the scroll, gave it back to the attendant and sat down. The eyes of everyone in the synagogue were fastened on him, and he began by saying to them, "Today this scripture is fulfilled in your hearing."

All spoke well of him and were amazed at the gracious words that came from his lips.

Everyone who hears these words of mine and puts them into practice is like a wise man who built his house on the rock.

Matthew 9:35. Mark 2:2. Mark 6:31. Luke 4:16-22. Matthew 7:24.

Jesus went through all the towns and villages healing every disease and sickness

The people all tried to touch him, because power was coming from him and healing them all.

He touched her hand ... the fever left. He touched their eyes... their sight was restored. He took him aside ... the man's ears were opened, his tongue was loosened and he began to speak plainly.

Many who were demon-possessed were brought to him, and he drove out the spirits with a word and healed all the sick. This was to fulfill what was spoken through the prophet Isaiah: "He took up our infirmities and carried our diseases."

Jesus came to them and said, "All authority in heaven and on earth has been given to me."

He is before all things, and in him all things hold together. Nothing is impossible with God.

Matthew 9:35. Luke 6:19. Matthew 8:15. Matthew 9:29. Mark 7:33, 35. Matthew 8:16, 17. Matthew 28:18. Colossians 1:17. Luke 1:37.

Lord ... you can make me clean

Jesus reached out his hand and touched the man, "I am willing," he said. "Be clean!" Immediately he was cured of his leprosy.

Naaman was commander of the army of the king of Aram. He was a valiant soldier, but he had leprosy. Elisha sent a messenger to say to him, "Go, wash yourself seven times in the Jordan, and your flesh will be restored and you will be cleansed. So he went down and dipped himself in the Jordan seven times, as the man of God had told him, and his flesh was restored and became clean like that of a young boy.

I will sprinkle clean water on you, and you will be clean; I will cleanse you from all your impurities and from all your idols.I will give you a new heart and put a new spirit in you. I will remove from you your heart of stone and give you a heart of flesh.

"Come now, let us reason together," says the Lord. "Though your sins are like scarlet, they shall be as white as snow; though they are red as crimson, they shall be like wool. If you are willing and obedient, you will eat the best from the land."

He whose walk is blameless is kept safe. A faithful man will be richly blessed.

Seek first his kingdom and his righteousness, and all these things will be given to you as well. For everyone who asks receives; he who seeks finds; and to him who knocks, the door will be opened.

Matthew 8:2, 3. 2 Kings 5:1, 10, 14. Ezekiel 36:25, 26. Isaiah 1:18, 19. Proverbs 28:18, 20. Matthew 6:33. Luke 11:10.

Just say the word...

Jesus came to them and said, "All authority in heaven and on earth has been given to me."

God ... has spoken to us by his Son, whom he appointed heir of all things, and through whom he made the universe. The Son is the radiance of God's glory and the exact representation of his being, sustaining all things by his powerful word.

He is able to save completely those who come to God through him, because he always lives to intercede for them. We did not follow cleverly invented stories when we told you about the power and coming of our Lord Jesus Christ, but we were eyewitnesses of his majesty.

See, the Sovereign Lord comes with power, and his arm rules for him.

In a loud voice they sang: "Worthy is the Lamb, who was slain, to receive power and wealth and wisdom and strength and honor and glory and praise!"

Matthew 8:8. Matthew 28:18. Hebrews 1:2, 3. Hebrews 7:25. 2 Peter 1:16. Isaiah 40:10. Revelation 5:12.

I have not found anyone in Israel with such great faith

The centurion replied, "Lord, I do not deserve to have you come under my roof. But just say the word, and my servant will be healed. Then Jesus said to the centurion, "Go! It will be done just as you believed it would." And his servant was healed at that very hour.

Faith is being sure of what we hope for and certain of what we do not see. By faith we understand that the universe was formed at God's command. And without faith it is impossible to please God, because anyone who comes to him must believe that he exists and that he rewards those who earnestly seek him. If you believe, you will receive whatever you ask for in prayer.

I will do whatever you ask in my name, so that the Son may bring glory to the Father. As the Scripture says, "Everyone who trusts in him will never be put to shame."

This is the victory that has overcome the world, even our faith.

Lord, my hope is in you.

Matthew 8:10, 8, 13. Hebrews 11:1, 3, 6. Matthew 21:22. John 14:13. Romans 10:11. 1 John 5:4. Psalm 39:7.

It will be done just as you believed it would

How great is your goodness which you have stored up for those who fear you, which you bestow in the sight of men on those who take refuge in you.

Those who trust in the Lord are like Mount Zion which cannot be shaken but endures forever. You will keep in perfect peace him whose mind is steadfast, because he trusts in you. Trust in the Lord forever, for the Lord, the Lord, is the Rock eternal.

Blessed is the man who trusts in the Lord, whose confidence is in him. He will be like a tree planted by the water that sends out its roots by the stream. It does not fear when heat comes; its leaves are always green. It has no worries in a year of drought and never fails to bear fruit.

Against all hope, Abraham in hope believed and so became the father of many nations, just as it had been said to him, "So shall your offspring be." He did not waver through unbelief regarding the promise of God, but was strengthened in his faith and gave glory to God, being fully persuaded that God had power to do what he had promised.

For no matter how many promises God has made, they are "Yes" in Christ. And so through him the "Amen" is spoken by us to the glory of God.

Matthew 8:13. Psalm 31:19. Psalm 125:1. Isaiah 26:3, 4. Jeremiah 17:7, 8. Romans 4:18, 20, 21. 2 Corinthians 1:20, 21.

Freely you have received, freely give

Give thanks to the Lord, for he is good; his love endures forever. Let the redeemed of the Lord say this-- those he redeemed from the hand of the foe, those he gathered from the lands, from east and west, from north and south.

Praise be to the God and Father of our Lord Jesus Christ, who has blessed us in the heavenly realms with every spiritual blessing in Christ. Everything comes from you, and we have given you only what comes from your hand.

We have different gifts, according to the grace given us. If a man's gift is prophesying, let him use it in proportion to his faith. If it is serving, let him serve; if it is teaching, let him teach; if it is encouraging, let him encourage; if it is contributing to the needs of others, let him give generously; if it is leadership, let him govern diligently; if it is showing mercy, let him do it cheerfully.

If the willingness is there, the gift is acceptable according to what one has, not according to what he does not have.

He who supplies seed to the sower and bread for food will also supply and increase your store of seed and will enlarge the harvest of your righteousness. You will be made rich in every way so that you can be generous on every occasion, and through us your generosity will result in thanksgiving to God. This service that you perform is not only supplying the needs of God's people but is also overflowing in many expressions of thanks to God.

Matthew 10:8. Psalm 107:1-3. Ephesians 1:3. 1 Chronicles 29:14. Romans 12:6-8. 2 Corinthians 8:12. 2 Corinthians 9:10-12.

I am sending you out like sheep among wolves

Therefore be as shrewd as snakes and as innocent as doves. Be self-controlled and alert. Your enemy the devil prowls around like a roaring lion looking for someone to devour. Resist him, standing firm in the faith. Put on the full armor of God so that you can take your stand against the devil's schemes.

Make your calling and election sure. For if you do these things, you will never fall. Be on your guard so that you may not be carried away by the error of lawless men and fall from your secure position. But grow in grace and knowledge of our Lord and Savior Jesus Christ.

Make every effort to add to your faith goodness; and to goodness, knowledge; and to knowledge, self-control; and to self-control, perseverance; and to perseverance, godliness; and to godliness, brotherly kindness; and to brotherly kindness, love. For if you possess these qualities in increasing measure, they will keep you from being ineffective and unproductive in your knowledge of our Lord Jesus Christ. Become mature, attaining to the whole measure of the fullness of Christ.

Who is wise? He will realize these things. Who is discerning?He will understand them. To the man who pleases him, God gives wisdom, knowledge and happiness.

Matthew 10:16. 1 Peter 5:8, 9. Ephesians 6:11. 2 Peter 1:10. 2 Peter 3:17, 18. 2 Peter 1:5-8. Ephesians 4:13. Hosea 14:9. Ecclesiastes 2:26.

You did not choose me, but I chose you to go and bear fruit--fruit that will last

He chose us in him before the creation of the world to be holy and blameless in his sight. We are God's workmanship, created in Christ Jesus to do good works, which God prepared in advance for us to do.

Remain in me [Christ], and I will remain in you. No branch can bear fruit by itself; it must remain in the vine. Neither can you bear fruit unless you remain in me.

I am the vine; you are the branches. If a man remains in me and I in him, he will bear much fruit; apart from me you can do nothing. If anyone does not remain in me, he is like a branch that is thrown away and withers; such branches are picked up, thrown into the fire and burned. If you remain in me and my words remain in you, ask whatever you wish, and it will be given you. This is to my Father's glory, that you bear much fruit, showing yourselves to be my disciples.

As God's chosen people, holy and dearly loved, clothe yourselves with compassion, kindness, humility, gentleness and patience. Bear with each other and forgive whatever grievances you may have against one another. Forgive as the Lord forgave you. Just as the Son of Man did not come to be served, but to serve, and to give his life as a ransom for many.

John 15:16. Ephesians 1:4. Ephesians 2:10. John 15:4-8. Colossians 3:12. Matthew 20:28.

God chose the weak ... to shame the strong

The message of the cross is foolishness to those who are perishing, but to us who are being saved it is the power of God. For it is written: "I will destroy the wisdom of the wise; the intelligence of the intelligent, I will frustrate."

Where is the wise man? Where is the scholar? Where is the philosopher of this age? Has not God made foolish the wisdom of the world? For the foolishness of God is wiser than man's wisdom, and the weakness of God is stronger than man's strength.

Brothers, think of what you were when you were called. Not many of you were wise by human standards; not many were influential; not many were of noble birth. But God chose the foolish things of the world to shame the wise; God chose the weak things of the world to shame the strong. He chose the lowly things of this world and the despised things--and the things that are not--to nullify the things that are, so that no one may boast before him.

Has not God chosen those who are poor in the eyes of the world to be rich in faith and to inherit the kingdom he promised those who love him?

He said to me, "My grace is sufficient for you, for my power is made perfect in weakness." Therefore I will boast all the more gladly about my weaknesses, so that Christ's power may rest on me. That is why, for Christ's sake, I delight in weaknesses, in insults, in hardships, in persecutions, in difficulties. For when I am weak, then I am strong.

---

1 Corinthians 1:27, 18-20, 25-29. James 2:5. 2 Corinthians 12:9, 10.

As you go, preach this message

The kingdom of heaven is near. Heal the sick, raise the dead, cleanse those who have leprosy, drive out demons.

I consider my life worth nothing to me, if only I may finish the race and complete the task the Lord Jesus has given me--the task of testifying to the gospel of God's grace. For I have not hesitated to proclaim to you the whole will of God. Keep watch over yourselves and all the flock of which the Holy Spirit has made you overseers.

For I resolved to know nothing while I was with you except Jesus Christ and him crucified. I came to you in weakness and fear, and with much trembling. My message and my preaching were not with wise and persuasive words, but with a demonstration of the Spirit's power, so that your faith might not rest on men's wisdom, but on God's power.

I pray that out of his glorious riches he may strengthen you with power through his Spirit in your inner being, so that Christ may dwell in your hearts through faith. And I pray that you, being rooted and established in love, may have power, together with all the saints, to grasp how wide and long and high and deep is the love of Christ, and to know this love that surpasses knowledge--that you may be filled to the measure of all the fullness of God.

Matthew 10:7, 8. Acts 20:24, 27, 28. 1 Corinthians 2:2-5. Ephesians 3:16-19.

Do not worry about what to say or how to say it

For it will not be you speaking, but the Spirit of your Father speaking through you. The Holy Spirit will teach you at that time what you should say. The Counselor, the Holy Spirit, whom the Father will send in my name, will teach you all things and will remind you of everything I have said to you.

This is what we speak, not in words taught us by human wisdom but in words taught by the Spirit, expressing spiritual truths in spiritual words. You will receive power when the Holy Spirit comes on you; and you will be my witnesses in Jerusalem, and in all Judea and Samaria, and to the ends of the earth.

I will give you words and wisdom that none of your adversaries will be able to resist or contradict. Be wise in the way you act toward outsiders; make the most of every opportunity. Let your conversation be always full of grace, seasoned with salt, so that you may know how to answer everyone.

Teach me to do your will, for you are my God; may your good Spirit lead me on level ground.

Now to him who is able to do immeasurably more than all we ask or imagine, according to his power that is at work within us, to him be glory in the church and in Christ Jesus throughout all generations, for ever and ever! Amen.

Matthew 10:19, 20. Luke 12:12. John 14:26. 1 Corinthians 2:13. Acts 1:8. Luke 21:15. Colossians 4:5, 6. Psalm 143:10. Ephesians 3:20.

The harvest is plentiful
but the workers are few

Ask the Lord of the harvest, therefore, to send out workers into his harvest field.

Do you not say, "Four months more and then the harvest"? I tell you, open your eyes and look at the fields! They are ripe for harvest. Even now the reaper draws his wages, even now he harveststhe crop for eternal life, so that the sower and the reaper may be glad together.

I planted the seed, Apollos watered it, but God made it grow.So neither he who plants nor he who waters is anything, but only God, who makes things grow. The man who plants and the man who waters have one purpose, and each will be rewarded according to his own labor. For we are God's fellow workers; you are God's field, God's building.

Those who are wise will shine like the brightness of the heavens, and those who lead many to righteousness, like the stars for ever and ever. Let us not become weary in doing good, for at the proper time we will reap a harvest if we do not give up.

The righteous will hold to their ways, and those with clean hands will grow stronger. Therefore, prepare your minds for action; be self-controlled; set your hope fully on the grace to be given you when Jesus Christ is revealed.

I am coming soon. Hold on to what you have, so that no one will take your crown.

Matthew 9:37, 38. John 4:35, 36. 1 Corinthians 3:6-9. Daniel 12:3. Galatians 6:9, 10. Job 17:9. 1 Peter 1:13. Revelation 3:11.

The kingdom of heaven is like a man who sowed good seed in his field

But while everyone was sleeping, his enemy came and sowed weeds among the wheat, and went away. When the wheat sprouted and formed heads, then the weeds also appeared. The owner's servants came to him and said, "Sir, didn't you sow good seed in your field? Where then did the weeds come from?"

The one who sowed the good seed is the Son of Man. The field is the world, and the good seed stands for the sons of the kingdom. The weeds are the sons of the evil one, and the enemy who sows them is the devil. The harvest is the end of the age, and the harvesters are angels.

As the weeds are pulled up and burned in the fire, so it will be at the end of the age. The Son of Man will send out his angels and they will weed out of his kingdom everything that causes sin and all who do evil. They will throw them into the fiery furnace, where there will be weeping and gnashing of teeth.

Since everything will be destroyed in this way, what kind of people ought you to be? You ought to live holy and godly lives as you look forward to the day of God and speed its coming. In keeping with his promise we are looking forward to a new heaven and a new earth, the home of the righteousness.

So then, dear friends, since you are looking forward to this, make every effort to be found spotless, blameless and at peace with him.

The righteous will shine like the sun in the kingdom of their Father.

Matthew 13:24-27. Matthew 13:37-42. 2 Peter 3:11-14. Matthew 13:43.

How blessed you will be,
sowing your seed by every stream

Those who sow in tears will reap with songs of joy. He who goes out weeping, carrying seed to sow, will return with songs of joy, carrying sheaves with him. He who sows righteousness reaps a sure reward.

Sow for yourselves righteousness, reap the fruit of unfailing love, and break up your unplowed ground; for it is time to seek the Lord, until he comes and showers righteousness on you. The one who sows to please his sinful nature, from that nature will reap destruction; the one who sows to please the Spirit, from the Spirit will reap eternal life.

The righteous will flourish like a palm tree, they will grow like a cedar of Lebanon; planted in the house of the Lord, they will flourish in the courts of our God. They will still bear fruit in old age, they will stay fresh and green, proclaiming, "The Lord is upright; he is my Rock, and there is no wickedness in him."

Isaiah 32:20. Psalm 126:5, 6. Proverbs 11:18. Hosea 10:12. Galatians 6:8. Psalm 92:12-15.

The kingdom of heaven is like treasure hidden in a field

When a man found it, he hid it again, and then in his joy went and sold all he had and bought that field.

Jesus answered, "If you want to be perfect, go, sell your possessions and give to the poor, and you will have treasure in heaven. Then come, follow me.

"No one who puts his hand to the plow and looks back is fit for service in the kingdom of God. And everyone who has left houses or brothers or sisters or father or mother or children or fields for my sake will receive a hundred times as much and will inherit eternal life. For whoever wants to save his life will lose it, but whoever loses his life for me will save it.

"I tell you the truth, unless a kernel of wheat falls to the ground and dies, it remains only a single seed. But if it does, it produces many seeds."

I consider everything a loss compared to the surpassing greatness of knowing Christ Jesus my Lord, for whose sake I have lost all things.

Store up for yourselves treasures in heaven, where moth and rust do not destroy, and where thieves do not break in and steal. For where your treasure is, there your heart will be also.

Matthew 13:44. Matthew 19:21. Luke 9:62. Matthew 19:29. Luke 9:24. John 12:24. Philippians 3:8. Matthew 6:20, 21.

Lay up treasure ... as a firm foundation

Do not store up for yourselves treasures on earth, where moth and rust destroy, and where thieves break in and steal.

Command those who are rich in this present world not to be arrogant nor to put their hope in wealth, which is so uncertain, but to put their hope in God, who richly provides us with everything for our enjoyment. Command them to do good, to be rich in good deeds, and to be generous and willing to share. In this way they will lay up treasure for themselves as a firm foundation for the coming age, so that they may take hold of the life that is truly life.

The Almighty will be your gold, the choicest silver for you. Surely then you will find delight in the Almighty and will lift up your face to God. You will pray to him, and he will hear you, and you will fulfill your vows.

Has not God chosen those who are poor in the eyes of the world to be rich in faith and to inherit the kingdom he promised those who love him?

---

1 Timothy 6:19. Matthew 6:19. 1 Timothy 6:17-19. Job 22:25-27. James 2:5.

The kingdom of heaven is like a merchant looking for fine pearls

When he found one of great value, he went away and sold everything he had and bought it.

Sell your possessions and give to the poor. Provide purses for yourselves that will not wear out, a treasure in heaven that will not be exhausted, where no thief comes near and no moth destroys. For where your treasure is, there your heart will be also.

The length of our days is seventy years--or eighty, if we have the strength; yet their span is but trouble and sorrow, for they quickly pass, and we fly away. All men are like grass, and all their glory is like the flowers of the field; the grass withers and the flowers fall. Man, despite his riches, does not endure; he is like the beasts that perish.

In the beginning you laid the foundations of the earth, and the heavens are the work of your hands. They will perish, but you remain; they will all wear out like a garment. Like clothing you will change them and they will be discarded. But you remain the same, and your years will never end.

His kingdom will never end. He was given authority, glory and sovereign power; all peoples, nations and men of every language worshiped him. His dominion is an everlasting dominion that will not pass away, and his kingdom is one that will never be destroyed.

The kingdom of the world has become the kingdom of our Lord and of his Christ, and he will reign for ever and ever.

Matthew 13:45, 46. Luke 12:33, 34. Psalm 90:10. 1 Peter 1:24.Psalm 49:12. Psalm 102:25-27. Luke 1:33. Daniel 7:14. Revelation 11:5.

A treasure in heaven
that will not be exhausted

Do not work for food that spoils, but for food that endures to eternal life, which the Son of Man will give you. On him God the Father has placed his seal of approval.

So we fix our eyes not on what is seen, but on what is unseen. For what is seen is temporary, but what is unseen is eternal.

The Lord will reward everyone for whatever good he does. Let the peace of Christ rule in your hearts, since as members of one body you were called to peace. And be thankful. Let the word of Christ dwell in you richly as you teach and admonish one another with all wisdom, and as you sing psalms, hymns and spiritual songs with gratitude in your hearts to God. And whatever you do, whether in word or deed, do it all in the name of the Lord Jesus, giving thanks to God the Father through him.

Whatever you do, work at it with all your heart, as working for the Lord, not for men, since you know that you will receive an inheritance from the Lord as a reward. It is the Lord Christ you are serving.

The Father ... has qualified you to share in the inheritance of the saints in the kingdom of light. ...An inheritance that can never perish, spoil or fade--kept in heaven for you, who through faith are shielded by God's power until the coming of the salvation that is ready to be revealed in the last time.

Luke 12:33. John 6:27. 2 Corinthians 4:18. Ephesians 6:8. Colossians 3:15-17. Colossians 3:23, 24. Colossians 1:2. 1 Peter 1:4, 5.

Declare his glory among the nations

Ask of me, and I will make the nations your inheritance, the ends of the earth your possession. All the ends of the earth will remember and turn to the Lord, and all the families of the nations will bow down before him.

It is like a mustard seed, which is the smallest seed you plant in the ground. Yet when planted, it grows and becomes the largest of all garden plants, with such big branches that the birds of the air can perch in its shade.

"My name will be great among the nations, from the rising to the setting of the sun. In every place incense and pure offerings will be brought to my name, because my name will be great among the nations," says the Lord Almighty.

The gospel of the kingdom will be preached in the whole world as a testimony to all nations, and then the end will come. Therefore go and make disciples of all nations. Open their eyes and turn them from darkness to light, and from the power of Satan to God, so that they may receive forgiveness of sins and a place among those who are sanctified by faith.

Psalm 96:3. Psalm 2:8. Psalm 22:27. Mark 4:31, 32. Malachi 1:11. Matthew 24:14. Matthew 28:19. Acts 26:18.

Who do you say I am?

Simon Peter answered, "You are the Christ, the Son of the living God."

In the beginning was the Word, and the Word was God. He was with God in the beginning. Through him all things were made; without him nothing was made that has been made. In him was life, and that life was the light of men. In Christ all the fullness of the Deity lives in bodily form.

Beyond all question, the mystery of godliness is great: He appeared in a body, was vindicated by the Spirit, was seen by angels, was preached among the nations, was believed on in the world, was taken up in glory.

The one who comes from above is above all. He is before all things, and in him all things hold together. And he is the head of the body, the church; he is the beginning and the first-born from among the dead, so that in everything he might have the supremacy.

And God placed all things under his feet. God exalted him to the highest place and gave him the name that is above every name.

There is but one Lord, Jesus Christ, through whom all things came and through whom we live. Jesus Christ, who has gone into heaven and is at God's right hand--with angels, authorities and powers in submission to him.

Matthew 16:15, 16. John 1:1-4. Colossians 2:9. 1 Timothy 3:16, 17. John 3:31. Colossians 1:18. Ephesians 1:22. Philippians 2:9. 1 Corinthians 8:6. 1 Peter 3:21, 22.

If any man will come after me

Your attitude should be the same as that of Christ Jesus: Who, being in very nature God, did not consider equality with God something to be grasped, but made himself nothing, taking the very nature of a servant, being made in human likeness. And being found in appearance as a man, he humbled himself and became obedient to death--even death on a cross!

A student is not above his teacher, nor a servant above his master. Christ suffered for you, leaving you an example, that you should follow in his steps.

Large crowds were traveling with Jesus, and turning to them he said: "If anyone comes to me and does not hate his father and mother, his wife and children, his brothers and sisters--yes, even his own life--he cannot be my disciple. And anyone who does not carry his cross and follow me cannot be my disciple.

"Suppose one of you wants to build a tower. Will he not first sit down and estimate the cost to see if he has enough money to complete it? For if he lays the foundation and is not able to finish it, everyone who sees it will ridicule him, saying, 'This fellow began to build and was not able to finish.'

"In the same way, any of you who does not give up everything he has cannot be my disciple.

"I tell you the truth," Jesus said to them, "no one who has left home or wife or brothers or parents or children for the sake of the kingdom of God will fail to receive many times as much in this age and, in the age to come, eternal life."

Matthew 16:24. Philippians 2:5-8. Matthew 10:24. 1 Peter 2:21. Luke 14:25-30, 33. Mark 18:29.

Let him... deny himself

Though I am free and belong to no man, I make myself a slave to everyone, to win as many as possible. To the Jews I became like a Jew, to win the Jews. To those under the law I became like one under the law (though I myself am not under the law), so as to win those under the law. To those not having the law I became like one not having the law (though I am not free from God's law but am under Christ's law), so as to win those not having the law. To the weak I became weak, to win the weak. I have become all things to all men so that by all possible means I might save some. I do all this for the sake of the gospel, that I may share in its blessings.

Do you not know that in a race all the runners run, but only one gets the prize? Run in such a way as to get the prize. Everyone who competes in the games goes into strict training. They do it to get a crown that will not last; but we do it to get a crown that will last forever. Therefore I do not run like a man running aimlessly; I do not fight like a man beating the air. No, I beat my body and make it my slave so that after I have preached to others, I myself will not be disqualified for the prize.

Let us throw off everything that hinders and the sin that so easily entangles, and let us run with perseverance the race marked out for us.

There is in store ... the crown of righteousness, which the Lord, the righteous Judge, will award ... to all who have longed for his appearance.

Matthew 16:24. 1 Corinthians 9:19-27. Hebrews 12:1. 2 Timothy 4:8.

Let him ... take up his cross

There was given to me a thorn in my flesh, a messenger of Satan, to torment me. Three times I pleaded with the Lord to take it away from me. But he said to me, "My grace is sufficient for you, for my power is made perfect in weakness." Therefore I will boast all the more gladly about my weaknesses, so that Christ's power may rest on me. That is why, for Christ's sake, I delight in weaknesses, in insults, in hardships, in persecutions, in difficulties. For when I am weak, then I am strong.

We do not lose heart. Though outwardly we are wasting away, yet inwardly we are being renewed day by day. For our light and momentary troubles are achieving for us an eternal glory that far outweighs them all.

See, I have refined you, though not as silver; I have tested you in the furnace of affliction. Do not be surprised at the painful trial you are suffering, as though something strange were happening to you. But rejoice that you participate in the sufferings of Christ, so that you may be overjoyed when his glory is revealed. Those who suffer according to God's will should commit themselves to their faithful Creator and continue to do good.

God ... after you have suffered a little while, will himself restore you and make you strong, firm and steadfast. To him be the power for ever and ever. Amen.

Matthew 16:24. 2 Corinthians 12:7-10. 2 Corinthians 4:16, 17. Isaiah 48:10. 1 Peter 4:12, 13, 19. 1 Peter 5:10.

Let him ... follow me

A teacher of the law came to him and said, "Teacher, I will follow you wherever you go."

Jesus replied, "Foxes have holes and birds of the air have nests, but the Son of Man has no place to lay his head."

Another man, one of his disciples, said to him, "Lord, first let me go and bury my father."

But Jesus told him, "Follow me, and let the dead bury their own dead."

He had no beauty or majesty to attract us to him, nothing in his appearance that we should desire him. He was despised and rejected by men, a man of sorrows, and familiar with suffering.

Jesus ... got up from the meal, took off his outer clothing, and wrapped a towel around his waist. After that, he poured water into a basin and began to wash his disciples' feet, drying them with the towel that was wrapped around him.

I am among you as one who serves. Take my yoke upon you and learn of me, for I am gentle and humble in heart, and you will find rest for your souls. For my yoke is easy and my burden is light.

Matthew 16:24. Matthew 8:19-22. Isaiah 53:2, 3, 7. John 3:3-5. Luke 22:27. Matthew 11:29.

Whoever loses his life for me will find it

If you live according to the sinful nature, you will die; but if by the Spirit you put to death the misdeeds of the body, you will live, because those who are led by the Spirit of God are sons of God.

Peter said to him, "We have left everything to follow you!" In the same way, any of you who does not give up everything he has cannot be my disciple.

Jesus said to his disciples: "Therefore I tell you, do not worry about your life, what you will eat; or about your body, what you will wear. Life is more than food, and the body more than clothes."

For you died, and your life is now hidden with Christ in God.When Christ, who is your life, appears, then you also will appear with him in glory.

Here is a trustworthy saying: If we died with him, we will also live with him; if we endure, we will also reign with him. If we disown him, he will also disown us; if we are faithless, he will remain faithful, for he cannot disown himself.

I would rather be a doorkeeper in the house of my God than dwell in the tents of the wicked. O Lord Almighty, blessed is the man who trusts in you.

Matthew 16:25. Romans 8:13, 14. Mark 10:28. Luke 14:33. Luke 12:22, 23. Colossians 3:3, 4. 2 Timothy 2:11-13. Psalm 84:10, 12.

What good will it be for a man if he gains the whole world, yet forfeits his soul?

You say, "I am rich; I have acquired wealth and do not need a thing." But you do not realize that you are wretched, pitiful, poor, blind and naked.

Be careful that you do not forget the Lord your God, failing to observe his commands, his laws and his decrees that I am giving you this day. Otherwise, when you eat and are satisfied, when you build fine houses and settle down, and when your herds and flocks grow large and your silver and gold increase and all you have is multiplied, then your heart will become proud and you will forget the Lord your God. Wealth is worthless in the day of wrath, but righteousness delivers from death.

Be careful, or your hearts will be weighed down with dissipation, drunkenness and the anxieties of life, and that day will close on you unexpectedly like a trap. Remember the Lord your God, for it is he who gives you the ability to produce wealth.

Do not conform any longer to the pattern of this world, but be transformed by the renewing of your mind. Set your minds on things above, not on earthly things.

Watch out! Be on your guard against all kinds of greed; a man's life does not consist in the abundance of his possessions.

Matthew 16:26. Revelation 3:17. Deuteronomy 8:11-14. Proverbs 11:4. Luke 21:34. Deuteronomy 8:18. Romans 12:2. Colossians 3:3. Luke 12:15.

He tends his flock like a shepherd

When he saw the crowds, he had compassion on them. They were harassed and helpless, like sheep without a shepherd.

My sheep wandered over all the mountains and on every high hill. They were scattered over the whole earth, and no one searched or looked for them.

See that you do not look down on one of these little ones. For I tell you that their angels in heaven always see the face of my Father in heaven.

What do you think? If a man owns a hundred sheep, and one of them wanders away, will he not leave the ninety-nine on the hills and go to look for the one that wandered off? And if he finds it, I tell you the truth, he is happier about that one sheep than about the ninety-nine that did not wander off. In the same way your Father in heaven is not willing that any of these little ones should be lost.

He said to them, "Go into all the world and preach the good news to all creation. I am sending you to open their eyes and turn them from darkness to light, and from the power of Satan to God, so that they may receive forgiveness of sins and a place among those who are sanctified by faith in me."

Keep watch over yourselves and all the flock of which the Holy Spirit has made you overseers. Be shepherds of the church of God, which he has bought with his own blood. You will be his witness to all men of what you have seen and heard.

And when the Chief Shepherd appears, you will receive the crown of glory that will never fade away.

Isaiah 40:11. Matthew 9:36. Ezekiel 34:6. Matthew 18:10-14. Mark 16:15. Acts 26:18. Acts 20:28. Acts 22:15. 1 Peter 5:4.

If your brother sins against you, go and show him his fault

...Just between the two of you. If he listens to you, you have won your brother over.

Like an earring of gold or an ornament of fine gold is a wise man's rebuke to a listening ear. Better is open rebuke than hidden love.

Therefore, if you are offering your gift at the altar and there remember that your brother has something against you, leave your gift there in front of the altar. First go and be reconciled to your brother; then come and offer your gift.

We who are strong ought to bear with the failings of the weak and not to please ourselves. Each of us should please his neighbor for his good, to build him up. You ought to forgive and comfort him, so that he will not be overwhelmed by excessive sorrow. I urge you, therefore, to reaffirm your love for him.

How good and pleasant it is when brothers live together in unity! It is like precious oil poured on the head, running down on the beard, down upon the collar of his robes. It is as if the dew of Hermon were falling on Mount Zion. For there the Lord bestows his blessing, even life forevermore.

Matthew 18:15. Proverbs 25:12. Proverbs 27:5. Matthew 5:23. Romans 15:1, 2. 2 Corinthians 2:7, 8. Psalm 133:1-3.

Warn a divisive person once, and then warn him a second time

If he will not listen, take one or two others along, so that 'every matter may be established by the testimony of two or three witnesses.' If he refuses to listen to them, tell it to the church; and if he refuses to listen even to the church, treat him as you would a pagan or a tax collector.

Watch out for those who cause divisions and put obstacles in your way that are contrary to the teaching you have learned. Keep away from them. For such people are not serving our Lord Christ, but their own appetites. By smooth talk and flattery they deceive the minds of naive people. For what do righteousness and wickedness have in common? Or what fellowship can light have with darkness?

A little yeast works through the whole batch of dough. ...The one who is throwing you into confusion will pay the penalty, whoever he may be.

Preach the Word: be prepared in season and out of season; correct, rebuke and encourage--with great patience and careful instruction. Aim for perfection, listen to my appeal, be of one mind, live in peace. And the God of love and peace will be with you.

Titus 3:10. Matthew 18:16, 17. Romans 16:17, 18. 2 Corinthians 6:14, 15. Galatians 5:9, 10. 2 Timothy 4:2. 2 Corinthians 13:11.

Warn ... encourage ... help

We urge you, brothers, warn those who are idle, encourage the timid, help the weak, be patient with everyone. Make sure that nobody pays back wrong for wrong, but always try to be kind to each other and to everyone else.

We hear that some among you are idle. They are not busy; they are busybodies. Such people we command and urge in the Lord Jesus Christ to settle down and earn the bread they eat. And as for you, brothers, never tire of doing what is right.

If someone is caught in a sin, you who are spiritual should restore him gently. But watch yourself, or you also may be tempted. Carry each other's burdens.
Above all, love each other deeply, because love covers over a multitude of sins.

Grant me a willing spirit, to sustain me. Then I will teach transgressors your ways, and sinners will turn back to you. Save me from blood guilt, O God, the God who saves me, and my tongue will sing of your righteousness. O Lord, open my lips, and my mouth will declare your praise. You do not delight in sacrifice, or I would bring it; you do not take pleasure in burnt offerings. The sacrifices of God are a broken spirit; a broken and contrite heart, O God, you will not despise.

Who is a God like you, who pardons sin and forgives the transgression of the remnant of his inheritance? You do not stay angry forever but delight to show mercy. You will again have compassion on us; you will tread our sins underfoot and hurl all our iniquities into the depths of the sea.

---

1 Thessalonians 5:14, 15. 2 Thessalonians 3:11-13. Galatians 6:1, 2. 1 Peter 4:8. Psalm 51:12-17. Micah 7:18, 19.

If two of you on earth agree

I tell you the truth, whatever you bind on earth will be bound in heaven, and whatever you loose on earth will be loosed in heaven. Again, I tell you that if two of you on earth agree about anything you ask for, it will be done for you by my Father in heaven. For where two or three come together in my name, there am I with them.

If you forgive anyone his sins, they are forgiven; if you do not forgive them, they are not forgiven.

I appeal to you, brothers, in the name of our Lord Jesus Christ, that all of you agree with one another so that there may be no divisions among you and that you may be perfectly united in mind and thought. Make every effort to keep the unity of the Spirit through the bond of peace.

Finally, all of you, live in harmony with one another; be sympathetic, love as brothers, be compassionate and humble. Do not repay evil with evil or insult with insult, but with blessing, because to this you were called so that you may inherit a blessing. For, "Whoever would love life and see good days must keep his tongue from evil and his lips from deceitful speech. He must turn from evil and do good; he must seek peace and pursue it.For the eyes of the Lord are on the righteous and his ears are attentive to their prayer, but the face of the Lord is against those who do evil.

Matthew 18:18-20. John 20:23. 1 Corinthians 1:10. Ephesians 4:3. Philippians 1:27. 1 Peter 3:8-12.

How many times shall I forgive?

Peter came to Jesus and asked, "Lord, how many times shall I forgive my brother when he sins against me? Up to seven times?"

Jesus answered, "I tell you, not seven times, but seventy-seven times. The kingdom of heaven is like a man who wanted to settle accounts with his servants. As he began the settlement, a man who owed him ten thousand talents was brought to him. Since he was not able to pay, the master ordered that he and his wife and his children and all that he had be sold to repay the debt.

"The servant fell on his knees before him. 'Be patient with me,' he begged, 'and I will pay back everything.' The servant's master took pity on him, canceled the debt and let him go.

"But when that servant went out, he found one of his fellow servants who owed him a hundred denarii. 'Pay back what you owe me!' he demanded.

"His fellow servant fell to his knees and begged him, 'Be patient with me, and I will pay you back.'

"But he refused. Instead, he went off and had the man thrown into prison until he could pay the debt.

"Then the master called the servant in. 'You wicked servant,' he said, `I canceled all that debt of yours because you begged me to. Shouldn't you have had mercy on your fellow servant just as I had on you?' In anger his master turned him over to the jailers.

"This is how my heavenly Father will treat each of you unless you forgive your brother from your heart."

Be kind and compassionate to one another, forgiving each other, just as in Christ God forgave you.

Matthew 18:21-35. Ephesians 4:32.

Where two or three come together in my name, there am I with them

You are no longer foreigners and aliens, but fellow citizens with God's people and members of God's household, built on the foundation of the apostles and prophets, with Christ Jesus himself as the chief cornerstone. In him the whole building is joined together and rises to become a holy temple in the Lord. And in him you too are being built together to become a dwelling in which God lives by his Spirit.

Our fellowship is with the Father and with his Son, Jesus Christ. God, who has called you into fellowship with his Son Jesus Christ our Lord, is faithful. I stand at the door and knock. If anyone hears my voice and opens the door, I will come in and eat with him, and he with me. You will realize that I am in my Father, and you are in me, and I am in you.

I pray that out of his glorious riches he may strengthen you with power through his Spirit in your inner being, so that Christ may dwell in your hearts through faith. And I pray that you, being rooted and established in love, may have power, together with all the saints, to grasp how wide and long and high and deep is the love of Christ, and to know this love that surpasses knowledge--that you may be filled to the measure of all the fullness of God.

Matthew 18:20. Ephesians 2:19-22. 1 John 1:3. 1 Corinthians 1:9. Revelation 3:20. John 14:20. Ephesians 3:16-19.

Seek righteousness, seek humility

She said, "Grant that one of these two sons of mine may sit at your right and the other at your left in your kingdom."

"You don't know what you are asking," Jesus said to them. ..."These places belong to those for whom they have been prepared by my Father."

Do not exalt yourself in the king's presence, and do not claim a place among great men; it is better for him to say to you,"Come up here," than for him to humiliate you before a nobleman. It is not good to eat too much honey, nor is it honorable to seek one's own honor.

For whoever exalts himself will be humbled, and whoever humbles himself will be exalted.

When pride comes, then comes disgrace, but with humility comes wisdom. Do nothing out of selfish ambition or vain conceit, but in humility consider others better than yourselves.

Seek the Lord, all you humble of the land, you who do what he commands. Seek righteousness, seek humility; perhaps you will be sheltered on the day of the Lord's anger.

The meek will inherit the land and enjoy great peace.

Zephaniah 2:3. Matthew 20:21-23. Proverbs 25:6, 7, 27. Matthew 23:12. Proverbs 11:2. Philippians 2:3. Zephaniah 2:3. Psalm 37:11.

Should you then seek great things for yourself? Seek them not

They said, "Come, let us build ourselves a city, with a tower that reaches to the heavens, so that we may make a name for ourselves and not be scattered over the face of the whole earth."

Adonijah ... said, "I will be king." So he got chariots and horses ready, with fifty men to run ahead of him.

"The pride of your heart has deceived you, you who live in the clefts of the rocks and make your home on the heights, you who say to yourself, 'Who can bring me down to the ground?' Though you soar like the eagle and make your nest among the stars, from there I will bring you down," declares the Lord.

Jesus called them together and said, "You know that the rulers of the Gentiles lord it over them, and their high officials exercise authority over them. Not so with you."

Does the ax raise itself above him who swings it, or the saw boast against him who uses it? As if a rod were to wield him who lifts it up, or a club brandish him who is not wood!

Unless the Lord builds the house, its builders labor in vain. I know, O Lord, that a man's life is not his own; it is not for man to direct his steps. A man can receive only what is given him from heaven.

[Jesus replied,] "I am the vine; you are the branches. If a man remains in me and I in him, he will bear much fruit; apart from me you can do nothing."

Jeremiah 45:5. Genesis 11:4. 1 Kings 1:5. Obadiah 3, 4. Matthew 20:25, 26. Isaiah 10:15. Psalm 127:1. Jeremiah 10:23. John 3:27. John 15:5.

The Son of Man did not come to be served, but to serve

[Jesus said,] "I am among you as one who serves."

Christ Jesus ... did not consider equality with God something to be grasped, but made himself nothing, taking the very nature of a servant.

"I am the good shepherd. The good shepherd lays down his life for the sheep."

"Come to me, all you who are weary and burdened, and I will give you rest."

While Jesus was in one of the towns, a man came along who was covered with leprosy. When he saw Jesus, he fell with his face to the ground and begged him, "Lord, if you are willing, you can make me clean." Jesus reached out his hand and touched the man, "I am willing," he said, "Be clean!" And immediately the leprosy left him.

When Jesus saw their faith he said, "Friend, your sins are forgiven."

Jesus began to explain ... that he must go to Jerusalem and suffer many things ... that he must be killed and on the third day be raised to life.

This is how we know what love is: Jesus Christ laid down his life for us. And we ought to lay down our lives for our brothers.

Matthew 20:28. Luke 22:27. Philippians 2:5-7. John 10:11. Matthew 11:28. Luke 5:12, 13, 20. Matthew 16:21. 1 John 3:16.

Whoever wants to become great among you must be your servant

What does the Lord require of you? To act justly and to love mercy and to walk humbly with your God.

Do not think of yourself more highly than you ought, but rather think of yourself with sober judgment, in accordance with the measure of faith God has given you. Humble yourselves before the Lord, and he will lift you up.

The Lord sends poverty and wealth; he humbles and he exalts. It is God who judges: He brings one down, he exalts another. He changes times and seasons; he sets up kings and deposes them. He gives wisdom to the wise and knowledge to the discerning.

"Now, O Lord my God, you have made your servant king in place of my father David. But I am only a little child and do not know how to carry out my duties. So give your servant a discerning heart to govern your people and to distinguish between right and wrong. For who is able to govern this great people of yours?"

The Lord was pleased that Solomon had asked for this. So God said to him, "Since you have asked for this and not for long life or wealth for yourself ... I will do what you have asked. I will give you a wise and discerning heart, so that there will never have been anyone like you, nor will there ever be. Moreover, I will give you what you have not asked for--both riches and honor--so that in your lifetime you will have no equal among kings. And if you walk in my ways and obey my statutes and commands as David your father did, I will give you a long life."

Matthew 20:26. Micah 6:8. Romans 12:3. James 4:10. 1 Samuel 2:7. Psalm 75:7. Daniel 2:21. 1 Kings 3:7, 9-14.

Each one should use whatever gift
he has received to serve others

If anyone serves, he should do it with the strength God provides.

We are God's fellow workers. As God's fellow workers we urge you not to receive God's grace in vain.

In Christ we who are many form one body, and each member belongs to all the others. We have different gifts, according to the grace given us. If a man's gift is prophesying, let him use it in proportion to his faith. If it is serving, let him serve; if it is teaching, let him teach; if it is encouraging, let him encourage; if it is contributing to the needs of others, let him give generously; if it is leadership, let him govern diligently; if it is showing mercy, let him do it cheerfully.

Give, and it will be given to you. A good measure, pressed down, shaken together and running over, will be poured into your lap. For with the measure you use, it will be measured to you. He who supplies seed to the sower and bread for food will also supply and increase your store of seed and will enlarge the harvest of your righteousness. You will be made rich in every way so that you can be generous on every occasion.

---

1 Peter 4:10, 11. 1 Corinthians 3:9. 2 Corinthians 6:1. Romans 12:5-8. Luke 6:38. 2 Corinthians 9:10, 11.

As God's chosen people ... clothe yourselves with compassion, kindness, humility, gentleness and patience

At that hour of the night the jailer took them and washed their wounds ... brought them into his house and set a meal before them. /Be kind and compassionate to one another.

The islanders showed us unusual kindness. The built a fire and welcomed us all because it was raining and cold. /Always try to be kind to each other and to everyone else.

King David went in and sat before the Lord, and he said: "Who am I, O Sovereign Lord, and what is my family, that you have brought me this far?" /Humble yourselves before the Lord, and he will lift you up.

Your king comes to you, gentle and riding on a donkey. /Let your gentleness be evident to all.

After waiting patiently, Abraham received what was promised. /Do not throw away your confidence; it will be richly rewarded. You need to persevere so that when you have done the will of God, you will receive what he has promised.

The fruit of the Spirit is love, joy, peace, patience, kindness, goodness, faithfulness, gentleness and self-control. Against such things there is no law.

Colossians 3:12. Acts 16:33, 34. Ephesians 4:32. Acts 28:2. 1 Thessalonians 5:15. 2 Samuel 7:18. James 4:10. Matthew 21:5. Philippians 4:5. Hebrews 6:15. Hebrews 10:36. Galatians 5:22.

Speak up for those
who cannot speak for themselves

Speak up and judge fairly; defend the rights of the poor and needy. Defend the cause of the weak and fatherless; maintain the rights of the poor and oppressed. Rescue the weak and needy; deliver them from the hand of the wicked.

Jesus said, "A man was going down from Jerusalem to Jericho, when he fell into the hands of robbers. They stripped him of his clothes, beat him and went away, leaving him half dead. But a Samaritan, as he traveled, came where the man was; and when he saw him, he took pity on him. He went to him and bandaged his wounds, pouring on oil and wine. Then he put the man on his own donkey, took him to an inn and took care of him. The next day he took out two silver coins and gave them to the innkeeper. 'Look after him,' he said, 'and when I return, I will reimburse you for any extra expense you may have.'"

The men designated by name took the prisoners, and from the plunder they clothed all who were naked. They provided them with clothes and sandals, food and drink, and healing balm. All those who were weak they put on donkeys. So they took them back to their fellow countrymen.

Carry each other's burdens, and in this way you will fulfill the law of Christ. We must help the weak, remembering the words the Lord Jesus himself said: "It is more blessed to give than to receive."

Proverbs 31:8, 9. Psalm 82:3, 4. Luke 10:30, 33-35. 2 Chronicles 28:15.
Galatians 6:2. Acts 20:35.

By their fruit you will recognize them

Do people pick grapes from thorn bushes, or figs from thistles? Likewise every good tree bears good fruit, but a bad tree bears bad fruit. A good tree cannot bear bad fruit, and a bad tree cannot bear good fruit. Every tree that does not bear good fruit is cut down and thrown into the fire. Thus, by their fruit you will recognize them.

Not everyone who says to me, "Lord, Lord," will enter the kingdom of heaven, but only he who does the will of my Father who is in heaven. Many will say to me on that day, "Lord, Lord, did we not prophesy in your name, and in your name drive out demons and perform many miracles?" Then I will tell them plainly, "I never knew you. Away from me, you evildoers!"

We must all appear before the judgment seat of Christ, that each one may receive what is due him for the things done while in the body, whether good or bad.

Therefore, prepare your minds for action: be self-controlled; set your hope fully on the grace to be given you when Jesus Christ is revealed. As obedient children, do not conform to the evil desires you had when you lived in ignorance. But just as he who called you is holy, so be holy in all you do; for it is written: "Be holy, because I am holy."

Since you call on a Father who judges each man's work impartially, live your lives as strangers here in reverent fear.

You understand, O Lord; remember me and care for me.

Matthew 7:16-23. 2 Corinthians 5:10. 1 Peter 1:13-17. Jeremiah 15:15.

The sheep ... and the goats

When the Son of Man comes in his glory, and all the angels with him, he will sit on his throne in heavenly glory. All the nations will be gathered before him, and he will separate the people one from another as a shepherd separates the sheep from the goats. He will put the sheep on his right and the goats on his left.

Then he will say to those on his left, "Depart from me, you who are cursed, into the eternal fire prepared for the devil and his angels. For I was hungry and you gave me nothing to eat, I was thirsty and you gave me nothing to drink, I was a stranger and you did not invite me in, I needed clothes and you did not clothe me, I was sick and in prison and you did not look after me. I tell you the truth, whatever you did not do for one of the least of these [brothers of mine], you did not do for me."

He never thought of doing a kindness, but hounded to death the poor and the needy and the brokenhearted. If a man shuts his ears to the cry of the poor, he too will cry out and not be answered. Woe to the worthless shepherd, who deserts the flock! May the sword strike his arm and his right eye! May his arm be completely withered, his right eye totally blinded! The way of the wicked is like deep darkness; they do not know what makes them stumble. Their path will become slippery; they will be banished to darkness and there will fall.

That is what some of you were. But you were washed, you were sanctified, you were justified in the name of the Lord Jesus Christ and by the Spirit of our God.

Matthew 25:31-33, 41-43, 45. Psalm 109:16. Proverbs 21:13. Zechariah 11:17. Proverbs 4:19. Jeremiah 23:12. 1 Corinthians 6:11.

A cup of cold water

If anyone gives a cup of cold water to one of these little ones because he is my disciple, I tell you the truth, he will certainly not lose his reward.

The King will say to those on his right, "Come, you who are blessed by my Father; take your inheritance, the kingdom prepared for you since the creation of the world. For I was hungry and you gave me something to eat, I was thirsty and you gave me something to drink, I was a stranger and you invited me in, I needed clothes and you clothed me, I was sick and you looked after me, I was in prison and you came to visit me."

Then the righteous will answer him, "Lord, when did we see you hungry and feed you, or thirsty and give you something to drink? When did we see you a stranger and invite you in, or needing clothes and clothe you? When did we see you sick or in prison and go to visit you?"

The King will reply, "I tell you the truth, whatever you did for one of the least of these brothers of mine, you did for me."

If you spend yourselves in behalf of the hungry and satisfy the needs of the oppressed, then your light will rise in the darkness, and your night will become like the noonday. The Lord will guide you always; he will satisfy your needs in a sun-scorched land and will strengthen your frame. You will be like a well-watered garden, like a spring whose waters never fail.

God is not unjust; he will not forget your work and the love you have shown him as you have helped his people and continue to help them.

Matthew 10:42. Matthew 25:34-40. Isaiah 58:10, 11. Hebrews 6:10.

The alien ... must be treated
as one of your native-born

There is no Greek or Jew, circumcised or uncircumcised, barbarian, Scythian, slave or free, but Christ is all, and is in all.

"Nazareth! Can anything good come from there?" Nathanael asked. "Come and see," said Philip.

Why do you judge your brother? Or why do you look down on your brother? Let us stop passing judgment on one another. Instead, make up your mind not to put any stumbling block or obstacle in your brother's way.

The Lord your God ... defends the cause of the fatherless and the widow, and loves the alien, giving him food and clothing. Consequently ... no longer foreigners and aliens, but fellow citizens with God's people and members of God's household. God is not ashamed to be called their God, for he has prepared a city for them.

Let love and faithfulness never leave you. Be merciful, just as your Father is merciful.

Leviticus 19:34. Colossians 3:11. John 1:46. Romans 14:10, 13. Deuteronomy 10:17, 18. Ephesians 2:19. Hebrews 11:16. Proverbs 3:3. Luke 6:36.

Defend the cause of the fatherless. Plead the case of the widow

Learn to do right! Seek justice, encourage the oppressed. Defend the cause of the fatherless, plead the case of the widow. Do not take advantage of a widow or an orphan. Do not deprive the alien or the fatherless of justice, or take the cloak of the widow as a pledge. When you are harvesting in your field and you overlook a sheaf, do not go back to get it. Leave it for the alien, the fatherless and the widow, so that the Lord your God may bless you in all the work of your hands.

Religion that God our Father accepts as pure and faultless is this: to look after orphans and widows in their distress and to keep oneself from being polluted by the world.

Give proper recognition to those widows who are really in need. But if a widow has children or grandchildren, these should learn first of all to put their religion into practice by caring for their own family and so repaying their parents and grandparents, for this is pleasing to God.

A father to the fatherless, a defender of widows, is God in his holy dwelling. God sets the lonely in families.

You, O God, do see trouble and grief; you consider it to take it in hand. The victim commits himself to you; you are the helper of the fatherless. You hear, O Lord, the desire of the afflicted; you encourage them, and you listen to their cry, defending the fatherless and the oppressed, in order that man, who is of the earth, may terrify no more.

Isaiah 1:17. Exodus 22:22. Deuteronomy 24:17, 19. James 1:27.1 Timothy 5:3, 4, 21. Psalm 68:5, 6. Psalm 10:14, 17, 18.

Bear with the failings of the weak

We who are strong ought to bear with the failings of the weak and not to please ourselves. We must help the weak, remembering the words the Lord Jesus himself said: "It is more blessed to give than to receive."

Be joyful in hope, patient in tribulation, faithful in prayer. Share with God's people who are in need. Practice hospitality. Bless those who persecute you; bless and do not curse. Rejoice with those who rejoice; mourn with those who mourn. Live in harmony with one another. Do not be proud, but be willing to associate with people of low position. Do not be conceited.

Remember those in prison as if you were their fellow prisoners, and those who are mistreated as if you yourselves were suffering. Show proper respect to everyone.

Don't show favoritism. Suppose a man comes into your meeting wearing a gold ring and fine clothes, and a poor man in shabby clothes also comes in. If you show special attention to the man wearing fine clothes and say, "Here's a good seat for you," but say to the poor man, "You stand there" or "Sit on the floor by my feet," have you not discriminated among yourselves and become judges with evil thoughts?

May the God who gives endurance and encouragement give you a spirit of unity among yourselves as you follow Christ Jesus, so that with one heart and mouth you may glorify the God and Father of our Lord Jesus Christ.

Accept one another, then, just as Christ accepted you, in order to bring praise to God.

Romans 15:1, 2. Acts 20:35. Romans 12:12-16. Hebrews 13:3. 1 Peter 2:17. James 2:1-4. Romans 15:5-7.

Do good to all people, especially to those who belong to the family of believers

For you are a people holy to the Lord your God. Out of all the peoples on the face of the earth, the Lord has chosen you to be his treasured possession.

If you have any encouragement from being united with Christ, if any comfort from his love, if any fellowship with the Spirit, if any tenderness and compassion, then make my joy complete by being like-minded, having the same love, being one in spirit and purpose. Do nothing out of selfish ambition or vain conceit, but in humility consider others better than yourselves. Each of you should look not only to your own interest, but also to the interests of others.

The disciples, each according to his ability, decided to provide help for the brothers living in Judea. There were no needy persons among them. For from time to time those who owned lands or houses sold them, brought the money from the sales... and it was distributed to anyone as he had need.

Out of the most severe trial, their (the Macedonian churches] overflowing joy and their extreme poverty welled up in rich generosity. For... they gave as much as they were able, and even beyond their ability.

Each man should give what he has decided in his heart to give, not reluctantly or under compulsion, for God loves a cheerful giver. Cast your bread upon the waters, for after many days you will find it again. Remember this: Whoever sows sparingly will also reap sparingly, and whoever sows generously will also reap generously.

Galatians 6:10. Deuteronomy 14:2. Philippians 2:1-4. Acts 11:29. Acts 4:34, 35. 2 Corinthians 8:2, 3. 2 Corinthians 9:7. Ecclesiastes 11:1. 2 Corinthians 9:6.

My appointed time is near

Look, the hour is near, and the Son of Man is betrayed into the hands of sinners.

Jesus replied, "The hour has come for the Son of Man to be glorified. I tell you the truth, unless a kernel of wheat falls to the ground and dies, it remains only a single seed. But if it dies, it produces many seeds. The man who loves his life will lose it, while the man who hates his life in this world will keep it for eternal life. Whoever serves me must follow me; and where I am, my servant also will be. My Father will honor the one who serves me.

"Now my heart is troubled, and what shall I say? 'Father, save me from this hour'? No, it was for this very reason I came to this hour. Father, glorify your name!"

Jesus knew that the time had come for him to leave this world and go to the Father. He looked toward heaven and prayed: "Father, the time has come. Glorify your Son, that your Son may glorify you. For you granted him authority over all people that he might give eternal life to all those you have given him. Now this is eternal life: that they may know you, the only true God and Jesus Christ, whom you have sent. I have brought you glory on earth by completing the work you gave me to do."

In a loud voice they sang: "Worthy is the Lamb, who was slain, to receive power and wealth and wisdom and strength and honor and glory and praise!"

God exalted him to the highest place and gave him the name that is above every name.

Matthew 26:18, 45. John 12:23-28. John 13:1. John 17:1-4. Revelation 5:12. Philippians 2:9.

One of you will betray me

They were very sad and began to say to him one after the other, "Surely not I, Lord?"

Jesus replied, "The one who has dipped his hand into the bowl with me will betray me. The Son of Man will go just as it is written about him. But woe to that man who betrays the Son of Man! It would be better for him if he had not been born."

Then Judas, the one who would betray him, said, "Surely not I, Rabbi?"

Jesus answered, "Yes, it is you."

Jesus had known from the beginning which of them did not believe and who would betray him.

Why do the nations rage and the peoples plot in vain? The kings of the earth take their stand and the rulers gather together against the Lord and against his Anointed One.

O Jerusalem, Jerusalem, you who kill the prophets and stone those sent to you, how often I have longed to gather your children together, as a hen gathers her chicks under her wings, but you were not willing!

But you are a chosen people, a royal priesthood, a holy nation, a people belonging to God, that you may declare the praises of him who called you out of darkness into his wonderful light.

Whoever follows me ... will have the light of life.

Matthew 26:21-25. John 6:64. Psalm 2:1, 2. Luke 13:34. 1 Peter 2:9. John 8:12.

Surely not I, Lord?

Jesus told them, "This very night you will all fall away on account of me, for it is written: "`I will strike the shepherd, and the sheep of the flock will be scattered."'

Peter replied, "Even if all fall away on account of you, I never will."

"I tell you the truth," Jesus answered, "this very night, before the rooster crows, you will disown me three times."

But Peter declared, "Even if I have to die with you, I will never disown you." And all the other disciples said the same.

Now Peter was sitting out in the courtyard, and a servant girl came to him. "You also were with Jesus of Galilee," she said. But he denied it before them all. "I don't know what you're talking about," he said. ...He denied it again, with an oath: "I don't know the man!" ...He began to call down curses on himself and he swore to them, "I don't know the man!" Immediately a rooster crowed. Then Peter remembered the words Jesus had spoken ...He went outside and wept bitterly.

Jesus said to them, "Can you drink the cup I am going to drink?"

We share in his sufferings in order that we may also share in his glory. Let us fix our eyes on Jesus, the author and perfector of our faith, who for the joy set before him endured the cross, scorning its shame, and sat down at the right hand of the throne of God. Consider him who endured such opposition from sinful men, so that you will not grow weary and lose heart.

Matthew 26:22, 31-35, 69-75. Matthew 20:22. Romans 8:17. Hebrews 12:2, 3.

Jesus took bread ... This is my body

I am the bread of life. Your forefathers ate the manna in the desert, yet they died. But here is the bread that comes down from heaven, which a man may eat and not die. I am the living bread that came down from heaven. If a man eats of this bread, he will live forever. This bread is my flesh, which I will give for the life of the world.

Is not the bread that we break a participation in the body of Christ?

Christ suffered for you, leaving you an example, that you should follow in his steps. He committed no sin, and no deceit was found in his mouth. When they hurled their insults at him, he did not retaliate; when he suffered, he made no threats. Instead, he entrusted himself to him who judges justly. He himself bore our sins in his body on the tree, so that we might die to sins and live for righteousness; by his wounds you have been healed.

The bread of God is he who comes down from heaven and gives life to the world. I am the bread of life. He who comes to me will never go hungry, and he who believes in me will never be thirsty.

Matthew 26:26. John 6:48-51. 1 Corinthians 10:16. 1 Peter 2:21-24. John 6:33, 35.

He took the cup ... This is my blood

Jesus said to them, "I tell you the truth, unless you eat the flesh of the Son of Man and drink his blood, you have no life in you. Whoever eats my flesh and drinks my blood has eternal life, and I will raise him up at the last day. For my flesh is real food and my blood is real drink. Whoever eats my flesh and drinks my blood remains in me, and I in him.

It was not with perishable things such as silver or gold that you were redeemed from the empty way of life handed down to you from your forefathers, but with the precious blood of Christ, a lamb without blemish or defect.

How much more, then, will the blood of Christ, who through the eternal Spirit offered himself unblemished to God, cleanse our consciences from acts that lead to death, so that we may serve the living God. If we walk in the light, as he is in the light, we have fellowship with one another, and the blood of Jesus, his Son, purifies us from all sin.

At just the right time, when we were still powerless, Christ died for the ungodly. Very rarely will anyone die for a righteous man, though for a good man someone might possibly dare to die. But God demonstrates his own love for us in this: While we were still sinners, Christ died for us.

Matthew 26:27, 28. John 6:53-56. 1 Peter 1:18, 19. Hebrews 9:14. 1 John 1:7. Romans 5:6-8.

...Anew with you in my Father's kingdom

I am among you as one who serves. You are those who have stood by me in my trials. And I confer on you a kingdom, just as my Father conferred one on me, so that you may eat and drink at my table in my kingdom and sit on thrones, judging the twelve tribes of Israel.

He made known to us the mystery of his will according to his good pleasure, which he purposed in Christ, to be put into effect when the times will have reached their fulfillment--to bring all things in heaven and on earth together under one head, even Christ.

You have come to Mount Zion, to the heavenly Jerusalem, the city of the living God. You have come to thousands upon thousands of angels in joyful assembly, to the church of the firstborn, whose names are written in heaven. You have come to God, the judge of all men, to the spirits of righteous men made perfect, to Jesus the mediator of a new covenant, and to the sprinkled blood that speaks a better word than the blood of Abel.

Therefore, since we are receiving a kingdom that cannot be shaken, let us be thankful, and so worship God acceptably with reverence and awe, for our God is a consuming fire.

Matthew 26:29. Luke 22:27-30. Ephesians 1:9, 10. Hebrews 12:22-24, 28, 29.

Until he comes...

Whenever you eat this bread and drink this cup, you proclaim the Lord's death until he comes.

"Men of Galilee," they said, "why do you stand here looking into the sky? This same Jesus, who has been taken from you into heaven, will come back in the same way you have seen him go into heaven."

In the future you will see the Son of Man sitting at the right hand of the Mighty One and coming on the clouds of heaven. No one knows about that day or hour, not even the angels in heaven, nor the Son, but only the Father. You ... must be ready, because the Son of Man will come at an hour when you do not expect him. For in just a very little while, "He who is coming will come and will not delay."

The Son of Man is going to come in his Father's glory with his angels, and then he will reward each person according to what he has done. When the Son of Man comes in his glory, and all the angels with him, he will sit on his throne in heavenly glory. All the nations will be gathered before him.

Hold on to what you have, so that no one will take your crown. To him who overcomes, I will give the right to sit with me on my throne.

---

1 Corinthians 11:26. Acts 1:11. Matthew 26:64. Matthew 24:36.Luke 12:40. Hebrews 10:37. Matthew 16:27. Matthew 25:31, 32. Revelation 3:11, 21.

My soul is overwhelmed with sorrow to the point of death. Stay here and keep watch with me

Save me, O God, for the waters have come up to my neck. I sink in the miry depths, where there is no foothold. I have come into the deep waters; the floods engulf me. I am worn out calling for help; my throat is parched. My eyes fail, looking for my God. Those who hate me without reason outnumber the hairs of my head; many are my enemies without cause, those who seek to destroy me.

Now my heart is troubled, and what shall I say? Father, save me from this hour? No, it was for this very reason I came to this hour. Father, glorify your name!

He fell with his face to the ground and prayed, "My Father, if it is possible, may this cup be taken from me. Yet not as I will, but as you will." Then he returned to his disciples and found them sleeping. "Could you men not keep watch with me for one hour?" he asked Peter.

He went away a second time and prayed. He ... went away once more and prayed the third time, saying the same thing.

Then he returned to the disciples and said to them, "Are you still sleeping and resting? Look, the hour is near."

We are going up to Jerusalem, and the Son of Man will be betrayed to the chief priests and the teachers of the law. They will condemn him to death and will turn him over to the Gentiles to be mocked and flogged and crucified. On the third day he will be raised to life!

I seek not to please myself but him who sent me.

Matthew 26:38. Psalm 69:1-4. John 12:27. Matthew 26:39, 40, 42, 44-45. Matthew 20:18, 19. John 5:30.

Could you men not keep watch with me for one hour?

He returned to his disciples and found them sleeping. He went away a second time. When he came back, he again found them sleeping, because their eyes were heavy. So he left them and went away once more. Then he returned to the disciples and said to them, "Are you still sleeping and resting?"

You will leave me all alone. Yet I am not alone, for my Father is with me.

From birth I was cast upon you; from my mother's womb you have been my God. Do not be far from me, for trouble is near and there is no one to help. O Lord, be not far off; O my Strength, come quickly to help me.

Commit your way to the Lord; trust in him and he will do this: He will make your righteousness shine like the dawn, the justice of your cause like the noonday sun. Be still before the Lord and wait patiently for him; do not fret when men succeed in their ways, when they carry out their wicked schemes.

If God is for us, who can be against us? He who did not spare his own Son, but gave him up for us all--how will he not also, along with him, graciously give us all things?

I pray that out of his glorious riches he may strengthen you with power through his Spirit in your inner being.

Matthew 26:40, 42-45. John 16:32. Psalm 22:10, 11, 19. Psalm 37:4-7. Romans 8:31, 32. Ephesians 3:16.

Watch and pray so that you will not fall into temptation. The spirit is willing, but the body is weak

Yes, Lord, walking in the way of your laws, we wait for you; your name and renown are the desire of our hearts. My soul yearns for you in the night; in the morning my spirit longs for you. When your judgments come upon the earth, the people of the world learn righteousness.

The sinful nature desires what is contrary to the Spirit, and the Spirit what is contrary to the sinful nature. They are in conflict with each other, so that you do not do what you want. I know that nothing good lives in me, that is, in my sinful nature. For I have the desire to do what is good, but I cannot carry it out. In my inner being I delight in God's law; but I see another law at work in the members of my body, waging war against the law of my mind and making me a prisoner of the law of sin at work within my members.

I can do everything through him who gives me strength. Our competence comes from God. He said to me, "My grace is sufficient for you, for my power is made perfect in weakness."

Matthew 26:41. Isaiah 26:8, 9. Galatians 5:17. Romans 7:18, 22, 23. Philippians 4:13. 2 Corinthians 3:5. 2 Corinthians 12:9.

Jesus told his disciples ... that they should always pray and not give up

I [Jesus] say to you: "Ask and it will be given to you; seek and you will find; knock and the door will be opened to you. For everyone who asks receives; he who seeks finds; and to him who knocks, the door will be opened. Which of you fathers, if your son asks for a fish, will give him a snake instead? Or if he asks for an egg, will give him a scorpion? If you then, though you are evil, know how to give good gifts to your children, how much more will your Father in heaven give the Holy Spirit to those who ask him!"

Do not be anxious about anything, but in everything, by prayer and petition, with thanksgiving, present your requests to God. And the peace of God, which transcends all understanding, will guard your hearts and your minds in Christ Jesus.

I want men everywhere to lift up holy hands in prayer, without anger or disputing. Let us then approach the throne of grace with confidence, so that we may receive mercy and find grace to help us in our time of need.

You hear, O Lord, the desire of the afflicted; you encourage them, and you listen to their cry.

Luke 18:1. Luke 11:9-13. Philippians 4:6, 7. 1 Timothy 2:8. Hebrews 4:16. Psalm 10:17.

Far be it from me that I should sin against the Lord by failing to pray for you

Abraham remained standing before the Lord. Then Abraham approached him and said: "Will you sweep away the righteous with the wicked? What if there are fifty righteous people in it? Far be it from you to do such a thing--to kill the righteous with the wicked, treating the righteous and the wicked alike. Far be it from you! Will not the Judge of all the earth do right?"

The Lord said, "If I find fifty righteous people in the city of Sodom, I will spare the whole place for their sake."

Then Abraham spoke up again: "What if the number of the righteous is five less than fifty? ...forty? ...thirty?...twenty? ...ten?" He answered, "For the sake of ten, I will not destroy it."

Moses said to Joshua, "Choose some of our men and go out to fight the Amalekites. Tomorrow, I will stand on top of the hill with the staff of God in my hands." As long as Moses held up his hands, the Israelites were winning, but whenever he lowered his hands, the Amalekites were winning. When Moses' hands grew tired, they took a stone and put it under him and he sat on it. Aaron and Hur held his hands up--one on one side, one on the other--so that his hands remained steady till sunset. So Joshua overcame the Amalekite army with the sword.

I have prayed for you, Simon, that your faith may not fail.

The eyes of the Lord are on the righteous and his ears are attentive to their cry.

Genesis 18:22-32. Exodus 17:9, 11-13. Luke 22:32. Psalm 34:15

Pray for each other

Samuel said, "Assemble all Israel at Mizpah and I will intercede with the Lord for you."

My servant Job will pray for you, and I will accept his prayer and not deal with you according to your folly. After Job had prayed for his friends, the Lord made him prosperous again and gave him twice as much as he had before.

Is any one of you sick? He should call the elders of the church to pray over him and anoint him with oil in the name of the Lord. And the prayer offered in faith will make the sick person well; the Lord will raise him up. If he has sinned, he will be forgiven. Therefore confess your sins to each other and pray for each other so that you may be healed. The prayer of a righteous man is powerful and effective.

Make every effort to do what leads to peace and to mutual edification. Nobody should seek his own good, but the good of others. Carry each other's burdens, and in this way you will fulfill the law of Christ.

I urge, then ... that requests, prayers, intercession and thanksgiving be made for everyone--for kings and all those in authority, that we may live peaceful and quiet lives in all godliness and holiness. This is good, and pleases God our Savior, who wants all men to be saved and to come to a knowledge of the truth.

James 5:16. 1 Samuel 7:5. Job 42:8, 10. James 5:14-16. Romans 14:19. 1 Corinthians 10:24. Galatians 6:2. 1 Timothy 2:1-4.

Keep on praying for all the saints

We always thank God, the Father of our Lord Jesus Christ, when we pray for you, because we have heard of your faith in Christ Jesus and of the love you have for all the saints. For this reason, since the day we heard about you, we have not stopped praying for you and asking God to fill you with the knowledge of his will through all spiritual wisdom and understanding.

I keep asking that the God of our Lord Jesus Christ, the glorious Father, may give you the Spirit of wisdom and revelation, so that you may know him better. I pray also that the eyes of your heart may be enlightened in order that you may know the hope to which he has called you, the riches of his glorious inheritance in the saints, and his incomparably great power for us who believe. That power is like the working of his mighty strength which he exerted in Christ when he raised him from the dead and seated him at his right hand in the heavenly realms, far above all rule and authority, power and dominion, and every title that can be given, not only in the present age but also in the one to come.

I pray that out of his glorious riches he may strengthen you with power through his Spirit in your inner being, so that Christ may dwell in your hearts through faith. And I pray that you, being rooted and established in love, may have power, together with all the saints, to grasp how wide and long and high and deep is the love of Christ, and to know this love that surpasses knowledge--that you may be filled to the measure of all the fullness of God.

Ephesians 6:18. Colossians 1:3, 4, 9. Ephesians 1:17-19. Ephesians 3:16-19.

Are you the king of the Jews?

"Yes, it is as you say," Jesus replied. "You are right in saying I am a king. In fact, for this reason I was born, and for this I came into the world, to testify to the truth. Everyone on the side of truth listens to me."

Who is this King of glory?

Great and marvelous are your deeds, Lord God Almighty. Just and true are your ways, King of the ages. Who will not fear you, O Lord, and bring glory to your name? For you alone are holy. All nations will come and worship before you, for your righteous acts have been revealed.

The Lord will be king over the whole earth. On that day there will be one Lord, and his name the only name. Of the increase of his government and peace there will be no end.

Worthy is the Lamb, who was slain, to receive power and wealth and wisdom and strength and honor and glory and praise! He must reign until he has put all his enemies under his feet. The last enemy to be destroyed is death.

Matthew 27:11. John 18:37. Psalm 24:8. Revelation 15:3, 4. Zechariah 14:9. Isaiah 9:7. Revelation 5:12. 1 Corinthians 15:25, 26.

Don't you hear how many things they are accusing you of?

Why does this fellow talk like that? He's blaspheming! Who can forgive sins but God alone?

It is only by Beelzebub, the prince of demons, that this fellow drives out demons.

The chief priests and the whole Sanhedrin were looking for false evidence against Jesus so that they could put him to death. But they did not find any, though many false witnesses came forward. Finally two came forward and declared, "This fellow said, I am able to destroy the temple of God and rebuild it in three days.'"

He has spoken blasphemy! Why do we need any more witnesses?

I endure scorn for your sake, and shame covers my face. I am a stranger to my brothers, an alien to my own mother's sons. Scorn has broken my heart and has left me helpless; I looked for sympathy, but there was none, for comforters, but I found none.

Now if we are children, then we are heirs--heirs of God and co-heirs with Christ, if indeed we share in his sufferings in order that we may also share in his glory.

I want to know Christ and the power of his resurrection and the fellowship of sharing in his sufferings, becoming like him in his death.

Matthew 27:13. Mark 2:7. Matthew 12:24. Matthew 26:59-61, 65.Psalm 69:7, 8, 20. Romans 8:17. Philippians 3:10.

Jesus made no reply,
not even to a single charge

Here is my servant whom I have chosen, the one I love, in whom I delight; I will put my Spirit on him, and he will proclaim justice to the nations. He will not quarrel or cry out; no one will hear his voice in the streets. A bruised reed he will not break, and a smoldering wick he will not snuff out, till he leads justice to victory. In his name the nations will put their hope.

He was oppressed and afflicted, yet he did not open his mouth; he was led like a lamb to the slaughter, and as a sheep before her shearers is silent, so he did not open his mouth.

"Put your sword back in its place," Jesus said to him, "for all who draw the sword will die by the sword. Do you think I cannot call on my Father, and he will at once put at my disposal more than twelve legions of angels?"

When they hurled their insults at him, he did not retaliate; when he suffered, he made no threats. Instead, he entrusted himself to him who judges justly. He himself bore our sins in his body on the tree, so that we might die to sins and live for righteousness; by his wounds you have been healed.

How is it to your credit if you receive a beating for doing wrong and endure it? But if you suffer for doing good and you endure it, this is commendable to God. To this you were called, because Christ suffered for you, leaving you an example, that you should follow in his steps. He committed no sin, and no deceit was found in his mouth.

Matthew 27:14. Matthew 12:18-21. Isaiah 53:7. Matthew 26:52, 53. 1 Peter 2:23, 24. 1 Peter 2:20-22.

What shall I do, then, with Jesus who is called Christ?

Simon Peter answered, "You are the Christ, the Son of the living God." Jesus replied, "Blessed are you, Simon son of Jonah, for this was not revealed to you by man, but by my Father in heaven."

Nathanael declared, "Rabbi, you are the Son of God; you are the King of Israel."

"Yes, Lord," she [Martha] told him, "I believe that you are the Christ, the Son of God, who was to come into the world."

Thomas said to him, "My Lord and my God!"

What about you? Who do you say I am?

How long will you waver between two opinions? If the Lord is God, follow him.

I set before you today life and prosperity, death and destruction. For I command you today to love the Lord your God, to walk in his ways, and to keep his commands, decrees and laws. Choose life, so that you and your children may live and that you may love the Lord your God, listen to his voice, and hold fast to him. For the Lord is your life. Choose for yourselves this day whom you will serve.

Trust in the Lord and do good; dwell in the land and enjoy safe pasture. Delight yourself in the Lord and he will give you the desires of your heart. Trust in the Lord forever, for the Lord, the Lord, is the Rock eternal.

Matthew 27:22. Matthew 16:16, 17. John 1:49. John 11:27. John 20:28. Matthew 16:15. 1 Kings 18:21. Deuteronomy 30:15, 16, 19, 20. Joshua 24:15. Psalm 37:3, 4. Isaiah 26:4.

Crucify him!

"Why? What crime has he committed?" asked Pilate. But they shouted all the louder, "Crucify him!

When Pilate saw that he has getting nowhere, but that instead an uproar was starting, he took water and washed his hands in front of the crowd. "I am innocent of this man's blood," he said. "It is your responsibility!" All the people answered, "Let his blood be on us and on our children!" Then he released Barabbas to them. But he had Jesus flogged, and handed him over to be crucified.

"This is my blood of the covenant, which is poured out for many," he said to them. He entered the Most Holy Place once for all by his own blood, having obtained eternal redemption. It is impossible for the blood of bulls and goats to take away sins.

It was not with perishable things such as silver or gold that you were redeemed from the empty way of life handed down to you from your forefathers, but with the precious blood of Christ, a lamb without blemish or defect.

I will sprinkle clean water on you, and you will be clean; I will cleanse you from all your impurities and from all your idols. I will give you a new heart and put a new spirit in you.

Let us draw near to God with a sincere heart in full assurance of faith, having our hearts sprinkled to cleanse us from a guilty conscience and having our bodies washed with pure water. Let us hold unswervingly to the hope we profess, for he who promised is faithful.

Matthew 27:22-26. Mark 14:24. Hebrews 9:12. Hebrews 10:4. 1 Peter 1:18, 19. Ezekiel 36:25, 26. Hebrews 10:22, 23.

Eloi, Eloi, lama sabachthani?

About the ninth hour Jesus cried out in a loud voice, "Eloi, Eloi, lama sabachthani?"--which means, "My God, my God, why have you forsaken me?"

Do not be far from me, for trouble is near and there is no one to help. How long, O Lord? Will you forget me forever? How long will you hide your face from me? How long must I wrestle with my thoughts and every day have sorrow in my heart? How long will my enemy triumph over me? Do not hide your face from me, do not turn your servant away in anger; you have been my helper. Do not reject me or forsake me, O God my Savior.

He will call upon me, and I will answer him; I will be with him in trouble, I will deliver him and honor him. The Lord is near to all who call on him, to all who call on him in truth. He fulfills the desires of those who fear him; he hears their cry and saves them.

God is our refuge and strength, an ever present help in trouble. Therefore we will not fear, though the earth give way and the mountains fall into the heart of the sea, though its waters roar and foam and the mountains quake with their surging.

Find rest, O my soul, in God alone; my hope comes from him. He alone is my rock and my salvation; he is my fortress, I will not be shaken.

Trust in him at all times, O people; pour out your hearts to him.

Matthew 27:46. Psalm 22:11. Psalm 13:1, 2. Psalm 27:9. Psalm 91:15. Psalm 145:18, 19. Psalm 46:1, 2. Psalm 62:5, 6, 8.

Jesus ... breathed his last

I have brought you glory on earth by completing the work you gave me to do. And now, Father, glorify me in your presence with the glory I had with you before the world began.

I will give him a portion among the great, and he will divide the spoils with the strong, because he poured out his life unto death, and was numbered with the transgressors. For he bore the sin of many, and made intercession for the transgressors.

The reason my Father loves me is that I lay down my life--only to take it up again. No one takes it from me, but I lay it down of my own accord. I have authority to lay it down and authority to take it up again.

By that will, we have been made holy through the sacrifice of the body of Jesus Christ once for all. Day after day every priest stands and performs his religious duties; again and again he offers the same sacrifices, which can never take away sins. But when this priest had offered for all time one sacrifice for sins, he sat down at the right hand of God. Since that time he waits for his enemies to be made his footstool, because by one sacrifice he has made perfect forever those who are being made holy.

Greater love has no one than this, that one lay down his life for his friends. Live a life of love, just as Christ loved us as a fragrant offering and sacrifice to God.

Mark 15:37. John 17:4. Isaiah 53:12. John 10:17, 18. Hebrews 10:10-14. John 15:13. Ephesians 5:2.

Go, make the tomb as secure as you know how

So they went and made the tomb secure by putting a seal on the stone and posting the guard.

Do not fight against the Lord, the God of your fathers, for you will not succeed. O Lord, you are our God; do not let man prevail against you.

Why do the nations rage and the peoples plot in vain? The kings of the earth take their stand and the rulers gather together against the Lord and against his Anointed One.

With God we will gain the victory, and he will trample down our enemies.

In my anguish I cried to the Lord, and he answered by setting me free. The Lord is with me; I will not be afraid. What can man do to me? The Lord is with me; he is my helper. I will look in triumph on my enemies.

It is better to take refuge in the Lord than to trust in man. It is better to take refuge in the Lord than to trust in princes.

All the nations surrounded me, but in the name of the Lord I cut them off. They surrounded me on every side, but in the name of the Lord I cut them off. They swarmed around me like bees, but they died out as quickly as burning thorns; in the name of the Lord I cut them off.

I will not die but live, and will proclaim what the Lord has done.

Matthew 27:65, 66. 2 Chronicles 13:12. 2 Chronicles 14:11. Psalm 2:1, 2. Psalm 108:13. Psalm 118:5-12, 17.

An angel of the Lord rolled back the stone

I will ransom them from the power of the grave; I will redeem them from death. Where, O death, are your plagues? Where, O grave, is your destruction? The last enemy to be destroyed is death.

God will redeem my soul from the grave; he will surely take me to himself. I waited patiently for the Lord; he turned to me and heard my cry. He lifted me out of the slimy pit, out of the mud and mire; he set my feet on a rock and gave me a firm place to stand. He put a new song in my mouth, a hymn of praise to our God. Many will see and fear and put their trust in the Lord.

When the perishable has been clothed with the imperishable, and the mortal with immortality, then the saying that is written will come true: "Death has been swallowed up in victory."

Thanks be to God! He gives us the victory through our Lord Jesus Christ. Therefore, my dear brothers, stand firm. Let nothing move you. Always give yourselves fully to the work of the Lord, because you know that your labor in the Lord is not in vain.

Your dead will live; their bodies will rise. You who dwell in the dust, wake up and shout for joy. Your dew is like the dew of the morning; the earth will give birth to her dead.

Matthew 28:2. Hosea 13:14. 1 Corinthians 15:26. Psalm 49:15. Psalm 40:1-3. 1 Corinthians 15:54, 57, 58. Isaiah 26:19.

I know that you are looking for Jesus

Do not be afraid.

Why are you downcast, O my soul? Why so disturbed within me? Put your hope in God, for I will yet praise him, my Savior and my God. I say to God my Rock, "Why have you forgotten me? Why must I go about mourning, oppressed by the enemy? My bones suffer mortal agony as my foes taunt me, saying to me all day long, "Where is your God?"

If ... you seek the Lord your God, you will find him if you look for him with all your heart and with all your soul. The Lord is with you when you are with him. If you seek him, he will be found by you, but if you forsake him, he will forsake you. They who seek the Lord will praise him.

In righteousness I will see your face; when I awake, I will be satisfied with seeing your likeness.

I consider everything a loss compared to the surpassing greatness of knowing Christ Jesus my Lord ... that I may gain Christ and be found in him not having a righteousness of my own that comes from the law, but that which is through faith in Christ--the righteousness that comes from God and is by faith.

Matthew 28:5. Psalm 42:5, 9, 10. Deuteronomy 4:29. 2 Chronicles 15:2. Psalm 22:26. Psalm 17:15. Philippians 3:8, 9.

He has risen from the dead

I am the resurrection and the life. He who believes in me will live, even though he dies; and whoever lives and believes in me will never die.

My heart is glad and my tongue rejoices; my body also will rest secure, because you will not abandon me to the grave, nor will you let your Holy One see decay.

We see Jesus, who was made a little lower than the angels, now crowned with glory and honor because he suffered death, so that by the grace of God he might taste death for everyone. But God raised him from the dead, freeing him from the agony of death, because it was impossible for death to keep its hold on him.

He will endure as long as the sun, as long as the moon, through all generations. He will be like rain falling on a mown field, like showers watering the earth. In his days the righteous will flourish; prosperity will abound till the moon is no more. He will rule from sea to sea and from the River to the ends of the earth.

I pray ... that the eyes of your heart may be enlightened in order that you may know the hope to which he has called you, the riches of his glorious inheritance in the saints, and his incomparably great power for us who believe. That power is like the working of his mighty strength, which he exerted in Christ when he raised him from the dead and seated him at his right hand in the heavenly realms, far above all rule and authority, power and dominion, and every title that can be given, not only in the present age but also in the one to come. And God placed all things under his feet and appointed him to be head over everything....

Matthew 28:7. John 11:25. Psalm 16:9, 10. Hebrews 2:9. Acts 2:24. Psalm 72:5-8. Ephesians 1:18-23.

Go quickly ... tell his disciples

He has risen from the dead and is going ahead of you into Galilee. There you will see him.

Weeping may remain for a night, but rejoicing comes in the morning. You turned my wailing into dancing; you removed my sackcloth and clothed me with joy, that my heart may sing to you and not be silent. O Lord my God, I will give you thanks forever.

Yes, Lord, walking in the way of your laws, we wait for you; your name and renown are the desire of our hearts. My soul yearns for you in the night; in the morning my spirit longs for you. When your judgments come upon the earth, the people of the world learn righteousness.

I will not leave you as orphans; I will come to you. Before long, the world will not see me anymore, but you will see me. Because I live, you also will live. On that day you will realize that I am in my Father, and you are in me, and I am in you.

If you confess with your mouth, "Jesus is Lord," and believe in your heart that God raised him from the dead, you will be saved. For it is with your heart that you believe and are justified, and it is with your mouth that you confess and are saved. As the Scripture says, "Everyone who trusts in him will never be put to shame."

You will be secure, because there is hope; you will look around you and take your rest in safety.

Matthew 28:7. Psalm 30:5, 11, 12. Isaiah 26:8, 9. John 14:18-20. Romans 10:9-11. Job 11:18.

Afraid yet filled with joy

The women hurried away from the tomb, afraid yet filled with joy, and ran to tell his disciples.

God did not give us a spirit of timidity, but a spirit of power, of love and of self-discipline. He was crucified in weakness, yet he lives by God's power. Likewise, we are weak in him, yet by God's power we will live with him to serve you.

Do not be afraid. I am the First and the Last. I am the Living One; I was dead, and behold I am alive for ever and ever! And I hold the keys of death and Hades.

You will keep in perfect peace him whose mind is steadfast, because he trusts in you. Trust in the Lord forever, for the Lord, the Lord, is the Rock eternal.

Peace I leave with you; my peace I give you. I do not give to you as the world gives. Do not let your hearts be troubled and do not be afraid. In this world you will have trouble. But take heart! I have overcome the world. And the peace of God, which transcends all understanding, will guard your hearts and your minds in Christ Jesus.

Jesus Christ ... the firstborn from the dead, and the ruler of the kings of the earth. To him who loves us and has freed us from our sins by his blood, and has made us to be a kingdom and priests to serve his God and Father--to him be glory and power forever and ever! Amen.

Matthew 28:8. 2 Timothy 1:7. 2 Corinthians 13:4. Revelation 1:17, 18. Isaiah 26:3, 4. John 14:27. John 16:33. Philippians 4:7.Revelation 1:5, 6.

Jesus met them

"Greetings," he said. They came to him, clasped his feet and worshiped him. Then Jesus said to them, "Do not be afraid. Go and tell my brothers to go to Galilee."

On the evening of that first day of the week, when the disciples were together, with the doors locked for fear of the Jews, Jesus came and stood among them and said, "Peace be with you." After he said this, he showed them his hands and side. The disciples were overjoyed when they saw the Lord. Again Jesus said, "Peace be with you! As the Father has sent me, I am sending you." And with that he breathed on them and said, "Receive the Holy Spirit."

The Counselor, the Holy Spirit, whom the Father will send in my name, will teach you all things and will remind you of everything I have said to you. Peace I leave with you; my peace I give you. I do not give to you as the world gives. Do not let your hearts be troubled and do not be afraid.

You heard me say, "I am going away and I am coming back to you." If you loved me, you would be glad that I am going to the Father, for the Father is greater than I. I have told you now before it happens, so that when it does happen you will believe.

From now on, the Son of Man will be seated at the right hand of the mighty God. ...With angels, authorities and powers in submission to him. In a loud voice they sang: "Worthy is the Lamb, who was slain, to receive power and wealth and wisdom and strength and honor and glory and praise!"

King of kings and Lord of lords.

———————

Matthew 28:9, 10. John 20:19-22. John 14:26-29. Luke 22:69. 1 Peter 3:22. Revelation 5:12. Revelation 19:16.

No one can serve two masters

Either he will hate the one and love the other, or he will be devoted to the one and despise the other. You cannot serve both God and Money.

The grace of God that brings salvation has appeared to all men. It teaches us to say "No" to ungodliness and worldly passions, and to live self-controlled, upright and godly lives in this present age. What good will it be for a man if he gains the whole world, yet forfeits his soul?

Jehu was not careful to keep the law of the Lord, the God of Israel, with all his heart. The high places ... were not removed, and the people still had not set their hearts on the God of their fathers. He [Amaziah] did what was right in the eyes of the Lord, but not whole-heartedly. He who is not with me is against me, and he who does not gather with me scatters.

Come near to God and he will come near to you. Wash your hands, you sinners, and purify your hearts, you double-minded. No one who puts his hand to the plow and looks back is fit for service in the kingdom of God.

Worship the Lord your God, and serve him only. What does the Lord your God ask of you but to fear the Lord your God, to walk in all his ways, to love him, to serve the Lord your God with all your heart and with all your soul? Serve wholeheartedly, as if you were serving the Lord, not men, because you know that the Lord will reward everyone for whatever good he does.

Matthew 6:24. Titus 2:11, 12. Matthew 16:26. 2 Kings 10:31. 2 Chronicles 20:33. 2 Chronicles 25:2. Matthew 12:30. James 4:8. Luke 9:62. Matthew 4:10. Deuteronomy 10:12. Ephesians 6:7, 8.

Do not worry about your life

Do not worry what you will eat or drink; or about your body, what you will wear. Is not life more important than food, and the body more important than clothes? Look at the birds of the air; they do not sow or reap or store away in barns, and yet your heavenly Father feeds them. Are you not much more valuable than they? So do not worry, saying, "What shall we eat?" or "What shall we drink?" or "What shall we wear?"

In vain you rise early and stay up late, toiling for food to eat--for he grants sleep to those he loves.

"Martha, Martha," the Lord answered, "you are worried and upset about many things." Cast all your anxiety on him because he cares for you. Do not be anxious about anything, but in everything, by prayer and petition, with thanksgiving, present your requests to God. And the peace of God, which transcends all understanding, will guard your hearts and your minds in Christ Jesus.

Godliness with contentment is great gain. I have learned to be content whatever the circumstances. I know what it is to be in need, and I know what it is to have plenty. I have learned the secret of being content in any and every situation, whether well fed or hungry, whether living in plenty or in want. I can do everything through him who gives me strength.

Be content with what you have. My God will meet all your needs according to his glorious riches in Christ Jesus.

Matthew 6:25, 26, 31. Psalm 127:2. Luke 10:41. 1 Peter 5:7. Philippians 4:6, 7. 1 Timothy 6:6. Philippians 4:11-13. Hebrews 13:5. Philippians 4:19.

Your heavenly Father knows

The Lord said, "I have indeed seen the misery of my people of Egypt. I have heard them crying out because of their slave drivers, and I am concerned about their suffering. As a father has compassion on his children, so the Lord has compassion on those who fear him; for he knows how we are formed, he remembers that we are dust.

To God belongs wisdom and power; counsel and understanding are his. All my longings lie open before you, O Lord; my sighing is not hidden from you. Does he not see my ways and count my every step? He will not let your foot slip--he who watches over you will not slumber; indeed, he who watches over Israel will neither slumber nor sleep.

Your Father knows what you need before you ask him. Oh, the depths of the riches of the wisdom and knowledge of God! How unsearchable his judgments, and his paths beyond tracing out! Who should not revere you, O King of the nations?

Matthew 6:32. Exodus 3:7. Psalm 103:13, 14. Job 12:13. Psalm 38:9. Job 31:4. Psalm 121:3, 4. Matthew 6:8. Romans 11:33. Jeremiah 10:7.

Seek first his [God's] kingdom and his righteousness

And all these things will be given to you as well.

"Bring the whole tithe into the storehouse, that there may be food in my house. Test me in this," says the Lord Almighty, "and see if I will not throw open the floodgates of heaven and pour out so much blessing that you will not have room enough for it." With honey from the rock I would satisfy you. A faithful man will be richly blessed.

You have ... set my feet in a spacious place. Those who seek the Lord lack no good thing. Though he stumble, he will not fall, for the Lord upholds him with his hand. His feet do not slip. He set my feet on a rock and gave me a firm place to stand. He put a new song in my mouth, a hymn of praise to our God. Wait for the Lord and keep his way. He will exalt you to possess the land. May your love and your truth always protect me. For this God is our God for ever and ever; he will be our guide even to the end.

Matthew 6:33. Malachi 3:10. Psalm 81:16. Proverbs 28:20. Psalm 31:8. Psalm 34:10. Psalm 37:24, 31. Psalm 40:2, 3. Psalm 37:34. Psalm 40:11. Psalm 48:14.

All authority in heaven and earth has been given to me

The crowds were amazed at his teaching, because he taught as one who had authority, and not as their teachers of the law. The people were all so amazed that they asked each other, "What is this? A new teaching--and with authority! He even gives orders to evil spirits and they obey him." The men were amazed and asked, "What kind of man is this? Even the winds and the waves obey him!" No one takes it [my life] from me, but I lay it down of my own accord. I have authority to lay it down and authority to take it up again.

He will be called Wonderful Counselor, Mighty God, Everlasting Father, Prince of Peace. He was given authority, glory and sovereign power; all peoples, nations and men of every language worshiped him. His dominion is an everlasting dominion that will not pass away, and his kingdom is one that will never be destroyed.

Gird your sword upon your side, O mighty one; clothe yourself with splendor and majesty. "I am the Alpha and the Omega," says the Lord God, "who is, and who was, and who is to come, the Almighty." God, the blessed and only Ruler, the King of kings and Lord of lords, who alone is immortal and who lives in unapproachable light, whom no one has seen or can see. To him be honor and might forever. Amen.

Matthew 28:18. Matthew 7:28, 29. Mark 1:27. Matthew 8:27. John 10:18. Isaiah 9:6, 7. Daniel 7:14. Psalm 45:3. Revelation 1:8. 1 Timothy 6:16.

Go and make disciples of all nations

Baptizing them in the name of the Father and of the Son and of the Holy Spirit, and teaching them to obey everything I have commanded you.

All the ends of the earth will remember and turn to the Lord, and all the families of the nations will bow down before him, for dominion belongs to the Lord and he rules over the nations. It is written: "'As surely as I live,' says the Lord, 'Every knee will bow before me; every tongue will confess to God.'"

In the presence of God and of Christ Jesus, who will judge the living and the dead, and in view of his appearing and his kingdom, I give you this charge: Preach the Word; be prepared in season and out of season; correct, rebuke and encourage--with great patience and careful instruction. For the time will come when men will not put up with sound doctrine. Instead, to suit their own desires, they will gather around them a great number of teachers to say what their itching ears want to hear. They will turn their ears away from the truth and turn aside to myths. But you, keep your head in all situations, endure hardship, do the work of an evangelist, discharge all the duties of your ministry.

All Scripture is God-breathed and is useful for teaching, rebuking, correcting and training in righteousness, so that the man of God may be thoroughly equipped for every good work.

The Sovereign Lord has given me an instructed tongue, to know the word that sustains the weary.

Matthew 28:19, 20. Psalm 22:27, 28. Romans 14:11. 2 Timothy 4:1-5. 2 Timothy 3:16. Isaiah 50:4.

I will be with you always, to the very end of the age

The Lord is God in heaven above and on the earth below. I am with you and will watch over you wherever you go. My Presence will go with you, and I will give you rest.

When you pass through the waters, I will be with you; and when you pass through the rivers, I will be with you; and when you pass through the fire, you will not be burned; the flames will not set you ablaze.

There is no one like the God of Jeshurun, who rides on the heavens to help you and on the clouds in his majesty. The eternal God is your refuge, and underneath are the everlasting arms. As the mountains surround Jerusalem, so the Lord surrounds his people both now and forevermore. I have set the Lord always before me. Because he is at my right hand, I will not be shaken.

Keep me as the apple of your eye; hide me in the shadow of your wings. He will cover you with his feathers, and under his wings you will find refuge; his faithfulness will be your shield and rampart.

If I go up to the heavens, you are there; if I make my bed in the depths, you are there. If I rise on the wings of the dawn, if I settle on the far side of the sea, even there your hand will guide me, your right hand will hold me fast.

Who shall separate us from the love of Christ?

Matthew 28:20. Deuteronomy 4:39. Genesis 28:15. Exodus 33:14.Isaiah 43:2. Deuteronomy 33:26, 27. Psalm 125:1, 2. Psalm 16:8. Psalm 17:8. Psalm 91:4. Psalm 139:8-10. Romans 8:35.

God ... has spoken to us by his Son

I will proclaim the decree of the Lord: He said to me, "You are my Son; today I have become your Father."

I am the way and the truth and the life. No one comes to the Father except through me. If you really knew me, you would know my Father as well. The words I say to you are not just my own. Rather, it is the Father, living in me, who is doing his work.

The Spirit of the Lord will rest on him--the Spirit of wisdom and of understanding, the Spirit of counsel and of power, the Spirit of knowledge and of the fear of the Lord--and he will delight in the fear of the Lord.

He will not judge by what he sees with his eyes, or decide by what he hears with his ears; but with righteousness he will judge the needy, with justice he will give decisions for the poor of the earth. He will strike the earth with the rod of his mouth; with the breath of his lips he will slay the wicked. Righteousness will be his belt and faithfulness the sash around his waist.

All this ... comes from the Lord Almighty, wonderful in counsel and magnificent in wisdom.

Hebrews 1:1, 2. Psalm 2:7. John 14:6, 7, 10. Isaiah 11:2-5. Isaiah 28:29.

His Son ... heir of all things

Ask of me, and I will make the nations your inheritance, the ends of the earth your possession.

He will rule from sea to sea and from the River to the ends of the earth. The desert tribes will bow before him and his enemies will lick the dust. The kings of Tarshish and of distant shores will bring tribute to him; the kings of Sheba and Seba will present him gifts. All kings will bow down to him and all nations will serve him.

He is the head of the body, the church; he is the beginning and the firstborn from among the dead, so that in everything he might have the supremacy. God exalted him to the highest place and gave him the name that is above every name, that at the name of Jesus every knee should bow, in heaven and on earth and under the earth, and every tongue confess that Jesus Christ is Lord, to the glory of God the Father. Jesus Christ, who has gone into heaven and is at God's right hand--with angels, authorities and powers in submission to him.

I heard every creature in heaven and on earth and under the earth and on the sea, and all that is in them, singing: "To him who sits on the throne and to the Lamb be praise and honor and glory and power for ever and ever!"

We are heirs--heirs of God and co-heirs with Christ, if indeed we share in his sufferings in order that we may also share in his glory.

Hebrews 1:2. Psalm 2:8. Psalm 72:8-11. Colossians 1:8. Philippians 2:9-11. 1 Peter 3:21, 22. Revelation 5:13. Romans 8:17.

His Son ... through whom he made the universe

Through him all things were made; without him nothing was made that has been made. By him all things were created; things in heaven and on earth, visible and invisible, whether thrones or powers or rulers or authorities; all things were created by him and for him. He is before all things, and in him all things hold together.

You made the heavens, even the highest heavens, and all their starry host, the earth and all that is on it, the seas and all that is in them. You give life to everything, and the multitudes of heaven worship you.

You care for the land and water it; you enrich it abundantly.The streams of God are filled with water to provide the people with grain, for so you have ordained it. You drench its furrows and level its ridges; you soften it with showers and bless its crops. You crown the year with your bounty, and your carts overflow with abundance. The grasslands of the desert overflow; the hills are clothed with gladness. The meadows are covered with flocks and the valleys are mantled with grain; they shout for joy and sing.

There is but one God, the Father, from whom all things came and for whom we live; and there is but one Lord, Jesus Christ, through whom all things came and through whom we live.

Hebrews 1:2. John 1:3. Colossians 1:16, 17. Nehemiah 9:6. Psalm 65:9-13. 1 Corinthians 8:6.

The Son ... the radiance of God's glory

In him was life, and that life was the light of men. The light shines in the darkness, but the darkness has not understood it.

I am the light of the world. Whoever follows me will never walk in darkness, but will have the light of life. For God, who said, "Let light shine out of darkness," made his light shine in our hearts to give us the light of the knowledge of the glory of God in the face of Christ.

We have seen his glory, the glory of the one and only Son, who came from the Father, full of grace and truth.

Father, I want those you have given me to be with me where I am, and to see my glory, the glory you have given me because you loved me before the creation of the world.

Then I saw a new heaven and a new earth, for the first heaven and the first earth had passed away, and there was no longer any sea. I saw the Holy City, the new Jerusalem, coming down out of heaven from God, prepared as a bride beautifully dressed for her husband. And I heard a loud voice from the throne saying, "Now the dwelling of God is with men, and he will live with them. They will be his people, and God himself will be with them and be their God. The city does not need the sun or the moon to shine on it, for the glory of God gives it light, and the Lamb is its lamp.

Hebrews 1:2. John 1:4, 5. John 8:12. 2 Corinthians 4:6. John 1:14. John 17:24. Revelation 21:1-3, 23.

The Son is ... the exact representation of his being

In Christ all the fullness of the Deity lives in bodily form. Beyond all question, the mystery of godliness is great: He appeared in a body, was vindicated by the Spirit, was seen by angels, was preached among the nations, was believed on in the world, was taken up in glory.

In the beginning was the Word, and the Word was with God, and the Word was God. He was with God in the beginning. From the fullness of his grace we have all received one blessing after another.

Jesus ... looked toward heaven and prayed: "Everything you have given me comes from you. All I have is yours, and all you have is mine. I have revealed you to those whom you gave me out of the world. I have given them the glory that you gave me, that they may be one as we are one. I in them and you in me. May they be brought to complete unity to let the world know that you sent me and have loved them even as you have loved me."

For the one whom God has sent speaks the words of God; to him God gives the Spirit without limit. The Father loves the Son and has placed everything in his hands. Whoever believes in the Son has eternal life, but whoever rejects the Son will not see life, for God's wrath remains on him.

And this is how we know that he lives in us: We know it by the Spirit he gave us.

Hebrews 1:3. Colossians 2:9. 1 Timothy 3:16. John 1:1, 2, 16.John 17:1, 7, 10, 6, 22, 23. John 3:34-36. 1 John 3:24.

The Son ... sustaining all things by his powerful word

About the Son he [God] says, "Your throne, O God, will last for ever and ever, and righteousness will be the scepter of your kingdom. You have loved righteousness and hated wickedness; therefore, God, your God, has set you above your companions by anointing you with the oil of joy."

He also says, "In the beginning, O Lord, you laid the foundations of the earth, and the heavens are the work of your hands. They will perish, but you remain; they will all wear out like a garment. You will roll them up like a robe; like a garment they will be changed. But you remain the same, and your years will never end."

The Lord remembers us and will bless us. Indeed, the very hairs of your head are all numbered.

The Lord is my strength and my shield; my heart trusts in him, and I am helped. My heart leaps for joy and I will give thanks to him in song. Yet I am poor and needy; may the Lord think of me. You are my help and my deliverer; O my God, do not delay.

I took you from the ends of the earth, from its farthest corners I called you. I said, "You are my servant;" I have chosen you and have not rejected you. So do not fear, for I am with you; do not be dismayed, for I am your God. I will strengthen you and help you; I will uphold you with my righteous right hand.

Even to your old age and gray hairs I am he, I am he who will sustain you. I have made you and I will carry you; I will sustain you and I will rescue you.

Hebrews 1:3. Hebrews 1:8-12. Psalm 115:12. Luke 12:7. Psalm 28:7. Psalm 40:17. Isaiah 41:9, 10. Isaiah 46:4.

The Son ... superior to the angels

He became as much superior to the angels as the name he has inherited is superior to theirs.

For to which of the angels did God ever say, "You are my Son; today I have become your Father?" Or again, "I will be his Father, and he will be my Son?" And again, when God brings his firstborn into the world, he says, "Let all God's angels worship him." To which of the angels did God ever say, "Sit at my right hand until I make your enemies a footstool...?"

Are not all angels ministering spirits sent to serve those who will inherit salvation?

I looked and heard the voice of many angels, numbering thousands upon thousands, and ten thousand times ten thousand. They encircled the throne and the living creatures and the elders. In a loud voice they sang: "Worthy is the Lamb, who was slain, to receive power and wealth and wisdom and strength and honor and glory and praise!"

After this I looked and there before me was a great multitude that no one could count, from every nation, tribe, people and language, standing before the throne and in front of the Lamb. They were wearing white robes and were holding palm branches in their hands. And they cried out in a loud voice: "Salvation belongs to our God, who sits on the throne, and to the Lamb." All the angels were standing around the throne and around the elders and the four living creatures. They fell down on their faces before the throne and worshiped God, saying: "Amen! Praise and glory and wisdom and thanks and honor and power and strength be to our God for ever and ever. Amen!"

Hebrews 1:3-7, 13, 14. Revelation 5:11, 12. Revelation 7:9-12. Luke 22:69.

Encourage one another daily ...
so that none of you may be hardened
by sin's deceit.

At one time we too were foolish, disobedient, deceived and enslaved by all kinds of passions and pleasures. We lived in malice and envy, being hated and hating one another. There is a way that seems right to a man, but in the end it leads to death.

When tempted, no one should say, "God is tempting me." For God cannot be tempted by evil nor does he tempt anyone; but each one is tempted when, by his own evil desire, he is dragged away and enticed. Then, after desire has conceived, it gives birth to sin; and sin, when it is full-grown, gives birth to death.

Brothers, if someone is caught in a sin, you who are spiritual should restore him gently. But watch yourself, or you also may be tempted. Carry each other's burdens, and in this way you will fulfill the law of Christ. We who are strong ought to bear with the failings of the weak and not to please ourselves.

Judas and Silas, who themselves were prophets, said much to encourage and strengthen the brothers.

Encourage one another and build each other up. Warn those who are idle, encourage the timid, help the weak, be patient with everyone. His divine power has given us everything we need for life and godliness through our knowledge of him.

Hebrews 3:13. Titus 3:3. Proverbs 14:12. James 1:13-15. Galatians 6:1, 2. Romans 15:1. Acts 15:32. 1 Thessalonians 5:11, 14. 2 Peter 1:3.

We have come to share in Christ
if we hold firmly till the end
the confidence we had at first

When the kindness and love of God our Savior appeared, he saved us, not because of righteous things we had done, but because of his mercy. He saved us through the washing of rebirth and renewal by the Holy Spirit whom he poured out on us generously through Jesus Christ our Savior, so that, having been justified by his grace, we might become heirs having the hope of eternal life. This is a trustworthy saying. And I want you to stress these things, so that those who have trusted in God may be careful to devote themselves to doing what is good. These things are excellent and profitable for everyone.

If we are children, then we are heirs--heirs of God and co-heirs with Christ, if indeed we share in his sufferings in order that we may also share in his glory. I consider that our present sufferings are not worth comparing with the glory that will be revealed in us.

If God is for us, who can be against us? He who did not spare his own Son, but gave him up for us all--how will he not alsograciously give us all things?

Who then is the faithful and wise servant, whom the master has put in charge of the servants in his household to give them their food at the proper time? It will be good for that servant whose master finds him doing so when he returns. I tell you the truth, he will put him in charge of all his possessions.

To him who overcomes, I will give the right to sit with me on my throne.

Hebrews 3:14. Titus 3:4-8. Romans 8:17, 18, 31, 32. Matthew 24:45-47. Revelation 3:21.

Since the promise of entering his rest still stands, let us be careful that none of you be found to have fallen short of it

Be at rest once more, O my soul, for the Lord has been good to you. Lord, you have assigned me my portion and my cup; you have made my lot secure. The boundary lines have fallen for me in pleasant places; surely I have a delightful inheritance.

Trust in the Lord and do good; dwell in the land and enjoy safe pasture. Delight yourself in the Lord and he will give you the desires of your heart. He will make your righteousness shine like the dawn, the justice of your cause like the noonday sun. Be still before the Lord and wait patiently for him; do not fret when men succeed in their ways, when they carry out their wicked schemes.

Take my yoke upon you and learn from me, for I am gentle and humble in heart, and you will find rest for your souls.

The fruit of the Spirit is love, joy, peace, kindness, goodness, faithfulness, gentleness and self-control. The fruit of righteousness will be peace; the effect of righteousness will be quietness and confidence forever.

Be still, and know that I am God; I will be exalted among the nations, I will be exalted in the earth.

Hebrews 4:1. Psalm 116:7. Psalm 16:5, 6. Psalm 37:3, 4, 6, 7. Matthew 11:29. Galatians 5:22, 23. Isaiah 32:17.

April 21

There remains, then, a Sabbath-rest
for the people of God.

Let us, therefore, make every effort to enter that rest.
Make every effort to enter through the narrow door,
because many, I tell you, will try to enter and will not
be able to.

There the wicked cease from turmoil, and there the
weary are at rest. Captives also enjoy their ease; they
no longer hear the slave driver's shout. The small and
the great are there, and the slave is freed from his
master. Blessed are the dead who die in the Lord ... they
will rest from their labor, for their deeds will follow
them. Meanwhile, we groan, longing to be clothed with
our heavenly dwelling. It is God who has made us for
this very purpose and has given us the Spirit as a
deposit, guaranteeing what is to come.

Ask where the good way is, and walk in it, and you
will find rest for your souls. Find rest, O my soul, in
God alone; my hope comes from him. He alone is my
rock and my salvation; he is my fortress, I will not be
shaken. My salvation and my honor depend on God; he
is my mighty rock, my refuge. Trust in him at all times,
O people; pour out your hearts to him, for God is our
refuge.

Wait for the Lord; be strong and take heart and wait
for the Lord.

*Hebrews 4:9, 11. Luke 13:24. Job 3:17-19. Revelation 14:13. 2 Corinthians
5:2, 5. Jeremiah 6:16. Psalm 62:5-8. Psalm 27:14.*

The word of God is living and active

O land, land, land, hear the word of the Lord!

Sharper than any double-edged sword, it penetrates even to dividing soul and spirit, joints and marrow. The sword of the Spirit, which is the word of God.

"Is not my word like fire," declares the Lord, "and like a hammer that breaks a rock in pieces?"

Everyone who hears these words of mine and puts them into practice is like a wise man who built his house on the rock. The rain came down, the streams rose, and the winds blew and beat against that house; yet it did not fall, because it had its foundations on the rock.

All Scripture is God-breathed and is useful for teaching, rebuking, correcting and training in righteousness, so that the man of God may be thoroughly equipped for every good work.

What does the Lord require of you? To act justly and to love mercy and to walk humbly with your God.

Speak, Lord, for your servant is listening.

Hebrews 4:12. Jeremiah 22:29. Hebrews 4:12. Ephesians 6:17. Jeremiah 23:29. Matthew 7:24, 25. 2 Timothy 3:16, 17. Micah 6:8. 1 Samuel 3:9.

The word of God judges the thoughts and attitudes of the heart

If anyone teaches false doctrines and does not agree to the sound instruction of our Lord Jesus Christ and to godly teaching, he is conceited and understands nothing. He has an unhealthy interest in controversies and arguments that result in envy, quarreling, malicious talk, evil suspicions and constant friction between men of corrupt mind, who have been robbed of the truth and who think that godliness is a means to financial gain.

Be strong in the grace that is in Christ Jesus. Here is a trustworthy saying: If we died with him, we will also live with him; if we endure, we will also reign with him. If we disown him, he will also disown us; if we are faithless, he will remain faithful, for he cannot disown himself.

Keep reminding them of these things. Warn them before God against quarreling about words, it is of no value, and only ruins those who listen. Do your best to present yourself to God as one approved, a workman who does not need to be ashamed and who correctly handles the word of truth.

The Spirit gives life; the flesh counts for nothing. The words I have spoken to you are spirit and they are life. If a man keeps my word, he will never see death.

Your word, O Lord, is eternal; it stands firm in the heavens.

Hebrews 4:12. 1 Timothy 6:3-5. 2 Timothy 2:1, 11-15. John 6:63. John 8:51. Psalm 119:89.

Nothing in all creation is hidden from God's sight

Everything is uncovered and laid bare before the eyes of him to whom we must give account.

O Lord, you have searched me and you know me. You know when I sit and when I rise; you perceive my thoughts from afar. You discern my going out and my lying down; you are familiar with all my ways. Even the darkness will not be dark to you; the night will shine like the day, for darkness is as light to you.

He reveals deep and hidden things; he knows what lies in darkness, and light dwells with him. "Can anyone hide in secret places so that I cannot see him?" declares the Lord. "Do not I fill heaven and earth?" declares the Lord.

Before a word is on my tongue you know it completely, O Lord. The eyes of the Lord are everywhere, keeping watch on the wicked and the good.

But because of his great love for us, God, who is rich in mercy, made us alive with Christ even when we were dead in transgressions--it is by grace you have been saved. And God raised us up with Christ and seated us with him in the heavenly realms in Christ Jesus, in order that in the coming ages he might show the incomparable riches of his grace, expressed in his kindness to us in Christ Jesus.

Hebrews 4:13. Psalm 139:1-3, 12. Daniel 2:22. Jeremiah 23:24.Psalm 139:4. Proverbs 15:3. Ephesians 2:4-7.

Jesus ... a high priest forever, in the order of Melchizedek

This Melchizedek was king of Salem and priest of God Most High. He met Abraham returning from the defeat of the kings and blessed him, and Abraham gave him a tenth of everything. First, his name means "king of righteousness"; then also, "king of peace." Without father or mother, without genealogy, without beginning of days or end of life, like the Son of God he remains a priest forever. Just think how great he was.

God exalted him [Jesus] to the highest place and gave him the name that is above every name. This is the name by which he will be called: The Lord Our Righteousness. For you who revere my name, the sun of righteousness will rise with healing in its wings. And you will go out and leap like calves released from the stall.

Prince of Peace. He himself is our peace. Lord, you establish peace for us; all that we have accomplished you have done for us. Whom have I in heaven but you? And being with you, I desire nothing on earth. My flesh and my heart may fail, but God is the strength of my heart and my portion forever.

We do have a high priest, who sat down at the right hand of the throne of the Majesty in heaven. The First and the Last, the Beginning and the End. From him and through him and to him are all things. To him be the glory forever! Amen.

Hebrews 6:20. Hebrews 7:1-4. Philippians 2:9. Jeremiah 23:6. Malachi 4:2. Isaiah 9:6. Ephesians 2:14. Isaiah 26:12. Psalm 73:25, 26. Hebrews 8:1. Revelation 22:13. Romans 11:36.

Such a high priest meets our need

Such a high priest meets our need--one who is holy, blameless, pure, set apart from sinners, exalted above the heavens.

One who is holy. Righteousness will be his belt and faithfulness the sash around his waist. God made him who had no sin to be sin for us, so that in him we might become the righteousness of God. Him who is holy and true, who holds the key of David.

One who is ... blameless. He had done no violence, nor was any deceit in his mouth. This man has done nothing wrong.

One who is .... pure. The blood of goats and bulls and the ashes of a heifer sprinkled on those who are ceremonially unclean sanctify them so that they are outwardly clean. How much more, then will the blood of Christ, who through the eternal Spirit offered himself unblemished to God, cleanse our consciences from acts that lead to death, so that we may serve the living God! A lamb without blemish or defect.

One who is ... set apart from sinners. Christ Jesus ... has become for us wisdom from God--that is, our righteousness, holiness and redemption. Jesus ... suffered outside the city gate to make the people holy through his own blood.

One who is ... exalted above the heavens. He raised him from the dead and seated him at his right hand in the heavenly realms, far above all rule and authority, power and dominion, and every title that can be given, not only in the present age but also in the one to come.

Hebrews 7:26. Isaiah 11:5. 2 Corinthians 5:21. Revelation 3:7. Hebrews 7:26. Psalm 45:2. Isaiah 53:9. Luke 23:41. Hebrews 7:26. Psalm 18:26. Hebrews 9:13, 14. 1 Peter 1:19. Hebrews 7:26. John 17:19. 1 Corinthians 1:30. Hebrews 13:12. Hebrews 7:26. Ephesians 1:20, 21.

We do not have a high priest who is unable to sympathize with our weaknesses

We have one who has been tempted in every way, just as we are--yet was without sin. Let us then approach the throne of grace with confidence, so that we may receive mercy and find grace to help us in our time of need.

For this reason he had to be made like his brothers in every way, in order that he might become a merciful and faithful high priest in service to God, and that he might make atonement for the sins of the people.

Jesus wept. In all their distress he too was distressed, and the angel of his presence saved them. In his love and mercy he redeemed them; he lifted them up and carried them all the days of old. When the Lord saw her, his heart went out to her and he said, "Don't cry."

The Lord has compassion on those who fear him; for he knows how we are formed, he remembers that we are dust. He said to me, "My grace is sufficient for you, for my power is made perfect in weakness." A bruised reed he will not break, and a smoldering wick he will not snuff out. For you know the grace of our Lord Jesus Christ, that though he was rich, yet for your sakes he became poor, so that you through his poverty might become rich.

May our Lord Jesus Christ himself and God our Father, who loved us and by his grace gave us eternal encouragement and good hope, encourage your hearts and strengthen you in every good deed and word.

Hebrews 4:15, 16. Hebrews 2:17. John 11:35. Isaiah 63:9. Luke 7:13. Psalm 103:13, 14. 2 Corinthians 12:9. Isaiah 42:3. 2 Corinthians 8:9. 2 Thessalonians 2:16, 17.

Jesus lives forever ... to intercede

Because Jesus lives forever, he has a permanent priesthood. Therefore he is able to save completely those who come to God through him, because he always lives to intercede for them. Christ Jesus ... is at the right hand of God and is also interceding for us. For Christ did not enter a man-made sanctuary that was only a copy of the true one; he entered heaven itself, now to appear for us in God's presence. For there is one God and one mediator between God and men, the man Christ Jesus.

He bore the sins of many, and made intercession for the transgressors. My prayer is ... that all of them may be one, Father, just as you are in me and I am in you.

I have prayed for you ... that your faith may not fail. But if anybody does sin, we have one who speaks to the Father in our defense--Jesus Christ, the Righteous One.

When I said, "My foot is slipping," your love, O Lord, supported me. Though a righteous man falls seven times, he rises again. Though he stumble, he will not fall, for the Lord upholds him with his hand. From six calamities he will rescue you; in seven no harm will befall you.

Surely God is my help; the Lord is the one who sustains me.

Hebrews 7:24, 25. Romans 8:34. Hebrews 9:24. 1 Timothy 2:5. Isaiah 53:12. John 17:20, 21. Luke 22:32. 1 John 2:1. Psalm 94:18.Proverbs 24:16. Psalm 37:24. Job 5:19. Psalm 54:4.

We have a great high priest who has gone through the heavens

When he had led them out to the vicinity of Bethany, he lifted up his hands and blessed them. While he was blessing them, he left them and was taken up into heaven. He sat down at the right hand of God.

In my Father's house are many rooms; if it were not so, I would have told you. I am going there to prepare a place for you. And if I go and prepare a place for you, I will come back and take you to be with me that you also may be where I am.

It is for your good that I am going away. Unless I go away, the Counselor will not come to you; but if I go, I will send him to you. The Counselor, the Holy Spirit, whom the Father will send in my name, will teach you all things and will remind you of everything I have said to you. Peace I leave with you; my peace I give you. I do not give to you as the world gives. Do not let your hearts be troubled and do not be afraid.

I came from the Father and entered the world; now I am leaving the world and going back to the Father.

He must remain in heaven until the time comes for God to restore everything, as he promised long ago through his holy prophets.

Hebrews 4:14. Luke 24:50, 51. Mark 16:19. John 14:2, 3. John 16:7. John 14:26, 27. John 16:28. Acts 3:21.

We have this hope as an anchor for the soul, firm and secure

Not one word has failed of all the good promises he gave through his servant Moses. May the Lord our God be with us as he was with our fathers; may he never leave or forsake us.

I lay a stone in Zion, a tested stone, a precious cornerstone for a sure foundation; the one who trusts will never be dismayed. For I am convinced that neither death nor life, neither angels nor demons, neither the present nor the future, nor any powers, neither height nor depth, nor anything else in all creation, will be able to separate us from the love of God that is in Christ Jesus our Lord.

Now we know that if the earthly tent we live in is destroyed, we have a building from God, an eternal house in heaven, not built by human hands. You will be secure, because there is hope; you will look about you and take your rest in safety. He set my feet on a rock and gave me a firm place to stand. He put a new song in my mouth, a hymn of praise to our God. When you lie down, you will not be afraid; when you lie down, your sleep will be sweet. So we say with confidence, "The Lord is my helper; I will not be afraid."

We wait for the blessed hope--the glorious appearing of our great God and Savior, Jesus Christ. Be strong and take heart, all you who hope in the Lord. The eyes of the Lord are on those who fear him, on those whose hope is in his unfailing love.

Hebrews 6:19. 1 Kings 8:56, 57. Isaiah 28:16. Romans 8:38, 39. 2 Corinthians 5:1. Job 11:18. Psalm 40:2, 3. Proverbs 3:24. Hebrews 13:6. Titus 2:13. Psalm 31:24. Psalm 33:18.

Let us hold firmly to the faith we profess

Remember, therefore, what you have received and heard; obey it, and repent. Christ is faithful as a son over God's house. And we are his house, if we hold on to our courage and the hope of which we boast.

Blessed is the man who perseveres under trial, because when he has stood the test, he will receive the crown of life that God has promised to those who love him. As you know, we consider blessed those who have persevered. You have heard of Job's perseverance and have seen what the Lord finally brought about. The Lord is full of compassion and mercy. For it is commendable if a man bears up under the pain of unjust suffering because he is conscious of God.

The righteous will hold to their ways, and those with clean hands will grow stronger. Since we are surrounded by such a great cloud of witnesses, let us throw off everything that hinders and the sin that so easily entangles, and let us run with perseverance the race marked out for us. Prepare your minds for action; be self-controlled; set your hope fully on the grace to be given you when Jesus Christ is revealed.

I am coming soon. Hold on to what you have, so that no one will take your crown. He who promised is faithful.

Hebrews 4:14. Revelation 3:3. Hebrews 3:6. James 1:12. James 5:11. 1 Peter 2:19. Job 17:9. Hebrews 12:1. 1 Peter 1:13. Revelation 3:11. Hebrews 10:23.

Man is destined to die once, and after that to face judgment

Like water spilled on the ground, which cannot be recovered, so we must die. But God does not take away life; instead, he devises ways so that a banished person may not remain estranged from him. For all can see that wise men die; the foolish and the senseless alike perish and leave their wealth to others. No man has power over the wind to contain it, so no one has power over the day of his death.

Sin entered the world through one man, and death through sin. The result of one trespass was condemnation for all men.

The Lord is coming with thousands upon thousands of his holy ones to judge everyone, and to convict all the ungodly of all the ungodly acts they have done in the ungodly way, and of all the harsh words ungodly sinners have spoken against him. All the nations will be gathered before him, and he will separate the people one from another as a shepherd separates the sheep from the goats.

If he rescued Lot, a righteous man, who was distressed by the filthy lives of lawless men (for that righteous man, living among them day after day, was tormented in his righteous soul by the lawless deeds he saw and heard)--if this is so, then the Lord knows how to rescue godly men.

The Lord will rescue me from every evil attack and will bring me safely to his heavenly kingdom. To him be glory for ever and ever. Amen.

Hebrews 9:27. 2 Samuel 14:14. Psalm 49:10. Ecclesiastes 8:8. Romans 5:12, 13. Romans 5:18. Jude 14, 15. Matthew 25:32. 2 Peter 2:7-9. 2 Timothy 4:18.

I will make a new covenant

The law is only a shadow of the good things that are coming--not the realities themselves. For this reason it can never, by the same sacrifices repeated endlessly year after year, make perfect those who draw near to worship. If it could, would they not have stopped being offered? For the worshipers would have been cleansed once for all, and would no longer have felt guilty for their sins. But those sacrifices are an annual reminder of sins, because it is impossible for the blood of bulls and goats to take away sins.

"The time is coming," declares the Lord, "when I will make a new covenant." If there had been nothing wrong with that first covenant, no place would have been sought for another. By calling this covenant "new," he has made the first one obsolete; and what is obsolete and aging will soon disappear.

The Holy Spirit also testifies to us about this. First he says: "This is the covenant I will make with them after that time, says the Lord. I will put my laws in their hearts, and I will write them on their minds." Then he adds: "Their sins and lawless acts I will remember no more."

I desire to do your will, O my God. The law of his God is in his heart; his feet do not slip. I will rejoice in doing them good and will assuredly plant them in this land with all my heart and soul.

Jeremiah 31:31. Hebrews 10:1-4. Jeremiah 31:31. Hebrews 8:7, 13. Hebrews 10:15-17. Psalm 40:8. Psalm 37:31. Jeremiah 32:41

Without shedding of blood
there is no forgiveness

This is why even the first covenant was not put into effect without blood. When Moses had proclaimed every commandment of the law to all the people, he took the blood of calves, together with water, scarlet wool and branches of hyssop, and sprinkled the scroll and all the people. He said, "This is the blood of the covenant, which God has commanded you to keep." In the same way, he sprinkled with the blood both the tabernacle and everything used in its ceremonies. In fact, the law requires that nearly everything be cleansed with blood.

They are to take some of the blood and put it on the sides and tops of the door frames of the houses where they eat the lambs. The blood will be a sign for you on the houses where you are; and when I see the blood, I will pass over you. It is the blood that makes atonement for one's life.

How much more, then, will the blood of Christ, who through the eternal Spirit offered himself unblemished to God, cleanse our consciences from acts that lead to death, so that we may serve the living God.

It was not with perishable things such as silver or gold that you were redeemed from the empty way of life handed down to you from your forefathers, but with the precious blood of Christ, a lamb without blemish or defect. Though him you believe in God, who raised him from the dead and glorified him, and so your faith and hope are in God.

Hebrews 9:22, 18-22. Exodus 12:7, 13. Leviticus 17:11. Hebrews 9:14. 1 Peter 1:18, 19, 21.

He appeared once for all ... to do away with sin by the sacrifice of himself

Every high priest is appointed to offer both gifts and sacrifices. They serve at a sanctuary that is a copy and shadow of what is in heaven. But the ministry Jesus has received is as superior to theirs as the covenant of which he is mediator is superior to the old one, and it is founded on better promises.

It was the Lord's will to crush him and cause him to suffer, and though the Lord makes his life a guilt offering, he will see his offspring and prolong his days, and the will of the Lord will prosper in his hand. After the suffering of his soul, he will see the light of life and be satisfied, by his knowledge my righteous servant will justify many, and he will bear their iniquities... For he bore the sin of many, and made intercession for the transgressors.

When Christ came as high priest of the good things that are already here, he went through the greater and more perfect tabernacle that is not man-made...he did not enter by means of the blood of goats and calves; but he entered the Most Holy Place once for all by his own blood, having obtained eternal redemption.

He will be clothed with majesty and will sit and rule on his throne. And he will be a priest on his throne.

Get rid of the old yeast that you may be a new batch without yeast--as you really are. For Christ, our Passover lamb, has been sacrificed. If a man cleanses himself ... he will be an instrument for noble purposes, made holy, useful to the Master and prepared to do any good work.

Hebrews 9:26. Hebrews 8:3, 5, 6. Isaiah 53:10-12. Hebrews 9:11, 12. Zechariah 6:13. 1 Corinthians 5:7. 2 Timothy 2:21.

Here I am, I have come to do your will

By that will, we have been made holy through the sacrifice of the body of Jesus Christ once for all. For just as through the disobedience of the one man the many were made sinners, so also through the obedience of the one man the many will be made righteous. The world must learn that I love the Father and that I do exactly what my Father has commanded me. Although he was a son, he learned obedience from what he suffered and once made perfect, he became the source of eternal salvation for all who obey him. It was fitting that God, for whom and through whom everything exists, should make the author of their salvation perfect through suffering.

Christ died for sins once for all, the righteous for the unrighteous, to bring you to God. He was put to death in the body but made alive by the Spirit. He died for all, that those who live should no longer live for themselves but for him who died for them and was raised again.

In the same way, count yourselves dead to sin but alive to God in Christ Jesus. I have been crucified with Christ and I no longer live, but Christ lives in me. The life I live in the body, I live by faith in the Son of God, who loved me and gave himself for me.

Hebrews 10:9, 10. Romans 5:19. John 14:31. Hebrews 5:8, 9. Hebrews 2:10. 1 Peter 3:18. 2 Corinthians 5:15. Romans 6:11. Galatians 2:20.

Christ did not enter a man-made sanctuary--he entered heaven itself now to appear for us in God's presence

The point of what we are saying is this: We do have such a high priest, who sat down at the right hand of the throne of the Majesty in heaven, and who serves in the sanctuary, the true tabernacle set up by the Lord, not by man.

He who descended is the very one who ascended higher than all the heavens, in order to fill the whole universe. We see Jesus, who was made a little lower than the angels, now crowned with glory and honor. Christ Jesus ... is at the right hand of God ... interceding for us.

Our citizenship is in heaven. And we eagerly await a Savior from there, the Lord Jesus Christ, who, by the power that enables him to bring everything under his control, will transform our lowly bodies so that they will be like his glorious body. For here we do not have an enduring city, but we are looking for the city that is to come. And you will receive a rich welcome into the eternal kingdom of our Lord and Savior Jesus Christ.

Let us lift up our hearts and our hands to God in heaven.

Hebrews 9:24. Hebrews 8:1, 2. Ephesians 4:10. Hebrews 2:9. Romans 8:34. Philippians 3:20, 21. Hebrews 13:14. 2 Peter 1:11. Lamentations 3:41.

Christ ... will appear a second time ... to bring salvation to those who are waiting for him

He will keep you strong to the end, so that you will be blameless on the day of our Lord Jesus Christ. God, who has called you into fellowship with his Son Jesus Christ our Lord, is faithful. May God himself, the God of peace, sanctify you through and through. May your whole spirit, soul and body be kept blameless at the coming of our Lord Jesus Christ.

Continue in him, so that when he appears we may be confident and unashamed before him at his coming. Our citizenship is in heaven. And we eagerly await a Savior from there, the Lord Jesus Christ, who, by the power that enables him to bring everything under his control, will transform our lowly bodies so that they will be like his glorious body.

And when the Chief Shepherd appears, you will receive the crown of glory that will never fade away. What we will be has not yet been made known. But we know that when he appears, we shall be like him, for we shall see him as he is.

When the Son of Man comes in his glory ... he will sit on his throne in heavenly glory. All the ends of the earth will remember and turn to the Lord, and all the families of the nations will bow down before him, for dominion belongs to the Lord and he rules over the nations.

Who will not fear you, O Lord, and bring glory to your name? For you alone are holy.

Hebrews 9:28. 1 Corinthians 1:5, 7-9. 1 Thessalonians 5:23. 1 John 2:28. Philippians 3:20, 21. 1 Peter 5:4. 1 John 3:2. Matthew 25:31. Psalm 22:27, 28. Revelation 15:4

My righteous one will live by faith

And if he shrinks back, I will not be pleased with him. But we are not of those who shrink back and are destroyed, but of those who believe and are saved.

Have faith in the Lord your God and you will be upheld; have faith in his prophets and you will be successful. Without faith it is impossible to please God, because anyone who comes to him must believe that he exists and that he rewards those who earnestly seek him. Let him who walks in the dark, who has no light, trust in the name of the Lord and rely on his God.

You, O Lord, keep my lamp burning; my God turns my darkness into light. With your help I can advance against a troop; with my God I can scale a wall.

As for God, his way is perfect; the word of the Lord is flawless. He is a shield for all who take refuge in him. For who is God besides the Lord? And who is the Rock except our God? It is God who arms me with strength and makes my way perfect. He makes my feet like the feet of a deer; he enables me to stand on the heights. You broaden the path beneath me, so that my ankles do not turn.

Increase our faith!

Hebrews 10:38, 39. 2 Chronicles 20:20. Hebrews 11:6. Isaiah 50:10. Psalm 18:28-33, 36. Luke 17:5.

Let us hold unswervingly to the hope we profess, for he who promised is faithful

Do not be afraid. Stand firm and you will see the deliverance the Lord will bring you today. The Lord will fight for you; you need only to be still. Be still before the Lord and wait patiently for him; do not fret when men succeed in their ways, when they carry out their wicked schemes.

Do not be afraid; do not be discouraged. For his compassions never fail. They are new every morning; great is your faithfulness. I say to myself, "The Lord is my portion; therefore I will wait for him."

The Lord is good to those whose hope is in him, to the one who seeks him; it is good to wait quietly for the salvation of the Lord. Not one word has failed of all the good promises he gave through his servant Moses.

Your love, O Lord, reaches to the heavens, your faithfulness to the skies. How priceless is your unfailing love! Both high and low among men find refuge in the shadow of your wings.

Let us not become weary in doing good, for at the proper time we will reap a harvest if we do not give up.

Hebrews 10:23. Exodus 14:13, 14. Psalm 37:7. 2 Chronicles 20:17. Lamentations 3:22-26. 1 Kings 8:56. Psalm 36:5, 7. Galatians 6:9.

Fight the good fight of the faith

Remember those earlier days after you had received the light, when you stood your ground in a great contest in the face of suffering. Sometimes you were publicly exposed to insult and persecution; at other times you stood side by side with those who were so treated. You sympathized with those in prison and joyfully accepted the confiscation of your property, because you knew that you yourselves had better and lasting possessions.

Be strong and courageous. Do not be afraid or discouraged because of the king of Assyria and the vast army with him, for there is a greater power with us than with him. With him is only the arm of flesh, but with us is the Lord our God to help us and to fight our battles.

O Sovereign Lord, you have begun to show to your servant your greatness and your strong hand. For what god is there in heaven or on earth who can do the deeds and mighty works you do?

The weapons we fight with are not the weapons of the world. On the contrary, they have divine power to demolish strongholds. Fight the good fight, holding on to faith and a good conscience. Some have rejected these and so have shipwrecked their faith.

I will be with you; I will never leave you or forsake you. Be strong and courageous. Do not be terrified; do not be discouraged, for the Lord your God will be with you wherever you go.

---

1 Timothy 6:12. Hebrews 10:32-34. 2 Chronicles 32:7, 8. Deuteronomy 3:22, 24. 2 Corinthians 10:4. 1 Timothy 1:18, 19. Joshua 1:5, 6, 9.

Do not throw away your confidence; it will be richly rewarded

Were not the Cushites and Libyans a mighty army with great numbers of chariots and horsemen? Yet when you relied on the Lord, he delivered them into your hand. For the eyes of the Lord range throughout the earth to strengthen those whose hearts are fully committed to him.

Jesus said to the centurion, "Go! It will be done just as you believed it would." And his servant was healed.

O Nebuchadnezzar, we do not need to defend ourselves before you in this matter. If we are thrown into the blazing furnace, the God we serve is able to save us from it, and he will rescue us from your hand, O king. Shadrach, Meschach and Abednego came out of the fire, and the satraps, prefects, governors and royal advisers crowded around them. They saw that the fire had not harmed their bodies, nor was a hair of their heads singed; their robes were not scorched, and there was no smell of fire on them.

What more shall I say? I do not have time to tell about Gideon, Barak, Samson, Japhthah, David, Samuel and the prophets, who through faith conquered kingdoms, administered justice, and gained what was promised; who shut the mouths of lions, quenched the fury of the flames, and escaped the edge of the sword; whose weakness was turned to strength; and who became powerful in battle and routed foreign armies.

As for you, be strong and do not give up, for your work will be rewarded. Remember the Lord, who is great and awesome.

Hebrews 10:35. 2 Chronicles 16:8, 9. Matthew 8:13. Daniel 3:16, 17, 26, 27. Hebrews 11:32-34. 2 Chronicles 15:7. Nehemiah 4:14.

You need to persevere so that when you have done the will of God, you will receive what he has promised

Be self-controlled and alert. Your enemy the devil prowls around like a roaring lion looking for someone to devour. Resist him, stand firm in the faith. Resist the devil, and he will flee from you.

Put on the full armor of God so that you can take your stand against the devil's schemes. For our struggle is not against flesh and blood, but against the rulers, against the authorities, against the powers of this dark world and against the spiritual forces of evil in the heavenly realms. Therefore put on the full armor of God, so that when the day of evil comes, you may be able to stand your ground, and after you have done everything, to stand. Stand firm then, with the belt of truth buckled around your waist, with the breastplate of righteousness in place, and with your feet fitted with the readiness that comes from the gospel of peace. In addition to all this, take up the shield of faith, with which you can extinguish all the flaming arrows of the evil one. Take the helmet of salvation and the sword of the Spirit, which is the word of God. And pray in the Spirit on all occasions with all kinds of prayers and requests. With this in mind, be alert and always keep on praying for all the saints.

And when the chief Shepherd appears, you will receive the crown of glory that will never fade away.

Hebrews 10:36. 1 Peter 5:8, 9. James 4:7. Ephesians 6:11-18. 1 Peter 5:4.

Faith is being sure of what we hope for

For in this hope we were saved. But hope that is seen is no hope at all. Who hopes for what he already has?

I pray ... that the eyes of your heart may be enlightened in order that you may know the hope to which he has called you, the riches of his glorious inheritance in the saints, and his incomparably great power for us who believe.

Since ancient times no one has heard, no ear has perceived, no eye has seen any God besides you, who acts on behalf of those who wait for him. You come to the help of those who gladly do right, who remember your ways. Against all hope, Abraham in hope believed and so became the father of many nations, just as it had been said to him, "So shall your offspring be."

Why are you downcast, O my soul? Why so disturbed within me? Put your hope in God, for I will yet praise him, my Savior and my God. We have this hope as an anchor for the soul, firm and secure. This is what the Sovereign Lord says: "See, I lay a stone in Zion, a tested stone, a precious cornerstone for a sure foundation; the one who trusts will never be dismayed.

Be strong and take heart, all you who hope in the Lord. For with the Lord is unfailing love and with him is full redemption.

Hebrews 11:1. Romans 8:24. Ephesians 1:18, 19. Isaiah 64:4, 5. Romans 4:18. Psalm 43:5. Hebrews 6:19. Isaiah 28:16. Psalm 31:24. Psalm 130:7.

Faith is being certain of what we do not see

Jesus told him [Thomas], "Because you have seen me, you have believed; blessed are those who have not seen and yet have believed."

Though you have not seen him, you love him; and even though you do not see him now, you believe in him and are filled with an inexpressible and glorious joy, for you are receiving the goal of your faith, the salvation of your souls. We live by faith, not by sight.

By faith Noah, when warned about things not yet seen, in holy fear built an ark to save his family. By faith Abraham, when called to go to a place he would later receive as his inheritance, obeyed and went, even though he did not know where he was going. By faith the people passed through the Red Sea as on dry land. By faith the walls of Jericho fell, after the people had marched around them for seven days.

It is better to take refuge in the Lord than to trust in man. Those who look to him are radiant; their faces are never covered with shame.

Now we see but a poor reflection; then we shall see face to face. Now I know in part; then I shall know fully, even as I am fully known. What we will be has not yet been made known. But we know that when he appears, we shall be like him, for we shall see him as he is. In his great mercy he has given us ... an inheritance that can never perish, spoil or fade--kept in heaven for you.

Hebrews 11:1. John 20:29. 1 Peter 1:8, 9. 2 Corinthians 5:7. Hebrews 11:7, 8, 29, 30. Psalm 118:8. Psalm 34:5. 1 Corinthians 13:12. 1 John 3:2. 1 Peter 1:3, 4.

Run with perseverance
race marked out for us

Let us throw off everything that hinders and the sin that so easily entangles. Make up your mind not to put any stumbling block or obstacle in your brother's way.

Let your eyes look straight ahead, fix your gaze directly before you. Make level paths for your feet and take only ways that are firm. Do not swerve to the right or to the left.

Do you not know that in a race all the runners run, but only one gets the prize? Run in such a way as to get the prize. Everyone who competes in the games goes into strict training. They do it to get a crown that will not last; but we do it to get a crown that will last forever.

I press on to take hold of that for which Christ Jesus took hold of me. Brothers, I do not consider myself yet to have taken hold of it. But one thing I do: Forgetting what is behind and straining toward what is ahead. I press on toward the goal to win the prize for which God has called me heavenward in Christ Jesus.

I have fought the good fight, I have finished the race, I have kept the faith. Now there is in store for me the crown of righteousness, which the Lord, the righteous Judge, will award to me on that day--and not only to me, but also to all who have longed for his appearing.

Hebrews 12:1. Romans 14:13. Proverbs 4:25-27. 1 Corinthians 9:24, 25. Philippians 3:12-14. 2 Timothy 4:7, 8.

Let us fix our eyes on Jesus

...the author and perfector of our faith, who for the joy set before him endured the cross, scorning its shame, and sat down at the right hand of the throne of God.

"I am the Alpha and the Omega," says the Lord God, "who is, and who was, and who is to come, the Almighty."

...Able to do immeasurably more than all we ask or imagine, according to his power that is at work within us.

...Able to keep you from falling and to present you before his glorious presence without fault and with great joy.

Christ's love compels us, because we are convinced that one died for all, and therefore all died. And he died for all, that those who live should no longer live for themselves but for him who died for them and was raised again. Therefore, if anyone is in Christ, he is a new creation; the old has gone, the new has come!

Remain in me, and I will remain in you. No branch can bear fruit by itself; it must remain in the vine. Neither can you bear fruit unless you remain in me. I am the vine; you are the branches. If a man remains in me and I in him, he will bear much fruit; apart from me you can do nothing. This is to my Father's glory, that you bear much fruit, showing yourselves to be my disciples.

The Lord will rescue me from every evil attack and will bring me safely to his heavenly kingdom. To him be glory for ever and ever. Amen.

Hebrews 12:2. Revelation 1:8. Ephesians 3:20. Jude 24. 2 Corinthians 5:14, 15, 17. John 15:4-8. 2 Timothy 4:18.

Consider him ... so that you will not grow weary and lose heart

In your struggle against sin, you have not yet resisted to the point of shedding your blood.

He was despised and rejected by men, a man of sorrows, and familiar with suffering. Like one from whom men hide their faces he was despised, and we esteemed him not. He was pierced for our transgressions, he was crushed for our iniquities; the punishment that brought us peace was upon him, and by his wounds we are healed. He was oppressed and afflicted, yet he did not open his mouth; he was led like a lamb to the slaughter, and as a sheep before her shearers is silent, so he did not open his mouth. Yet it was the Lord's will to crush him and cause him to suffer.

And so Jesus also suffered outside the city gate to make the people holy through his own blood.

Christ suffered for you, leaving you an example, that you should follow in his steps. He committed no sin, and no deceit was found in his mouth. When they hurled their insults at him, he did not retaliate; when he suffered, he made no threats. Instead, he entrusted himself to him who judges justly. He himself bore our sins in his body on the tree, so that we might die to sins and live for righteousness; by his wounds you have been healed.

Therefore, since Christ suffered in his body, arm yourselves also with the same attitude, because he who has suffered in his body is done with sin. As a result, he does not live the rest of his earthly life for evil human desires, but rather for the will of God.

Hebrews 12:3, 4. Isaiah 53:3, 5, 7, 10. Hebrews 2:10. Hebrews 13:12. 1 Peter 2:21-24. 1 Peter 4:1, 2.

The Lord disciplines those he loves

Know then in your heart that as a man disciples his son, so the Lord your God disciplines you.

Blessed is the man whom God corrects; so do not despise the discipline of the Almighty. Do not lose heart when he rebukes you. For he wounds, but he also binds up; he injures, but his hands also heal. Our light and momentary troubles are achieving for us an eternal glory that far outweighs them all.

The God of all grace, who called you to his eternal glory in Christ, after you have suffered a little while, will himself restore you and make you strong, firm and steadfast. ...An instrument for noble purposes made holy, useful to the Master and prepared to do any good work.

He knows the way that I take; when he has tested me, I will come forth as gold. It was good for me to be afflicted so that I might learn your decrees. The law from your mouth is more precious to me than thousands of pieces of silver and gold.

Those I love I rebuke and discipline. I will refine them like silver and test them like gold. They will call on my name and I will answer them; I will say, "They are my people," and they will say, "The Lord is our God."

Hebrews 12:6. Deuteronomy 8:5. Job 5:17. Hebrews 12:5. Job 5:18. 2 Corinthians 4:17. 1 Peter 5:10. 2 Timothy 2:21. Job 23:10. Psalm 119:71, 72. Revelation 3:19. Zechariah 13:9.

Endure hardship as discipline;
God is treating you as sons.

My son, do not despise the Lord's discipline and do not resent his rebuke, because the Lord disciplines those he loves, as a father the son he delights in. Do not make light of the Lord's discipline.

For what son is not disciplined by his father? If you are not disciplined (and everyone undergoes discipline), then you are illegitimate children and not true sons. Moreover, we have all had human fathers who disciplined us and we respected them for it. How much more should we submit to the Father of our spirits and live! Our fathers disciplined us for a little while as they thought best; but God disciplines us for our good, that we may share in his holiness.

Abba Father ... everything is possible for you. Take this cup from me. Yet not what I will, but what you will.

I know, O Lord, that your laws are righteousness, and in faithfulness you have afflicted me. May your unfailing love be my comfort, according to your promise to your servant. Let your compassion come to me that I may live, for your law is my delight. Though he brings grief, he will show compassion, so great is his unfailing love.

I know, O Lord, that a man's life is not his own; it is not for man to direct his steps. Correct me, Lord, but only with justice--not in your anger, lest you reduce me to nothing.

As a mother comforts her child, so will I comfort you.

Hebrews 12:7. Proverbs 3:11, 12. Hebrews 12:5, 7-10. Mark 14:36. Psalm 119:75-77. Lamentations 3:32, 33. Jeremiah 10:23, 24.Isaiah 66:13.

God disciplines us for our good that we may share in his holiness

No discipline seems pleasant at the time, but painful. Later on, however, it produces a harvest of righteousness and peace for those who have been trained by it.

I cried like a swift or thrush, I moaned like a mourning dove. My eyes grew weak as I looked to the heavens. I am troubled;O Lord, come to my aid!

But what can I say? He has spoken to me, and he himself has done this. I will walk humbly all my years because of this anguish of my soul. Lord, by such things men live; and my spirit finds life in them too. You restored me to health and let me live. Surely it was for my benefit that I suffered such anguish. In your love you kept me from the pit of destruction; you have put all my sins behind your back.

For the grace of God...teaches us to say "no" to ungodliness and worldly passions, and to live self-controlled, upright and godly lives in this present age.

Praise be to the God and Father of our Lord Jesus Christ! In his great mercy he has given us new birth into a living hope... In this you greatly rejoice, though now for a little while you may have had to suffer grief in all kinds of trials. These have come so that your faith--of greater worth than gold, which perishes even though refined by fire--may be proved genuine and may result in praise, glory and honor.

What kind of people ought you to be? You ought to live holy and godly lives. Without holiness no one will see the Lord.

Hebrews 12:10, 11. Isaiah 38:14-17. Titus 2:11, 12. 1 Peter 1:3-7. 2 Peter 3:11. Hebrews 12:14.

No discipline seems pleasant at the time, but painful

Later on, however, it produces a harvest of right-eousness and peace for those who have been trained by it. Therefore, strengthen your feeble arms and weak knees. Make level paths for your feet, so that the lame may not be disabled, but rather healed.

Blessed is the man you discipline, O Lord, the man you teach from your law. Sorrow is better than laughter, because a sad face is good for the heart. The heart of the wise is in the house of mourning, but the heart of fools is in the house of pleasure. Before I was afflicted I went astray, but now I obey your word.

Praise be to the God and Father of our Lord Jesus Christ, the Father of compassion and the God of all comfort, who comforts us in all our troubles, so that we can comfort those in any trouble with the comfort we ourselves have received from God. For just as the sufferings of Christ flow over into our lives, so also through Christ our comfort overflows. If we are distressed, it is for your comfort and salvation; if we are comforted, it is for your comfort, which produces in you patient endurance of the same sufferings we suffer. And our hope for you is firm, because we know that just as you share in our sufferings, so also you share in our comfort.

Hebrews 12:11-13. Psalm 94:12. Ecclesiastes 7:3, 4. Psalm 119:67. 2 Corinthians 1:3-7.

Keep on loving each other as brothers

All men will know that you are my disciples if you love one another. My command is this: Love each other as I have loved you.

Love must be sincere. Love one another deeply, from the heart.

Love is patient, love is kind. It does not envy, it does not boast, it is not proud. It is not rude, it is not self-seeking, it is not easily angered, it keeps no record of wrongs. Love does not delight in evil but rejoices with the truth. It always protects, always trusts, always hopes, always perseveres. Love never fails.

Greater love has no man than this, that one lay down his life for his friend. A friend loves at all times, and a brother is born for adversity.

Hebrews 13:1. John 13:35. John 15:12. Romans 12:9. 1 Peter 1:22. 1 Corinthians 13:4-8. John 15:13. Proverbs 17:17.

Do not forget to entertain strangers

For the Lord your God is God of gods and Lord of lords, the great God, mighty and awesome, who ... loves the alien, giving him food and clothing. And you are to love those who are aliens. Fear the Lord your God and serve him.

Do not mistreat an alien or oppress him. The alien living with you must be treated as one of your native-born. Love him as yourself. If one of your countrymen becomes poor and is unable to support himself among you, help him as you would an alien or a temporary resident, so he can continue to live among you.

Whatever you did for one of the least of these brothers of mine, you did for me [Christ].

We who are strong ought to bear with the failings of the weak and not to please ourselves. Each of us should please his neighbor for his good, to build him up. For even Christ did not please himself. If you really keep the royal law found in Scripture, "Love your neighbor as yourself," you are doing right.

Some people have entertained angels without knowing it.

Hebrews 13:2. Deuteronomy 10:17-20. Exodus 22:21. Leviticus 19:34. Leviticus 25:35. Matthew 25:40. Romans 15:1-3. James 2:8. Hebrews 13:2.

Remember those in prison

I, the Lord, have called you in righteousness; I will take hold of your hand. I will keep you and will make you to be a covenant for the people and a light for the Gentiles, to open eyes that are blind, to free captives from prison and to release from the dungeon those who sit in darkness.

Blessed is he whose help is the God of Jacob, whose hope is in the Lord his God, the Maker of heaven and earth, the sea, and everything in them--the Lord, who remains faithful forever. He upholds the cause of the oppressed and gives food to the hungry. The Lord sets prisoners free.

Joseph said to him ... "When all goes well with you, remember me and show me kindness; mention me to Pharaoh and get me out of this prison." The chief cupbearer, however, did not remember Joseph; he forgot him.

When my spirit grows faint with me, it is you who know my way. In the path where I walk men have hidden a snare for me. Look to my right and see; no one is concerned for me. I have no refuge; no one cares for my life. I cry to you, O Lord; I say, "You are my refuge, my portion in the land of the living. Set me free from my prison, that I may praise your name. Then the righteous will gather about me because of your goodnes."
God sets the lonely in families, he leads forth the prisoners with singing. They feast on the abundance of your house; you give them drink from your river of delights. I have come that they may have life, and have it to the full.

Hebrews 13:3. Isaiah 42:6, 7. Psalm 146:5-7. Genesis 40:12, 14, 23. Psalm 142:3-5, 7. Psalm 68:6. Psalm 36:8. John 10:10.

Remember your leaders

Obey your leaders and submit to their authority. They keep watch over you as men who must give an account. Obey them so that their work will be a joy, not a burden, for that would be of no advantage to you.

Respect those who work hard among you, who are over you in the Lord and who admonish you. Hold them in the highest regard in love because of their work. The elders who direct the affairs of the church well are worthy of double honor....

Everyone must submit himself to the governing authorities, for there is no authority except that which God has established. The authorities that exist have been established by God. Consequently, he who rebels against the authority is rebelling against what God has instituted, and those who do so will bring judgment on themselves.

This is also why you pay taxes, for the authorities are God's servants, who give their full time to governing. Give everyone what you owe him: If you owe taxes, pay taxes; if revenue, then revenue; if respect, then respect; if honor, then honor.

Remind the people to be subject to rulers and authorities, to be obedient, to be ready to do whatever is good. Submit yourselves for the Lord's sake to every authority instituted among men: whether to the king, as the supreme authority, or to governors, who are sent by him to punish those who do wrong and to commend those who do right. Show proper respect to everyone: Love the brotherhood of believers, fear God, honor the king.

Hebrews 13:7, 17. 1 Thessalonians 5:12, 13. 1 Timothy 5:17. Romans 13:1, 2, 6, 7. Titus 3:1. 1 Peter 2:13, 14, 17.

Marriage should be honored by all

Two are better than one, because they have a good return for their work: If one falls down, his friend can help him up. But pity the man who falls and has no one to help him up! Also, if two lie down together, they will keep warm. But how can one keep warm alone?

He satisfies my desires with good things, so that my youth is renewed like the eagle's.

Wives, submit to your husbands as to the Lord. For the husband is the head of the wife as Christ is the head of the church, his body, of which he is the Savior. Now as the church submits to Christ, so also wives should submit to their husbands in everything. Husbands, love your wives, just as Christ loved the church and gave himself up for her to make her holy, cleansing her by the washing with water through the word, and to present her to himself as a radiant church, without stain or wrinkle or any other blemish, but holy and blameless.

Live a life of love. Let us consider how we may spur one another on toward love and good deeds.

Choose for yourselves this day whom you will serve ... as for me and my household, we will serve the Lord.

Hebrews 13:4. Ecclesiastes 4:9-11. Psalm 103:5. Ephesians 5:22-27, 2. Hebrews 10:24. Joshua 24:15.

Keep your lives free of the love of money

When you have eaten and are satisfied, praise the Lord your God for the good land he has given you. Be careful that you do not forget the Lord your God, failing to observed his commands, his laws and his decrees that I am giving you this day.

Otherwise, when you eat and are satisfied, when you build fine houses and settle down, and when your herds and flocks grow large and your silver and gold increase and all you have is multiplied, then your heart will become proud and you will forget the Lord your God. Remember the Lord your God, for it is he who gives you the ability to produce wealth.

When God gives any man wealth and possessions, and enables him to enjoy them, to accept his lot and be happy in his work--this is a gift of God.

Jesus said to his disciples, "I tell you the truth, it is hard for a rich man to enter the kingdom of heaven."

People who want to get rich fall into temptation and a trap and into many foolish and harmful desires that plunge men into ruin and destruction. Cast but a glance at riches, and they are gone, for they will surely sprout wings and fly off to the sky like an eagle. For riches do not endure forever, and a crown is not secure for all generations. For we brought nothing into the world, and we can take nothing out of it.

Be content with what you have. The blessing of the Lord brings wealth, and he adds no trouble with it. With me are riches and honor, enduring wealth and prosperity.

Hebrews 13:5. Deuteronomy 8:10-14, 18. Ecclesiastes 5:19. Matthew 19:23. 1 Timothy 6:9. Proverbs 23:5. Proverbs 27:24. 1 Timothy 6:7. Hebrews 13:5. Proverbs 10:22. Proverbs 8:18.

Do not forget to do good and to share with others, for with such sacrifices God is pleased

Give to the one who asks you, and do not turn away from the one who wants to borrow from you. Sell your possessions and give to the poor. Provide purses for yourselves that will not wear out, a treasure in heaven that will not be exhausted, where no thief comes near and no moth destroys. The Lord Jesus himself said, "It is more blessed to give than to receive."

A generous man will prosper; he who refreshes others will himself be refreshed. If you spend yourselves in behalf of the hungry and satisfy the needs of the oppressed, then your light will rise in the darkness, and your night will become like the noonday.

Give, and it will be given to you. A good measure, pressed down, shaken together and running over, will be poured into your lap. For with the measure you use, it will be measured to you. Remember this: Whoever sows sparingly will also reap sparingly, and whoever sows generously will also reap generously.

Command those who are rich in this present world not to be arrogant nor to put their hope in wealth, which is so uncertain, but to put their hope in God, who richly provides us with everything for our enjoyment.

Command them to do good, to be rich in good deeds, and to be generous and willing to share. In this way they will lay up treasure for themselves as a firm foundation for the coming age, so that they may take hold of the life that is truly life.

Hebrews 13:16. Matthew 5:42. Luke 12:33. Acts 20:35. Proverbs 11:25. Isaiah 58:10. Luke 6:38. 2 Corinthians 9:6. 1 Timothy 6:17-19.

This is one of the Hebrew babies

The girl went and got the baby's mother. Pharaoh's daughter said to her, "Take this baby and nurse him for me, and I will pay you." So the woman took the baby and nursed him. When the child grew older, she took him to Pharaoh's daughter and he became her son. She named him Moses, saying, "I drew him out of the water."

Moses ... was no ordinary child. Moses was educated in all the wisdom of the Egyptians and was powerful in speech and action.

Who is like the Lord our God, the One who sits enthroned on high, who stoops down to look on the heavens and the earth? He raises the poor from the dust and lifts the needy from the ash heap. You have been a refuge for the poor, a refuge for the needy in his distress, a shelter from the storm and a shade from the heat. For the breath of the ruthless is like a storm driving against a wall and like the heat of the desert. You silence the uproar of foreigners; as heat is reduced by the shadow of a cloud, so the song of the ruthless is stilled.

Has not God chosen those who are poor in the eyes of the world to be rich in faith and to inherit the kingdom he promised those who love him?

No prophet has risen in Israel like Moses, whom the Lord knew face to face, who did all those miraculous signs and wonders the Lord sent him to do in Egypt--to Pharaoh and to all his officials and to his whole land. Moses was a hundred and twenty years old when he died, yet his eyes were not weak nor his strength gone.

Exodus 2:6, 8, 9. Acts 7:20, 22. Psalm 113:5-7. Isaiah 25:4, 5. James 2:5. Deuteronomy 34:10, 11, 7

From birth I have relied on you

You brought me forth from my mother's womb. I will ever praise you. I have become like a portent to many, but you are my strong refuge. My mouth is filled with your praise, declaring your splendor all day long.

My mouth will tell of your righteousness, of your salvation all day long, though I know not its measure. I will come and proclaim your mighty acts, O Sovereign Lord; I will proclaim your righteousness, yours alone.

Since my youth, O God, you have taught me, and to this day I declare your marvelous deeds. Even when I am old and gray, do not forsake me, O God, till I declare your power to the next generation, your might to all who are to come.

Your righteousness reaches to the skies, O God, you who have done great things. Who, O God, is like you? Though you have made me see troubles, many and bitter, you will restore my life again; from the depths of the earth you will again bring me up. You will increase my honor and comfort me once again.

Through you we push back our enemies; through your name we trample our foes.

For you who revere my name, the sun of righteousness will rise with healing in its wings. And you will go out and leap like calves released from the stall. For everyone born of God overcomes the world. This is the victory that has overcome the world, even our faith.

Psalm 71:6-8, 15-21. Psalm 44:5. Malachi 4:2. 1 John 5:4.

He brought his people out like a flock; he led them like sheep through the desert

He guided them safely, so they were unafraid; but the sea engulfed their enemies. Thus he brought them to the border of his holy land, to the hill country his right hand had taken. He drove out nations before them and allotted their lands to them as an inheritance; he settled the tribes of Israel in their homes.

We have heard with our ears, O God; our fathers have told us what you did in their days, in days long ago. With your hand you drove out the nations and planted our fathers; you crushed the peoples and made our fathers flourish. It was not by their sword that they won the land, nor did their arm bring them victory; it was your right hand, your arm, and the light of your face, for you loved them.

The Lord foils the plans of the nations; he thwarts the purposes of the peoples. But the plans of the Lord stand firm forever, the purposes of his heart through all generations.

Many, O Lord my God, are the wonders you have done. The things you planned for us no one can recount to you; were I to speak and tell of them, they would be too many to declare.

Psalm 78:52-55. Psalm 44:1-3. Psalm 33:10, 11. Psalm 40:5.

With us is the Lord our God to help us and to fight our battles

The Lord will fight for you; you need only to be still. He will be a spirit of justice to him who sits in judgment, a source of strength to those who turn back the battle at the gate. Though you search for your enemies, you will not find them. Those who wage war against you will be as nothing at all. For I am the Lord, your God, who takes hold of your right hand and says to you, "Do not fear; I will help you."

I took you from the ends of the earth, from its farthest corners I called you. I said, "You are my servant; I have chosen you and have not rejected you. So do not fear, for I am with you; do not be dismayed, for I am your God. I will strengthen you and help you; I will uphold you with my righteous right hand."

When you pass through the waters, I will be with you; and when you pass through the rivers, they will not sweep over you. When you walk through the fire, you will not be burned; the flames will not set you ablaze.

Even the very hairs of your head are all numbered. So don't be afraid. Those who hope in the Lord will renew their strength. They will soar on wings like eagles; they will run and not grow weary, they will walk and not be faint.

I pray that out of his glorious riches he may strengthen you with power through his Spirit in your inner being.

---

2 Chronicles 32:8. Exodus 14:14. Isaiah 28:6. Isaiah 41:12, 13. Isaiah 41:9, 10. Isaiah 43:2. Matthew 10:30, 31. Isaiah 40:31. Ephesians 3:16.

Merchants on the mighty waters ... they saw the works of the Lord, his wonderful deeds in the deep

For he spoke and stirred up a tempest that lifted high the waves. They mounted up to the heavens and went down to the depths;in their peril their courage melted away. They reeled and staggered like drunken men; they were at their wits' end. Then they cried out to the Lord in their trouble, and he brought them out of their distress. He stilled the storm to a whisper; the waves of the sea were hushed. They were glad when it grew calm, and he guided them to their desired haven. Let them give thanks to the Lord for his unfailing love and his wonderful deeds for men.

Who has gathered up the wind in the hollow of his hands? Who has wrapped up the waters in his cloak? Who has established all the ends of the earth? What is his name, and the name of his son? Tell me if you know!

Praise the Lord from the earth, you great sea creatures and all ocean depths, lightning and hail, snow and clouds, stormy winds that do his bidding, you mountains and all hills, fruit trees and all cedars, wild animals and all cattle, small creatures and flying birds, kings of the earth and all nations, you princes and all rulers on earth, young men and maidens, old men and children. Let them praise the name of the Lord, for his name alone is exalted; his splendor is above the earth and the heavens.

Psalm 107:23-31. Proverbs 30:4. Psalm 148:7-13.

He turned the desert into pools of water and the parched ground into flowing springs

Blessed are those whose strength is in you, who have set their hearts on pilgrimage. As they pass through the Valley of Baca, they make it a place of springs; the autumn rains also cover it with pools.

Forget the former things; do not dwell on the past. See, I am doing a new thing! Now it springs up; do you not perceive it? I am making a way in the desert and streams in the wasteland. I dry up the green tree and make the dry tree flourish.

The Lord will guide you always; he will satisfy your needs in a sun-scorched land and will strengthen your frame. You will be like a well-watered garden, like a spring whose waters never fail. Water will gush forth in the wilderness and streams in the desert. The burning sand will become a pool, the thirsty ground bubbling springs.

Every valley shall be raised up, every mountain and hill made low; the rough ground shall become level, the rugged places a plain. Stand firm. Let nothing move you. Always give yourselves fully to the work of the Lord, because you know that your labor in the Lord is not in vain.

Psalm 107:35. Psalm 84:5, 6. Isaiah 43:18, 19. Ezekiel 17:24.Isaiah 58:11. Isaiah 35:6, 7. Isaiah 40:4, 5. 1 Corinthians 15:58.

Know that the Lord is God

I will remember the deeds of the Lord; yes, I will remember your miracles of long ago. I will meditate on all your works and consider all your mighty deeds. Your ways, O God, are holy. What god is so great as our God? You are the God who performs miracles;you display your power among the peoples. Your path led through the sea, your way through the mighty waters, though your footprints were not seen. I know that you can do all things; no plan of yours can be thwarted.

O Lord God Almighty, who is like you? You are mighty, O Lord,and your faithfulness surrounds you. You rule over the surging sea; when its waves mount up, you still them. You crushed Rahab like one of the slain; with your strong arm you scattered your enemies. The heavens are yours, and yours also the earth; you founded the world and all that is in it.

You created the north and the south; Tabor and Hermon sing for joy at your name. Your arm is endued with power; your hand is strong, your right hand exalted.

Righteousness and justice are the foundation of your throne; love and faithfulness go before you. Blessed are those who have learned to acclaim you, who walk in the light of your presence, O Lord. They rejoice in your name all day long; they exult in your righteousness. For you are their glory and strength.

Psalm 100:3. Psalm 77:11-14, 19. Job 42:2. Psalm 89:8-17

Moses ... chose to be mistreated

By faith Moses, when he had grown up, refused to be known as the son of Pharaoh's daughter. He chose to be mistreated along with the people of God rather than to enjoy the pleasures of sin for a short time. He regarded disgrace for the sake of Christ as of greater value than the treasures of Egypt, because he was looking ahead to his reward.

One day, after Moses had grown up, he went out to where his own people were and watched them at their hard labor. He saw an Egyptian beating a Hebrew, one of his own people. Glancing this way and that and seeing no one, he killed the Egyptian and hid him in the sand. Moses thought that his own people would realize that God was using him to rescue them, but they did not.

We all stumble in many ways. There is not a righteous man on earth who does what is right and never sins. But he gives us more grace. That is why Scripture says: "God opposes the proud but gives grace to the humble."

Submit yourselves, then, to God. Resist the devil, and he will flee from you. Come near to God and he will come near to you. Wash your hands, you sinners, and purify your hearts, you double-minded. Grieve, mourn and wail. Change your laughter to mourning and your joy to gloom. Humble yourselves before the Lord, and he will lift you up.

Though your sins are like scarlet, they shall be as white as snow; though they are red as crimson, they shall be like wool.

Hebrews 11:24, 25. Exodus 2:11, 12. Acts 7:25. James 3:2. Ecclesiastes 7:20. James 4:6-10. Isaiah 1:18.

Because of the Lord's great love we are not consumed

I remember my affliction and my wandering, the bitterness and the gall. I well remember them, and my soul is downcast within me.Yet this I call to mind and therefore I have hope: Because of the Lord's great love we are not consumed, for his compassions never fail. They are new every morning; great is your faithfulness. I say to myself, "The Lord is my portion; therefore I will wait for him."

The Lord is good to those whose hope is in him, to the one who seeks him; it is good to wait quietly for the salvation of the Lord. This is a trustworthy saying that deserves full acceptance ... that we have put our hope in the living God, who is the Savior of all men, and especially of those who believe.

The Lord your God is with you, he is mighty to save. He will take great delight in you, he will quiet you with his love, he will rejoice over you with singing.

Therefore, my brothers, be all the more eager to make your calling and election sure. For if you do these things, you will never fall, and you will receive a rich welcome into the eternal kingdom of our Lord and Savior Jesus Christ.

Lamentations 3:22, 19-26. 1 Timothy 4:9, 10. Zephaniah 3:17. 2 Peter 1:10, 11.

He knows how we are formed, he remembers that we are dust

The Lord God formed the man from the dust of the ground and breathed into his nostrils the breath of life, and the man became a living being.

Their hearts were not loyal to him, they were not faithful to his covenant. Yet he was merciful; he forgave their iniquities and did not destroy them. Time after time he restrained his anger and did not stir up his full wrath. He remembered that they were but flesh, a passing breeze that does not return.

If the Lord delights in a man's way, he makes his steps firm;though he stumble, he will not fall, for the Lord upholds him with his hand. The Lord is compassionate and gracious, slow to anger, abounding in love. He will not always accuse, nor will he harbor his anger forever; he does not treat us as our sins deserve or repay us according to our iniquities. For as high as the heavens are above the earth, so great is his love for those who fear him. As a father has compassion on his children, so the Lord has compassion on those who fear him. A bruised reed he will not break, and a smoldering wick he will not snuff out.

O Lord, be gracious to us; we long for you. Be our strength every morning, our salvation in time of distress.

Psalm 103:14. Genesis 2:7. Psalm 78:37-39. Psalm 37:23, 24. Psalm 103:8-11, 13. Isaiah 42:3. Isaiah 33:2.

"Woe to me!" I cried. "I am ruined!"

"I am a man of unclean lips, and I live among a people of unclean lips, and my eyes have seen the King, the Lord Almighty." Then one of the seraphs flew to me [Isaiah] with a live coal in his hand, which he had taken with tongs from the altar. With it he touched my mouth and said, "See, this has touched your lips; your guilt is taken away and your sin atoned for."

Since we have these promises, dear friends, let us purify ourselves from everything that contaminates body and spirit, perfecting holiness out of reverence for God. As far as the east is from the west, so far has he removed our transgressions from us.

If a man cleanses himself ... he will be an instrument for noble purposes, made holy, useful to the Master and prepared to do any good work.

If we claim to have fellowship with him yet walk in the darkness, we lie and do not live by the truth. But if we walk in the light, as he is in the light, we have fellowship with one another, and the blood of Jesus, his Son, purifies us from all sin. If we claim to be without sin, we deceive ourselves and the truth is not in us. If we confess our sins, he is faithful and just and will forgive us our sins and purify us from all unrighteousness.

For men are not cast off by the Lord forever. Though he brings grief, he will show compassion, so great is his unfailing love. For he does not willingly bring affliction or grief to the children of men.

Isaiah 6:5-7. 2 Corinthians 7:1. Psalm 103:12. 2 Timothy 2:21. 1 John 1:6-9. Lamentations 3:31-33.

A broken and contrite heart, O God, you will not despise

Have mercy on me, O God, according to your unfailing love; according to your great compassion blot out my transgressions. Wash away all my iniquity and cleanse me from my sin. For I know my transgressions, and my sin is always before me. Against you, you only, have I sinned and done what is evil in your sight, so that you are proved right when you speak and justified when you judge.

Surely I was sinful at birth, sinful from the time my mother conceived me. Surely you desire truth in the inner parts; you teach me wisdom in the inmost place.

Cleanse me with hyssop, and I will be clean; wash me, and I will be whiter than snow. Let me hear joy and gladness; let the bones you have crushed rejoice. Hide your face from my sins and blot out all my iniquity.

Create in me a pure heart, O God, and renew a steadfast spirit within me. Do not cast me from your presence or take your Holy Spirit from me. Restore to me the joy of your salvation and grant me a willing spirit, to sustain me. Then I will teach transgressors your ways, and sinners will turn back to you.

Though I have fallen, I will rise.

Not by might nor by power, but by my Spirit, says the Lord Almighty

God chose the foolish things of the world to shame the wise; God chose the weak things of the world to shame the strong. He chose the lowly things of this world and the despised things--and the things that are not--to nullify the things that are, so that no one may boast before him.

My Spirit remains among you. Do not fear. The battle is not yours, but God's. My grace is sufficient for you, for my power is made perfect in weakness.

He will keep you strong to the end, so that you will be blameless on the day of our Lord Jesus Christ. God, who has called you into fellowship with his Son Jesus Christ our Lord, is faithful. If we are faithless, he will remain faithful, for he cannot disown himself.

See to it, brothers, that none of you has a sinful, unbelieving heart that turns away from the living God. But encourage one another daily, as long as it is called Today, so that none of you may be hardened by sin's deceitfulness. We have come to share in Christ if we hold firmly till the end the confidence we had at first.

Zechariah 4:6. 1 Corinthians 1:27-29. Haggai 2:5. 2 Chronicles 20:15. 2 Corinthians 12:9. 1 Corinthians 1:8, 9. 2 Timothy 2:13. Hebrews 3:12-14.

"My thoughts are not your thoughts neither are your ways my ways," declares the Lord

In my alarm I said, "I am cut off from your sight!" Yet you heard my cry for mercy when I called to you for help.

Surely it was for my benefit that I suffered such anguish. In your love you kept me from the pit of destruction; you have put all my sins behind your back.

O Lord, you have searched me and you know me. You know when I sit and when I rise; you perceive my thoughts from afar. You discern my going out and my lying down; you are familiar with all my ways. Before a word is on my tongue you know it completely, O Lord.

The Lord searches every heart and understands every motive behind the thoughts. "Can anyone hide in secret places so that I cannot see him?" declares the Lord. "Do not I fill heaven and earth?"

He knew what was in a man. Death and Destruction lie open before the Lord--how much more the hearts of men!

Therefore let everyone who is godly pray to you while you maybe found; surely when the mighty waters rise, they will not reach him. You are my hiding place; you will protect me from trouble and surround me with songs of deliverance. I will instruct you and teach you in the way you should go; I will counsel you and watch over you. Many are the woes of the wicked, but the Lord's unfailing love surrounds the man who trusts him.

Isaiah 55:8. Psalm 31:22. Isaiah 38:17. Psalm 139:1-4. 1 Chronicles 28:9. Jeremiah 23:24. John 2:25. Proverbs 5:11. Psalm 32:6-8, 10.

The Lord said ... "I am sending you."

You did not choose me, but I chose you and appointed you to go and bear fruit--fruit that will last. I took you from the ends of the earth, from its farthest corners I called you. I said, "You are my servant; I have chosen you and have not rejected you. So do not fear, for I am with you; do not be dismayed, for I am your God. I will strengthen you and help you; I will uphold you with my righteous right hand."

You will receive power when the Holy Spirit comes on you; and you will be my witnesses in Jerusalem, and in all Judea and Samaria, and to the ends of the earth.

Those who hope in the Lord will renew their strength. They will soar on wings like eagles; they will run and not grow weary, they will walk and not be faint.

The ordinances of the Lord are sure and altogether righteous.In keeping them there is great reward. Love the Lord, all his saints! The Lord preserves the faithful.

Be faithful, even to the point of death, and I will give you the crown of life. I am coming soon. Hold on to what you have, so that no one will take your crown.

Exodus 3:7, 10. John 15:16. Isaiah 41:9, 10. Acts 1:8. Isaiah 40:31. Psalm 19:9, 11. Psalm 31:23. Revelation 2:10. Revelation 3:11.

Moses said to God, "Who am I, that I should go ?"

Moses said to the Lord, "O Lord, I have never been eloquent, neither in the past nor since you have spoken to your servant. I am slow of speech and tongue." The Lord said to him, "Who gave man his mouth? Who makes him deaf or mute? Who gives him sight or makes him blind? Is it not I, the Lord? Now go; I will help you speak and will teach you what to say."

The Lord does not look at the things man looks at. Man looks at the outward appearance, but the Lord looks at the heart.

He [the Lord] said to me, "My grace is sufficient for you, for my power is made perfect in weakness." Therefore I will boast all the more gladly about my weaknesses, so that Christ's power may rest on me. That is why, for Christ's sake, I delight in weaknesses, in insults, in hardships, in persecutions, in difficulties. For when I am weak, then I am strong. We have this treasure in jars of clay to show that this all-surpassing power is from God and not from us.

As for me, I will always have hope; I will praise you more and more. My mouth will tell of your righteousness, of your salvation all day long, though I know not its measure. I will come and proclaim your mighty acts, O Sovereign Lord; I will proclaim your righteousness, yours alone. Even when I am old and gray, do not forsake me, O God, till I declare your power to the next generation, your might to all who are to come.

I can do everything through him who gives me strength.

Exodus 3:11. Exodus 4:10-12. 1 Samuel 16:7. 2 Corinthians 12:9, 10. 2 Corinthians 4:7. Psalm 71:14-18. Philippians 4:13.

O Lord, please send someone else

"Ah, Sovereign Lord," I [Jeremiah] said, "I do not know how to speak; I am only a child."

"But Lord," Gideon asked, "how can I save Israel? My clan is the weakest in Manasseh, and I am the least in my family."

Jonah ran away from the Lord and headed for Tarshish.

No one who puts his hand to the plow and looks back is fit for service in the kingdom of God. Open your eyes and look at the fields! They are ripe for harvest.

Does the Lord delight in burnt offerings and sacrifices as much as in obeying the voice of the Lord? To obey is better than sacrifice, and to heed is better than the fat of rams.

Obey me, and I will be your God and you will be my people. Walk in all the ways I command you, that it may go well with you. Do not merely listen to the word, and so deceive yourselves. Do what it says. Anyone who listens to the word but does not do what it says is like a man who looks at his face in a mirror and, after looking at himself, goes away and immediately forgets what he looks like. But the man who looks intently into the perfect law that gives freedom, and continues to do this, not forgetting what he has heard, but doing it--he will be blessed in what he does.

Exodus 4:13. Jeremiah 1:6. Judges 6:15. Jonah 1:3. Luke 9:62 John 4:35. 1 Samuel 15:22. Jeremiah 7:23. James 1:22-25.

I will help you speak
and will teach you what to say

Think of what you were when you were called. Not many of you were wise by human standards; not many were influential; not many were of noble birth. But God chose the foolish things of the world to shame the wise; God chose the weak things of the world to shame the strong. He chose the lowly things of this world and the despised things--and the things that are not--to nullify the things that are, so that no one may boast before him. It is because of him that you are in Christ Jesus, who has become for us wisdom from God--that is, our righteousness, holiness and redemption. Therefore, as it is written: "Let him who boasts boast in the Lord."

My message and my preaching were not with wise and persuasive words, but with a demonstration of the Spirit's power, so that your faith might not rest on men's wisdom, but on God's power.

The Sovereign Lord has given me an instructed tongue, to know the word that sustains the weary. He wakens me morning by morning,wakens my ear to listen like one being taught. Because the Sovereign Lord helps me, I will not be disgraced. Therefore have I set my face like flint, and I know I will not be put to shame.

Preach the Word; be prepared in season and out of season; correct, rebuke and encourage--with great patience and careful instruction.

Exodus 4:12. 1 Corinthians 1:26-31. 1 Corinthians 2:4, 5. Isaiah 50:4, 7. 2 Timothy 4:2.

Wait for the Lord; be strong and take heart and wait for the Lord

Do you not know? Have you not heard? The Lord is the everlasting God, the Creator of the ends of the earth. He will not grow tired or weary, and his understanding no one can fathom. He gives strength to the weary and increases the power of the weak. Even youths grow tired and weary, and young men stumble and fall; but those who hope in the Lord will renew their strength.

Come, all you who are thirsty, come to the waters; and you who have no money, come, buy and eat! Come, buy wine and milk without money and without cost. His bread will be supplied, and water will not fail.

The path of the righteous is level; O upright One, you make the way of the righteous smooth. Yes, Lord, walking in the way of your laws, we wait for you; your name and renown are the desire of our hearts.

As the rain and the snow come down from heaven, and do not return to it without watering the earth and make it bud and flourish, so that it yields seed for the sower and bread for the eater, so is my word that goes out from my mouth: It will not return to me empty, but will accomplish what I desire and achieve the purpose for which I sent it. You will go out in joy and be led forth in peace; the mountains and hills will burst into song before you, and all the trees of the field will clap their hands.

Since ancient times no one has heard, no ear has perceived, no eye has seen any God besides you, who acts on behalf of those who wait for him.

Psalm 27:14. Isaiah 40:28-31. Isaiah 55:1. Isaiah 33:16. Isaiah 26:7, 8. Isaiah 55:10-12. Isaiah 64:4, 5.

In your hands are strength and power to exalt and give strength to all

He does as he pleases with the powers of heaven and the peoples of the earth. No one can hold back his hand or say to him: "What have you done?" Everything he does is right and all his ways are just. And those who walk in pride he is able to humble.

Live a life worthy of the Lord and ... please him in every way: bearing fruit in every good work, growing in the knowledge of God, being strengthened with all power according to his glorious might so that you may have great endurance and patience, and joyfully giving thanks to the Father, who has qualified you to share in the inheritance of the saints in the kingdom of light.

Just as you received Christ Jesus as Lord, continue to live in him, rooted and built up in him, strengthened in the faith as you were taught, and overflowing with thankfulness. For in Christ all the fullness of the Deity lives in bodily form, and you have been given fullness in Christ, who is the head over every power and authority.

Whatever you do, work at it with all your heart, as working for the Lord, not for men, since you know that you will receive an inheritance from the Lord as a reward. It is the Lord Christ you are serving.

---

1 Chronicles 29:12. Daniel 4:35, 37. Colossians 1:10-12. Colossians 2:6, 7, 9, 10. Colossians 3:23, 24.

Be strong in the Lord and in his mighty power

Put on the full armor of God so that you can take your stand against the devil's schemes. For our struggle is not against flesh and blood, but against the rulers, against the authorities, against the powers of this dark world and against the spiritual forces of evil in the heavenly realms. Therefore put on the full armor of God, so that when the day of evil comes, you may be able to stand your ground, and after you have done everything, to stand.

To him who overcomes, I will give the right to eat from the tree of life, which is in the paradise of God.

To him who overcomes, I will give some of the hidden manna. I will also give him a white stone with a new name written on it....

To him who overcomes, and does my will to the end, I will give authority over the nations.

He who overcomes will ... be dressed in white. I will never blot out his name from the book of life, but will acknowledge his name before my Father and his angels.

Him who overcomes I will make a pillar in the temple of my God.

To him who overcomes, I will give the right to sit with me on my throne, just as I overcame and sat down with my Father on his throne.

I consider my life worth nothing to me, if only I may finish the race and complete the task the Lord Jesus has given me--the task of testifying to the gospel of God's grace.

Ephesians 6:10-13. Revelation 2:7, 17, 26. Revelation 3:5, 12, 21. Acts 20:24.

By faith ... he [Moses] persevered because he saw him who is invisible

Let us fix our eyes on Jesus. Fight the good fight, holding on to faith and a good conscience. Some have rejected these and so have shipwrecked their faith.

Be all the more eager to make your calling and election sure. For if you do these things, you will never fall, and you will receive a rich welcome into the eternal kingdom of our Lord and Savior Jesus Christ.

Do not let your hearts be troubled. Trust in God; trust also in me. In my Father's house are many rooms; if it were not so, I would have told you. I am going there to prepare a place for you. And if I go and prepare a place for you, I will come back and take you to be with me that you also may be where I am.

If you love me, you will obey what I command. And I will ask the Father, and he will give you another Counselor to be with you forever--the Spirit of truth. The world cannot accept him, because it neither sees him nor knows him. But you know him, for he lives with you and will be in you. I will not leave you as orphans; I will come to you. Before long, the world will not see me anymore, but you will see me. Because I live, you also will live.

Be faithful, even to the point of death, and I will give you the crown of life. Hold on to what you have until I come.

Hebrews 11:27. Hebrews 12:2. 1 Timothy 1:18, 19. 2 Peter 1:10, 11. John 14:1-3, 15-19. Revelation 2:10, 25.

Look to the Lord and his strength; seek his face always

Sow for yourselves righteousness, reap the fruit of unfailing love, and break up your unplowed ground; for it is time to seek the Lord, until he comes and showers righteousness on you.

Fan into flame the gift of God, which is in you through the laying on of my hands. For God did not give us a spirit of timidity, but a spirit of power, of love and of self-discipline. That power is like the working of his mighty strength, which he exerted in Christ when he raised him from the dead and seated him at his right hand in the heavenly realms.

Come to me, all you who are weary and burdened, and I will give you rest. Take my yoke upon you and learn from me, for I am gentle and humble in heart, and you will find rest for your souls. For my yoke is easy and my burden is light. Wait for the Lord; be strong and take heart and wait for the Lord. Be still before the Lord and wait patiently for him; do not fret when men succeed in their ways, when they carry out their wicked schemes.

Praise be to the Lord, to God our Savior, who daily bears our burdens. Sing to God, O kingdoms of the earth, sing praise to the Lord, to him who rides the ancient skies above, who thunders with mighty voice. You are awesome, O God, in your sanctuary; the God of Israel gives power and strength to his people.

Praise be to God!

---

1 Chronicles 16:11. Hosea 10:12. 2 Timothy 1:6, 7. Ephesians 1:19, 20. Matthew 11:28-30. Psalm 27:14. Psalm 37:7. Psalm 68:19, 32, 33, 35.

Let us not become weary in doing good, for at the proper time we will reap a harvest if we do not give up

In the presence of God and of Christ Jesus, who will judge the living and the dead, and in view of his appearing and his kingdom, I give you this charge: Preach the Word; be prepared in season and out of season; correct, rebuke and encourage--with great patience and careful instruction. For the time will come when men will not put up with sound doctrine. Instead, to suit their own desires, they will gather around them a great number of teachers to say what their itching ears want to hear. They will turn their ears away from the truth and turn aside to myths. But you, keep your head in all situations, endure hardship, do the work of an evangelist, discharge all the duties of your ministry.

In fact, everyone who wants to live a godly life in Christ Jesus will be persecuted, while evil men and impostors will go from bad to worse, deceiving and being deceived. But as for you, continue in what you have learned and have become convinced of, because you know those from whom you learned it, and how from infancy you have known the holy Scriptures, which are able to make you wise for salvation through faith in Christ Jesus. All Scripture is God-breathed and is useful for teaching, rebuking, correcting and training in righteousness, so that the man of God may be thoroughly equipped for every good work.

Those who are wise will shine like the brightness of the heavens, and those who lead many to righteousness, like the stars for ever and ever.

2 Timothy 4:1-5. 2 Timothy 3:12-16. Daniel 12:3.

He who began a good work in you will carry it on to completion until the day of Christ Jesus

If God is for us, who can be against us? The Lord is with me; I will not be afraid. What can man do to me? The Lord is with me; he is my helper.

The Lord is my light and my salvation--whom shall I fear? The Lord is the stronghold of my life--of whom shall I be afraid? When evil men advance against me to devour my flesh, when my enemies and my foes attack me, they will stumble and fall. Though an army besiege me, my heart will not fear; though war break out against me, even then will I be confident. God is with us; he is our leader.

He guides me in paths of righteousness for his name's sake. Even though I walk through the valley of the shadow of death, I will fear no evil, for you are with me; your rod and staff, they comfort me. You prepare a table before me in the presence of my enemies. You anoint my head with oil; my cup overflows. Surely goodness and love will follow me all the days of my life, and I will dwell in the house of the Lord forever.

Trust in the Lord forever, for the Lord, the Lord, is the Rock eternal.

Philippians 1:6. Romans 8:31. Psalm 118:6, 7. Psalm 27:1-3. 2 Chronicles 13:12. Psalm 23:3-6. Isaiah 26:4.

Be strong in the grace
that is in Christ Jesus

Endure hardship with us like a good soldier of Christ Jesus. No one serving as a soldier gets involved in civilian affairs--he wants to please his commanding officer. Similarly, if anyone competes as an athlete, he does not receive the victor's crown unless he competes according to the rules. The hard-working farmer should be the first to receive a share of the crops. Reflect on what I am saying, for the Lord will give you insight into all this.

Remember Jesus Christ, raised from the dead, descended from David. This is my gospel, for which I am suffering even to the point of being chained like a criminal. But God's word is not chained. Therefore I endure everything for the sake of the elect, that they too may obtain the salvation that is in Christ Jesus, with eternal glory.

Whatever happens, conduct yourselves in a manner worthy of the gospel of Christ ... contending as one man for the faith of the gospel.

One thing I do: Forgetting what is behind and straining toward what is ahead, I press on toward the goal to win the prize for which God has called me heavenward in Christ Jesus. All of us who are mature should take such a view of things. And if on some point you think differently, that too God will make clear to you. Only let us live up to what we have already attained.

---

2 Timothy 2:1, 3-10. Philippians 1:27. Philippians 3:13-16.

To him who overcomes...

The Lord will fight for you; you need only to be still. I will send my terror ahead of you and throw into confusion every nation you encounter. I will make all your enemies turn their backs and run. As soon as you hear the sound of marching in the tops of the balsam trees, move quickly, because that will mean the Lord has gone out in front of you to strike the Philistine army. The fear of God came upon all the kingdom of the countries when they heard how the Lord had fought against the enemies of Israel. With him is only the arm of flesh, but with us is the Lord our God to help us and to fight our battles.

In this world you will have trouble. But take heart! I have overcome the world. To him who overcomes, I will give the right to sit with me on my throne, just as I overcame and sat down with my Father on his throne. For everyone born of God overcomes the world. This is the victory that has overcome the world, even our faith.

This gospel of the kingdom will be preached in the whole world as a testimony to all nations, and then the end will come.   The end will come, when he hands over the kingdom to God and Father after he has destroyed all dominion, authority and power. For he must reign until he has put all his enemies under his feet.

Revelation 2:7. Exodus 14:14. Exodus 23:27. 2 Samuel 5:24. 2 Chronicles 20:29. 2 Chronicles 32:8. John 16:33. Revelation 3:21. 1 John 5:4. Matthew 24:14. 1 Corinthians 15:24, 25.

An inheritance that can never perish, spoil or fade--kept in heaven for you

In this you greatly rejoice, though now for a little while you may have had to suffer grief in all kinds of trials.

You must understand that in the last days scoffers will come, scoffing and following their own evil desires. They will say, "Where is this coming' he promised? Ever since our fathers died, everything goes on as it has since the beginning of creation." But they deliberately forget that long ago by God's word the heavens existed and the earth was formed out of water and by water. By these waters also the world of that time was deluged and destroyed. By the same word the present heavens and earth are reserved for fire, being kept for the day of judgment and destruction of ungodly men.

Consider it pure joy, my brothers, whenever you face trials of many kinds, because you know that the testing of your faith develops perseverance. Perseverance must finish its work so that you may be mature and complete, not lacking anything.

Be on your guard; stand firm in the faith; be men of courage; be strong. Night is coming, when no one can work. Hold on to what you have, so that no one will take your crown.

---

1 Peter 1:4, 6. 2 Peter 3:3-7. James 1:2-4. 1 Corinthians 16:13. John 9:4. Revelation 3:11.

This is a day you are to commemorate.

Celebrate the Feast of Unleavened Bread, because it was on this very day that I brought your divisions out of Egypt. Celebrate this day as a lasting ordinance for the generations to come. For seven days they celebrated with joy the Feast of Unleavened Bread, because the Lord had filled them with joy by changing the attitude of the king of Assyria, so that he assisted them in the work on the house of God, the God of Israel.

When the Lord brought back the captives to Zion, we were like men who dreamed. Our mouths were filled with laughter, our tongues with songs of joy. Then it was said among the nations, "The Lord has done great things for them." The Lord has done great things for us, and we are filled with joy.

You are a chosen people, a royal priesthood, a holy nation, a people belonging to God, that you may declare the praises of him who called you out of darkness into his wonderful light. Once you were not a people, but now you are the people of God; once you had not received mercy, but now you have received mercy.

You were once darkness, but now you are light in the Lord. Live as children of light (for the fruit of the light consists in all goodness, righteousness and truth) and find out what pleases the Lord. Be filled with the Spirit. Speak to one another with psalms, hymns and spiritual songs. Sing and make music in your heart to the Lord, always giving thanks to God the Father for everything, in the name of our Lord Jesus Christ.

Exodus 12:14, 17. Ezra 6:22. Psalm 126:1-3. 1 Peter 2:9, 10. Ephesians 5:8-10, 18-20.

This day is sacred to the Lord your God

So the wall was completed on the twenty-fifth of Elul, in fifty-two days. When all our enemies heard about this, all the surrounding nations were afraid and lost their self-confidence, because they realized that this work had been done with the help of our God.

Nehemiah said, "Go and enjoy choice food and sweet drinks, and send some to those who have nothing prepared. This day is sacred to our Lord. Do not grieve, for the joy of the Lord is your strength."

Those who sow in tears will reap with songs of joy. He who goes out weeping, carrying seed to sow, will return with songs of joy, carrying sheaves with him.

Shout for joy, O heavens; rejoice, O earth; burst into song, O mountains! For the Lord comforts his people and will have compassion on his afflicted ones. I delight greatly in the Lord; my soul rejoices in my God. For he has clothed me with garments of salvation and arrayed me in a robe of righteousness, as a bridegroom adorns his head like a priest, and as a bride adorns herself with her jewels.

I glory in Christ Jesus in my service to God. I will not venture to speak of anything except what Christ has accomplished through me in leading the Gentiles to obey God by what I have said and done.

I will extol the Lord at all times; his praise will always be on my lips. My soul will boast in the Lord; let the afflicted hear and rejoice. Glorify the Lord with me; let us exalt his name together.

Nehemiah 8:9. Nehemiah 6:15, 16. Nehemiah 8:10. Psalm 126:5, 6. Isaiah 49:13. Isaiah 61:10. Romans 15:17, 18. Psalm 34:1-3.

Let us come before him with thanksgiving

Celebrate the Feast of Weeks with the firstfruits of the wheat harvest, and the Feast of Ingathering at the turn of the year. Celebrate the Feast of Tabernacles for seven days after you have gathered the produce of your threshing floor and your winepress. Be joyful at your Feast--you, your sons and daughters, your menservants and maidservants, and the Levites, the aliens, the fatherless and the widows who live in your towns. For seven days celebrate the Feast to the Lord your God at the place the Lord will choose. For the Lord your God will bless you in all your harvest and in all the work of your hands, and your joy will be complete.

How priceless is your unfailing love! Both high and low among men find refuge in the shadow of your wings. They feast on the abundance of your house; you give them drink from your river of delights. As long as the earth endures, seedtime and harvest, cold and heat, summer and winter, day and night will never cease.

You care for the land and water it; you enrich it abundantly. The streams of God are filled with water to provide the people with grain, for so you have ordained it. You drench its furrows and level its ridges; you soften it with showers and bless its crops. You crown the year with your bounty, and your carts overflow with abundance. The grasslands of the desert overflow; the hills are clothed with gladness. The meadows are covered with flocks and the valleys are mantled with grain; they shout for joy and sing.

Let heaven and earth praise him, the seas and all that move in them.

Psalm 95:2. Exodus 34:22. Deuteronomy 16:13-15. Psalm 36:7, 8. Genesis 8:22. Psalm 65:9-13. Psalm 69:34 .

A time to laugh

May the righteous be glad and rejoice before God; may they be happy and joyful. A cheerful heart is good medicine. A heart at peace gives life to the body.

I know that there is nothing better for men than to be happy and do good while they live. That everyone may eat and drink, and find satisfaction in all his toil--this is the gift of God. For without him, who can eat or find enjoyment? To the man who pleases him, God gives wisdom, knowledge and happiness.

Rejoice in the Lord always. I will say it again: Rejoice!

You turned my wailing into dancing; you removed my sackcloth and clothed me with joy, that my heart may sing to you and not be silent. O Lord my God, I will give you thanks forever.

Shout for joy to the Lord, all the earth, burst into jubilant song with music; make music to the Lord with the harp, with the harp and the sound of singing, with trumpets and the blast of the ram's horn--shout for joy before the Lord, the King.

There is a time for everything, and a season for every activity under heaven.

Ecclesiastes 3:4. Psalm 68:3. Proverbs 17:22. Proverbs 14:30. Ecclesiastes 3:12, 13. Ecclesiastes 2:25, 26. Philippians 4:4. Psalm 30:11, 12. Psalm 98:4-6. Ecclesiastes 3:1.

Where morning dawns and evening fades you call forth songs of joy

Our mouths were filled with laughter, our tongues with songs of joy. Then it was said among the nations, "The Lord has done great things for them."

You have filled my heart with greater joy than when their grain and new wine abound. Let all who take refuge in you be glad; let them ever sing for joy. Spread your protection over them, that those who love your name may rejoice in you. For surely, O Lord, you bless the righteous; you surround them with your favor as with a shield.

Come, let us sing for joy to the Lord; let us shout aloud to the Rock of our salvation. Let us come before him with thanksgiving and extol him with music and song.

Let the word of Christ dwell in you richly as you teach and admonish one another with all wisdom, and as you sing psalms, hymns and spiritual songs with gratitude in your hearts to God. And whatever you do, whether in word or deed, do it all in the name of the Lord Jesus, giving thanks to God the Father through him.

Praise God in his sanctuary; praise him in his mighty heavens. Praise him for his acts of power, praise him for his surpassing greatness. Praise him with the sounding of the trumpet, praise him with the harp and lyre, praise him with tambourine and dancing, praise him with the strings and flute, praise him with the clash of cymbals, praise him with resounding cymbals.

Let everything that has breath praise the Lord.

Psalm 65:8. Psalm 126:2, 3. Psalm 4:7. Psalm 5:11, 12. Psalm 95:1, 2. Colossians 3:16, 17. Psalm 150:1-6.

Thanks be to God for his indescribable gift

For God so loved the world that he gave his one and only Son, that whoever believes in him shall not perish but have eternal life. It is by grace you have been saved, through faith--and this not from yourselves, it is the gift of God. I, even I, am he who blots out your transgressions, for my own sake, and remembers your sins no more.

I delight greatly in the Lord; my soul rejoices in my God. For he has clothed me with garments of salvation and arrayed me in a robe of righteousness, as a bridegroom adorns his head like a priest, and as a bride adorns herself with her jewels.

See, your king comes to you, righteous and having salvation. Of the increase of his government and peace there will be no end. His dominion is an everlasting dominion that will not pass away, and his kingdom is one that will never be destroyed.

I looked and heard the voice of many angels, numbering thousands upon thousands, and ten thousand times ten thousand. They encircled the throne and the living creatures and the elders. In a loud voice they sang: "Worthy is the Lamb, who was slain, to receive power and wealth and wisdom and strength and honor and glory and praise!" Then I heard every creature in heaven and on earth and under the earth and on the sea, and all that is in them, singing: "To him who sits on the throne and to the Lamb be praise and honor and glory and power, for ever and ever!"

---

2 Corinthians 9:15. John 3:16. Ephesians 2:8. Isaiah 43:25. Isaiah 61:10.
Zechariah 9:9. Isaiah 9:7. Daniel 7:14. Revelation 5:11-13.

Clap your hands, all you nations; shout to God with cries of joy

Though the fig tree does not bud and there are no grapes on the vines, though the olive crop fails and the fields produce no food, though there are no sheep in the pen and no cattle in the stalls, yet I will rejoice in the Lord, I will be joyful in God my Savior. The Sovereign Lord is my strength; he makes my feet like the feet of a deer, he enables me to go on the heights.

By day the Lord directs his love, at night his song is with me--a prayer to the God of my life. For the Lord God is a sun and shield; the Lord bestows favor and honor; no good thing does he withhold from those whose walk is blameless.

How awesome is the Lord Most High, the great King over all the earth! He subdued nations under us, peoples under our feet. He chose our inheritance for us, the pride of Jacob, whom he loved. God has ascended amid shouts of joy, the Lord amid the sounding of trumpets. Sing praises to God, sing praises; sing praises to our King, sing praises.

For God is the King of all the earth; sing to him a psalm of praise. God reigns over the nations; God is seated on his holy throne. The nobles of the nations assemble as the people of the God of Abraham, for the kings of the earth belong to God; he is greatly exalted. The Lord will reign for ever and ever.

You rule over all the kingdoms of the nations. Power and might are in your hand, and no one can withstand you.

·

Psalm 47:1. Habakkuk 3:17-19. Psalm 42:8. Psalm 84:11. Psalm 47:2-9. Exodus 15:18. 2 Chronicles 20:6.

Do not be afraid.
Stand firm and you will see the deliverance the Lord will bring you today

The Lord is a warrior; the Lord is his name. Pharaoh's chariots and his army he has hurled into the sea.

The Lord who delivered me [David] from the paw of the lion and the paw of the bear will deliver me from the hand of this Philistine.

My God sent his angel, and he shut the mouths of the lions. They have not hurt me [Daniel], because I was found innocent in his sight.

Suddenly an angel of the Lord appeared and a light shone in the cell. He struck Peter on the side and woke him up. "Quick, get up!" he said, and the chains fell off Peter's wrists.

The Lord knows how to rescue godly men from trials. The Sovereign Lord will wipe away the tears from all faces; he will remove the disgrace of his people from all the earth. The Lord has spoken. In that day they will say, "Surely this is our God; we trusted in him, and he saved us. This is the Lord, we trusted in him; let us rejoice and be glad in his salvation."

There will be no more death or mourning or crying or pain. A righteous man may have many troubles, but the Lord delivers him from them all. The Lord himself goes before you and will be with you; he will never leave you nor forsake you. Do not be afraid; do not be discouraged.

•

Exodus 14:13. Exodus 15:3, 4. 1 Samuel 17:37. Daniel 6:22. Acts 12:7. 2 Peter 2:9. Isaiah 25:8, 9. Revelation 21:4. Psalm 34:19. Deuteronomy 31:8.

The Lord will fight for you; you need only to be still

I will send my terror ahead of you and throw into confusion every nation you encounter. I will make all your enemies turn their backs and run.

As soon as you hear the sound of marching in the tops of the balsam trees, move quickly, because that will mean the Lord has gone out in front of you to strike the Philistine army.

With him is only the arm of flesh, but with us is the Lord our God to help us and to fight our battles. Through you we push back our enemies; through your name we trample our foes.

We are more than conquerors through him who loved us. Yes, Lord, walking in the way of your laws, we wait for you; your name and renown are the desire of our hearts. O Lord, be gracious to us; we long for you. Be our strength every morning, our salvation in time of distress.

I waited patiently for the Lord; he turned to me and heard my cry. He lifted me out of the slimy pit, out of the mud and mire; he set my feet on a rock and gave me a firm place to stand. He put a new song in my mouth, a hymn of praise to our God. Many will see and fear and put their trust in the Lord. Many, O Lord my God, are the wonders you have done. The things you planned for us no one can recount to you; were I to speak and tell of them, they would be too many to declare.

Exodus 14:14. Exodus 23:27. 2 Samuel 5:24. 2 Chronicles 32:8. Psalm 44:5. Romans 8:37. Isaiah 26:8. Isaiah 33:2. Psalm 40:1-3, 5.

In your unfailing love you will lead the people you have redeemed

In your strength you will guide them to your holy dwelling. You guide me with your counsel, and afterward you will take me into glory. Whom have I in heaven but you? And earth has nothing I desire besides you. My flesh and my heart may fail, but God is the strength of my heart and my portion forever. For this God is our God for ever and ever; he will be our guide even to the end.

Whether you turn to the right or to the left, your ears will hear a voice behind you, saying, "This is the way; walk in it." Remember how the Lord your God led you all the way in the desert these forty years, to humble you and to test you in order to know what was in your heart, whether or not you would keep his commands.

Like an eagle that stirs up its nest and hovers over its young, that spreads its wings to catch them and carries them on its pinions. The Lord alone led him; no foreign god was with him. If I rise on the wings of the dawn, if I settle on the far side of the sea, even there your hand will guide me, your right hand will hold me fast.

Praise the Lord, O my soul; all my inmost being, praise his holy name. Praise the Lord, O my soul, and forget not all his benefits--who forgives all your sins and heals all your diseases, who redeems your life from the pit and crowns you with love and compassion, who satisfies your desires with good things so that your youth is renewed like the eagle's.

Exodus 15:13. Psalm 73:24-26. Psalm 48:14. Isaiah 30:21. Deuteronomy 8:2. Deuteronomy 32:11, 12. Psalm 139:9, 10. Psalm 103:1-6.

Stretch out your hand

Raise your staff and stretch out your hand over the sea to divide the water so that the Israelites can go through the sea on dry ground. And when the Israelites saw the great power the Lord displayed against the Egyptians, the people feared the Lord and put their trust in him and in Moses his servant.

I will lead the blind by ways they have not known, along unfamiliar paths I will guide them; I will turn the darkness into light before them and make the rough places smooth. I will not forsake them.

This is what the Lord says--he who made a way through the sea, a path through the mighty waters, who drew out the chariots and horses, the army and reinforcements together, and they lay there, never to rise again, extinguished, snuffed out like a wick: "Forget the former things; do not dwell on the past. See, I am doing a new thing! Now it springs up; do you not perceive it? I am making a way in the desert and streams in the wasteland. Every valley shall be raised up, every mountain and hill made low; the rough ground shall become level, the rugged places a plain. I will turn all my mountains into roads, and my highways will be raised up."

When I said, "My foot is slipping," your love, O Lord, supported me. When anxiety was great within me, your consolation brought joy to my soul. You have been a refuge for the poor, a refuge for the needy in his distress, a shelter from the storm and a shade from the heat. The Lord has become my fortress, and my God the rock in whom I take refuge.

Exodus 14:16, 31. Isaiah 42:16. Isaiah 43:16-19. Isaiah 40:4.Isaiah 49:11. Psalm 94:18, 19. Isaiah 25:4. Psalm 94:22.

The Lord is with me; I will not be afraid. What can man do to me?

Was it not you who dried up the sea, the waters of the great deep, who made a road in the depths of the sea so that the redeemed might cross over?

In my anguish I cried to the Lord, and he answered by setting me free. The Lord is with me; he is my helper. I will look in triumph on my enemies. It is better to take refuge in the Lord than to trust in man. It is better to take refuge in the Lord than to trust in princes. I was pushed back and about to fall, but the Lord helped me. The Lord is my strength and my song; he has become my salvation.

I delight in weaknesses, in insults, in hardships, in persecutions, in difficulties. For when I am weak, then I am strong. My God has been my strength. David said to the Philistine, "You come against me with sword and spear and javelin, but I come against you in the name of the Lord Almighty, the God of the armies of Israel, whom you have defied."

Contend, O Lord, with those who contend with me; fight against those who fight against me. Take up shield and buckler; arise and come to my aid.

Psalm 118:6. Isaiah 51:10. Psalm 118:5, 7-9, 13, 14. 2 Corinthians 12:10. Isaiah 49:5. 1 Samuel 17:45. Psalm 35:1, 2.

I will never leave you or forsake you

Even to your old age and gray hairs I am he, I am he who will sustain you. I have made you and I will carry you; I will sustain you and I will rescue you.

"Though the mountains be shaken and the hills be removed, yet my unfailing love for you will not be shaken nor my covenant of peace be removed," says the Lord, who has compassion on you.

There is no one like the God of Jeshurun, who rides on the heavens to help you and on the clouds in his majesty. The eternal God is your refuge, and underneath are the everlasting arms.

So do not fear, for I am with you; do not be dismayed, for I am your God. I will strengthen you and help you; I will uphold you with my righteous right hand. For he guards the course of the just and protects the way of his faithful ones.

You have been my hope, O Sovereign Lord, my confidence since my youth. From birth I have relied on you; you brought me forth from my mother's womb. I will ever praise you. I have become like a portent to many, but you are my strong refuge. My mouth is filled with your praise, declaring your splendor all day long.

You give me your shield of victory, and your right hand sustains me; you stoop down to make me great. You broaden the path beneath me, so that my ankles do not turn.

The Lord will rescue me from every evil attack and will bring me safely to his heavenly kingdom. To him be glory for ever and ever. Amen.

Joshua 1:5. Isaiah 46:4. Isaiah 54:10. Deuteronomy 33:26, 27. Isaiah 41:10. Proverbs 2:8. Psalm 71:5-8. Psalm 18:35, 36. 2 Timothy 4:18.

From the Lord comes deliverance

You are a shield around me, O Lord; you bestow glory on me and lift up my head. To the Lord I cry aloud, and he answers me from his holy hill.

Great is the Lord in Zion; he is exalted over all the nations. Let them praise your great and awesome name--he is holy. The Lord your God, who is among you, is a great and awesome God. He is your praise; he is your God, who performed for you those great and awesome wonders.

Say to God, "How awesome are your deeds! So great is your power that your enemies cringe before you. All the earth bows down to you; they sing praise to you, they sing praise to your name."

Come and see what God has done, how awesome his works in man's behalf! He turned the sea into dry land, they passed through the waters on foot--come, let us rejoice in him. He rules forever by his power, his eyes watch the nations--let not the rebellious rise up against him.

Praise our God, O peoples, let the sound of his praise be heard; he has preserved our lives and kept our feet from slipping. For you, O God, tested us; you refined us like silver. You brought us into prison and laid burdens on our backs. You let men ride over our heads; we went through fire and water, but you brought us to a place of abundance.

Psalm 3:8, 3, 4. Psalm 99:2, 3. Deuteronomy 7:21. Deuteronomy 10:21. Psalm 66:3-12.

Be careful that you don't fall!

In the desert the whole community grumbled against Moses and Aaron. I do not want you to be ignorant of the fact, brothers, that our forefathers were all under the cloud and that they all passed through the sea. They were all baptized into Moses in the cloud and in the sea. They all ate the same spiritual food and drank the same spiritual drink; for they drank from the spiritual rock that accompanied them, and that rock was Christ. Nevertheless, God was not pleased with most of them; their bodies were scattered over the desert.

We should not test the Lord, as some of them did-- and were killed by snakes. And do not grumble, as some of them did--and were killed by the destroying angel.

So, if you think you are standing firm, be careful that you don't fall. No temptation has seized you except what is common to man. And God is faithful; he will not let you be tempted beyond what you can bear. And when you are tempted, he will also provide a way out so that you can stand up under it.

Do not test the Lord your God. Consider what God has done: Who can straighten what he has made crooked? When times are good, be happy; but when times are bad, consider: God has made the one as well as the other.

I know what it is to be in need, and I know what it is to have plenty. I have learned the secret of being content in any and every situation, whether well fed or hungry, whether living in plenty or in want. I can do everything through him who gives me strength.

---

1 Corinthians 10:12. Exodus 16:2. 1 Corinthians 10:1-6, 9, 10, 12, 13.
Deuteronomy 6:16. Ecclesiastes 7:13, 14. Philippians 4:12, 13.

There is no bread! There is no water! And we detest this miserable food!

When our fathers were in Egypt, they gave no thought to your miracles; they did not remember your many kindnesses, and they rebelled by the sea, the Red Sea. In the desert they gave in to their craving; in the wasteland they put God to the test. So he gave them what they asked for, but sent a wasting disease upon them.

Since the creation of the world God's invisible qualities--his eternal power and divine nature--have been clearly seen, being understood from what has been made, so that men are without excuse. For although they knew God, they neither glorified him as God nor gave thanks to him, but their thinking became futile and their foolish hearts were darkened.

When you eat and are satisfied, be careful that you do not forget the Lord, who brought you out of Egypt, out of the land of slavery. A man can do nothing better than to eat and drink and find satisfaction in his work. This too, I see, is from the hand of God, for without him, who can eat or find enjoyment?

He makes grass grow for the cattle, and plants for man to cultivate--bringing forth food from the earth: wine that gladdens the heart of man, oil to make his face shine, and bread that sustains his heart.

Look at the birds of the air; they do not sow or reap or store away in barns, and yet your heavenly Father feeds them. Are you not much more valuable than they? Give thanks to the God of heaven. His love endures forever.

Numbers 21:5. Psalm 106:7, 14, 15. Romans 1:20, 21. Deuteronomy 6:11, 12. Ecclesiastes 2:24, 25. Psalm 104:14, 15. Matthew 6:26, 27. Psalm 136:26.

You are not grumbling against us, but against the Lord

They forgot what he had done, the wonders he had shown them. He did miracles in the sight of their fathers in the land of Egypt, in the region of Zoan. He divided the sea and led them through; he made the water stand firm like a wall. He guided them with the cloud by day and with light from the fire all night. He split the rocks in the desert and gave them water as abundant as the seas; he brought streams out of a rocky crag and made water flow down like rivers.

But they continued to sin against him, rebelling in the desert against the Most High. They willfully put God to the test by demanding the food they craved. They did not keep his statutes. Like their fathers they were disloyal and faithless, as unreliable as a faulty bow.

Who can discern his errors? Forgive my hidden faults. Keep your servant also from willful sins; may they not rule over me. Then will I be blameless, innocent of great transgression. If you, O Lord, kept a record of sins, O Lord, who could stand? But with you there is forgiveness; therefore you are feared.

The Lord has compassion on those who fear him; for he knows how we are formed, he remembers that we are dust. He does not treat us as our sins deserve or repay us according to our iniquities. For as high as the heavens are above the earth, so great is his love for those who fear him. As far as the east is from the west, so far has he removed our transgressions from us.

Exodus 16:8. Psalm 78:11-18, 56, 57. Psalm 19:12, 13. Psalm 130:3, 4. Psalm 103:13, 14, 10-12.

Who are you, O man to talk back to God?

Shall what is formed say to him who formed it, "Why did you make me like this?" Does not the potter have the right to make out of the same lump of clay some pottery for noble purposes and some for common use?

Though one wished to dispute with him, he could not answer him one time out of a thousand. His wisdom is profound, his power is vast. Who has resisted him and come out unscathed? He moves mountains without their knowing it and overturns them in his anger. He shakes the earth from its place and makes its pillars tremble. He speaks to the sun and it does not shine; he seals off the light of the stars. He alone stretches out the heavens and treads on the waves of the sea. He is the Maker of the Bear and Orion, the Pleiades and the constellations of the south. He performs wonders that cannot be fathomed, miracles that cannot be counted. When he passes me, I cannot see him; when he goes by, I cannot perceive him. If he snatches away, who can stop him? Who can say to him, "What are you doing?"

O Lord, God of our fathers, are you not the God who is in heaven? You rule over all the kingdoms of the nations. Power and might are in your hand, and no one can withstand you.

Romans 9:20, 21. Job 9:3-12. 2 Chronicles 20:6.

As a mother comforts her child, so will I comfort you

Are God's consolations not enough for you, words spoken gently to you? Why has your heart carried you away, and why do your eyes flash, so that you vent your rage against God and pour out such words from your mouth?

I went down to the potter's house, and I saw him working at the wheel. But the pot he was shaping from the clay was marred in his hands; so the potter formed it into another pot, shaping it as seemed best to him. Then the word of the Lord came to me: "O house of Israel, can I not do with you as this potter does?" declares the Lord. "Like clay in the hand of the potter, so are you in my hand, O house of Israel."

We know that in all things God works for the good of those who love him, who have been called according to his purpose. For our light and momentary troubles are achieving for us an eternal glory that far outweighs them all. My grace is sufficient for you, for my power is made perfect in weakness. Do not let your hearts be troubled. Trust in God; trust also in me.

Rejoice that you participate in the sufferings of Christ, so that you may be overjoyed when his glory is revealed. He will wipe every tear from their eyes. There will be no more death or mourning or crying or pain.

Isaiah 66:13. Job 15:11-13. Jeremiah 18:3-6. Romans 8:28. 2 Corinthians 4:7. 2 Corinthians 12:9. John 14:1. 1 Peter 4:13. Revelation 21:4.

Do everything without complaining or arguing

So that you may become blameless and pure, children of God without fault in a crooked and depraved generation, in which you shine like stars in the universe as you hold out the word of life.

A hot-tempered man stirs up dissension, but a patient man calms a quarrel. As charcoal to embers and as wood to fire, so is a quarrelsome man for kindling strife.

Do nothing out of selfish ambition or vain conceit, but in humility consider others better than yourselves. Starting a quarrel is like breaching a dam; so drop the matter before a dispute breaks out. The Lord's servant must not quarrel; instead, he must be kind to everyone, able to teach, not resentful. In everything set them an example by doing what is right. For we are God's workmanship, created in Christ Jesus to do good works, which God prepared in advance for us to do.

Trust in the Lord and do good; dwell in the land and enjoy safe pasture. Delight yourself in the Lord and he will give you the desires of your heart. Commit your way to the Lord; trust in him and he will do this: He will make your righteousness shine like the dawn, the justice of your cause like the noonday sun.

Philippians 2:14-16. Proverbs 15:18. Proverbs 26:21. Philippians 2:3. Proverbs 17:14. 2 Timothy 2:24. Titus 2:7. Ephesians 2:10. Psalm 37:3-6.

Joyfully giving thanks to the Father

Let the peace of Christ rule in your hearts, since as members of one body you were called to peace. And be thankful. Give thanks in all circumstances, for this is God's will for you in Christ Jesus. You are a chosen people, a royal priesthood, a holy nation, a people belonging to God, that you may declare the praises of him who called you out of darkness into his wonderful light.

For us there is but one God, the Father, from whom all things came and for whom we live; and there is but one Lord, Jesus Christ, through whom all things came and through whom we live. Through Jesus, therefore, let us continually offer to God a sacrifice of praise--the fruit of lips that confess his name.

I waited patiently for the Lord; he turned to me and heard my cry. He lifted me out of the slimy pit, out of the mud and mire; he set my feet on a rock and gave me a firm place to stand. He put a new song in my mouth, a hymn of praise to our God. Many will see and fear and put their trust in the Lord. Many, O Lord my God, are the wonders you have done. The things you planned for us no one can recount to you; were I to speak and tell of them, they would be too many to declare.

My soul will rejoice in the Lord and delight in his salvation. My whole being will exclaim, "Who is like you, O Lord? You rescue the poor from those too strong for them, the poor and needy from those who rob them." I will give you thanks in the great assembly; among throngs of people I will praise you.

Colossians 1:11, 12. Colossians 3:15. 1 Thessalonians 5:1 1 Peter 2:9. 1 Corinthians 8:6. Hebrews 13:15. Psalm 40:1-3, 5. Psalm 35:9, 10, 18.

Come to me, all you who are weary and burdened, and I will give you rest

When his father-in-law saw all that Moses was doing for the people, he said, "What is this you are doing for the people? Why do you alone sit as judge, while all these people stand around you from morning till evening? ... What you are doing is not good. You and these people who come to you will only wear yourselves out. The work is too heavy for you; you cannot handle it alone."

Moses heard the people of every family wailing, each at the entrance to his tent. The Lord became exceedingly angry, and Moses was troubled. He asked the Lord, "Why have you brought this trouble on your servant? What have I done to displease you that you put the burden of all these people on me? Did I conceive all these people? Did I give them birth? Why do you tell me to carry them in my arms, as a nurse carries an infant, to the land you promised on oath to their forefathers? Where can I get meat for all these people? They keep wailing to me, 'Give us meat to eat!' I cannot carry all these people by myself; the burden is too heavy for me...." Trouble came to Moses because of them.

If any of you lacks wisdom, he should ask God, who gives generously to all without finding fault, and it will be given to him. The heart of the discerning acquires knowledge; the ears of the wise seek it out. Listen to advice and accept instruction, and in the end you will be wise.

Matthew 11:28. Exodus 18:14, 17, 18. Numbers 11:10-15. Psalm 106:32. James 1:5. Proverbs 18:15. Proverbs 19:20.

Carry each other's burdens, and in this way you will fulfill the law of Christ

Select capable men from all the people. ... That will make your load lighter, because they will share it with you. If you do this and God so commands, you will be able to stand the strain, and all these people will go home satisfied.

Jesus went out to a mountainside to pray, and spent the night praying to God. When morning came, he called his disciples to him and chose twelve of them, whom he also designated apostles.

Tychicus will tell you all the news about me. He is a dear brother, a faithful minister and fellow servant in the Lord. It was good of you to share in my troubles. Even when I was in Thessalonica, you sent me aid again and again when I was in need. Onesimus ... formerly he was useless to you, but now he has become useful both to you and to me. Timothy has proved himself, because as a son with his father he has served with me in the work of the gospel.

Be sympathetic, love as brothers, be compassionate and humble. Each of you should look not only to your own interests, but also to the interest of others.

Galatians 6:2. Exodus 18:21-23. Luke 6:12, 13. Colossians 4:7. Philippians 4:14, 16. Philemon 1:10, 11. 1 Peter 3:8. Philippians 2:4.

In vain you rise early and stay up late

Do not worry about your life, what you will eat or drink; or about your body, what you will wear. Is not life more important than food, and the body more important than clothes? "Martha, Martha," the Lord answered, "you are worried and upset about many things, but only one thing is needed. Mary has chosen what is better, and it will not be taken away from her."

Be careful, or your hearts will be weighed down with dissipation, drunkenness and the anxieties of life. Do not be anxious about anything, but in everything, by prayer and petition, with thanksgiving, present your requests to God.

Man is a mere phantom as he goes to and fro: He bustles about, but only in vain; he heaps up wealth, not knowing who will get it. "For whom am I toiling," he asked, "and why am I depriving myself of enjoyment?"

Godliness with contentment is great gain. For we brought nothing into the world, and we can take nothing out of it. But if we have food and clothing, we will be content with that.

Blessed is the man who trusts in the Lord, whose confidence is in him. He will be like a tree planted by the water that sends out its roots by the stream. It does not fear when heat comes; its leaves are always green. It has no worries in a year of drought and never fails to bear fruit.

Cast all your anxiety on him because he cares for you.

Psalm 127:2. Matthew 6:25. Luke 10:41. Luke 21:34. Philippians 4:6. Psalm 39:6. Ecclesiastes 4:8. 1 Timothy 6:6-8. Jeremiah 17:7, 8. 1 Peter 5:7.

Why is my pain unending?

O Lord, you deceived me, and I was deceived; you overpowered me and prevailed. I am ridiculed all day long; everyone mocks me. Whenever I speak, I cry out proclaiming violence and destruction. So the word of the Lord has brought me insult and reproach all day long. But if I say, "I will not mention him or speak any more in his name," his word is in my heart like a fire, a fire shut up in my bones. I am weary of holding it in; indeed, I cannot. Cursed be the day I was born! May the day my mother bore me not be blessed! Why did I ever come out of the womb to see trouble and sorrow and to end my days in shame?

My heart is in anguish within me; the terrors of death assail me. Fear and trembling have beset me; horror has overwhelmed me. I said, "Oh, that I had the wings of a dove! I would fly away and beat rest--I would flee far away and stay in the desert; I would hurry to my place of shelter, far from the tempest and storm. My God, my God, why have you forsaken me? Why are you so far from saving me, so far from the words of my groaning? O my God, I cry out by day, but you do not answer, by night, and am not silent.

All the days of the oppressed are wretched. This poor man called, and the Lord heard him; he saved him out of all his troubles. The angel of the Lord encamps around those who fear him, and he delivers them.

The God of all grace, who called you to his eternal glory in Christ, after you have suffered a little while, will himself restore you and make you strong, firm and steadfast. To him be the power for ever and ever.

Jeremiah 15:18. Jeremiah 20:7-9, 14, 18. Psalm 55:4-8. Psalm 22:1, 2. Proverbs 15:15. Psalm 34:6, 7. 1 Peter 5:10.

Call upon me in the day of trouble;
I will deliver you, and you will honor me

Elijah was afraid and ran for his life. When he came to Beer-sheba in Judah, he left his servant there, while he himself went a day's journey into the desert. He came to a broom tree, sat down under it and prayed that he might die. "I have had enough, Lord," he said. "Take my life; I am no better than my ancestors." Then he lay down under the tree and fell asleep.

All at once an angel touched him and said, "Get up and eat." He looked around, and there by his head was a cake of bread baked over hot coals, and a jar of water. He ate and drank and then lay down again.

The angel of the Lord came back a second time and touched him and said, "Get up and eat, for the journey is too much for you." So he got up and ate and drank.

My God will meet all your needs according to his glorious riches in Christ Jesus. Be still before the Lord and wait patiently for him.

It is not good to have zeal without knowledge, nor to be hasty and miss the way. A man's own folly ruins his life.

Jesus often withdrew to lonely places and prayed. Seek first his kingdom and his righteousness, and all these things will be given to you as well. Therefore, do not worry about tomorrow.

Ask and it will be given to you; seek and you will find; knock and the door will be opened to you. For everyone who asks receives; he who seeks finds; and to him who knocks, the door will be opened.

Psalm 50:15. 1 Kings 19:3-8. Philippians 4:9. Psalm 37:7. Proverbs 19:2, 3. Luke 5:16. Matthew 6:33, 34. Matthew 7:7, 8.

Be still before the Lord
and wait patiently for him

The apostles gathered around Jesus and reported to him all they had done and taught. Then, because so many people were coming and going that they did not even have a chance to eat, he said to them, "Come with me by yourselves to a quiet place and get some rest."

The news about him spread all the more, so that crowds of people came to hear him and to be healed of their sicknesses. But Jesus often withdrew to lonely places and prayed.

This is what the Lord says: "Stand at the crossroads and look; ask for the ancient paths, ask where the good way is, and walk in it, and your will find rest for your souls. You will keep in perfect peace him whose mind is steadfast, because he trusts in you.

The Lord gives strength to his people; the Lord blesses his people with peace.

You hold me by my right hand. You guide me with your counsel, and afterward you will take me into glory. Whom have I in heaven but you? And earth has nothing I desire besides you. My flesh and my heart may fail, but God is the strength of my heart and my portion forever. Those who are far from you will perish; you destroy all who are unfaithful to you. But as for me, it is good to be near God.

How great is the love the Father has lavished on us, that we should be called children of God! And that is what we are!

Psalm 37:7. Mark 6:30-32. Luke 5:15, 16. Jeremiah 6:16. Isaiah 26:3. Psalm 29:11. Psalm 73:23-26, 28. 1 John 3:1.

Rejoice in the Lord always

I will say it again: Rejoice! Let your gentleness be evident to all. The Lord is near. Do not be anxious about anything, but in everything, by prayer and petition, with thanksgiving, present your requests to God. And the peace of God, which transcends all understanding, will guard your hearts and your minds in Christ Jesus.

I have learned to be content whatever the circumstances. I know what it is to be in need, and I know what it is to have plenty. I have learned the secret of being content in any and every situation, whether well fed or hungry, whether living in plenty or in want. I can do everything through him who gives me strength.

Now to him who is able to do immeasurably more than all we ask or imagine, according to his power that is at work within us. "I know the plans I have for you," declares the Lord, "plans to prosper you and not to harm you, plans to give you hope and a future. Then you will call upon me and come and pray to me, and I will listen to you. You will seek me and find me when you seek me with all your heart."

Finally, brothers, whatever is true, whatever is noble, whatever is right, whatever is pure, whatever is lovely, whatever is admirable--if anything is excellent or praiseworthy--think about such things.

Philippians 4:4-7, 11-13. Ephesians 3:20. Jeremiah 29:11-13. Philippians 4:8.

Moses led the people out of the camp to meet with God

They stood at the foot of the mountain. Mount Sinai was covered with smoke, because the Lord descended on it in fire. The smoke billowed up from it like smoke from a furnace, the whole mountain trembled violently, and the sound of the trumpet grew louder and louder.

And God spoke all these words:

You shall have no other gods before me. You shall not make for yourself an idol. You shall not misuse the name of the Lord your God. Remember the Sabbath day by keeping it holy. Honor your father and your mother. You shall not murder. You shall not commit adultery. You shall not steal. You shall not give false testimony against your neighbor. You shall not covet your neighbor's house.

Love the Lord your God with all your heart and with all your soul and with all your strength. These commandments that I give you today are to be upon your hearts. Impress them on your children. Talk about them when you sit at home and when you walk along the road, when you lie down and when you get up. Tie them as symbols on your hands and bind them on your foreheads. Write them on the door frames of your houses and on your gates.

A man came up to Jesus and asked, "Teacher, what good thing must I do to get eternal life?"

Jesus replied. "... If you want to enter life, obey the commandments....Sell your possessions and give to the poor, and you will have treasure in heaven. Then come, follow me.

Exodus 19:17-20. Exodus 20:1, 3-17. Deuteronomy 6:5-9. Matthew 19:16-19, 21, 29.

The voice of the Lord is powerful

The voice of the Lord is majestic. The voice of the Lord strikes with flashes of lightning. The voice of the Lord shakes the desert; the Lord shakes the Desert of Kadesh. The voice of the Lord twists the oaks and strips the forests bare. And in his temple all cry, "Glory!"

A great and powerful wind tore the mountains apart and shattered the rocks before the Lord, but the Lord was not in the wind. After the wind there was an earthquake, but the Lord was not in the earthquake. After the earthquake came a fire, but the Lord was not in the fire. And after the fire came a gentle whisper.

Come, let us bow down in worship, let us kneel before the Lord our Maker; for he is our God and we are the people of his pasture, the flock under his care.

So, as the Holy Spirit says: "Today, if you hear his voice, do not harden your hearts." I stand at the door and knock. If anyone hears my voice and opens the door, I will come in and eat with him, and he with me.

You will realize that I am in my Father, and you are in me, and I am in you. Those who obey his commands live in him, and he in them. And this is how we know that he lives in us: We know it by the Spirit he gave us. ...Filled to the measure of all the fullness of God.

Psalm 29:4, 7-9. 1 Kings 19:11, 12. Psalm 95:6, 7. Hebrews 3:7, 8. Revelation 3:20. John 14:20. 1 John 3:24. Ephesians 3:19.

The Lord reigns

He is robed in majesty; the Lord is robed in majesty and is armed with strength. Out of the north he comes in golden splendor; God comes in awesome majesty. The Almighty is beyond our reach and exalted in power; in his justice and great righteousness, he does not oppress. Therefore, men revere him, for does he not have regard for all the wise in heart?

The eyes of the Lord range throughout the earth to strengthen those whose hearts are fully committed to him. The Lord is with you when you are with him. If you seek him, he will be found by you, but if you forsake him, he will forsake you. Be strong and do not give up, for your work will be rewarded.

Take to heart all the words I have solemnly declared to you this day, so that you may command your children to obey carefully all the words of this law. They are not just idle words for you--they are your life.

Do not let this Book of the Law depart from your mouth; meditate on it day and night, so that you may be careful to do everything written in it. Then you will be prosperous and successful. Those who hope in the Lord will renew their strength. They will soar on wings like eagles; they will run and not grow weary, they will walk and not be faint.

My flesh and my heart may fail, but God is the strength of my heart and my portion forever.

Psalm 93:1. Job 37:22-24. 2 Chronicles 16:9. 2 Chronicles 15:2, 7. Deuteronomy 32:46, 47. Joshua 1:8. Isaiah 40:31. Psalm 73:26.

Ascribe to the Lord glory and strength

Ascribe to the Lord the glory due his name; bring an offering and come into his courts. Worship the Lord in the splendor of his holiness; tremble before him, all the earth.

Let us not give up meeting together, as some are in the habit of doing, but let us encourage one another. I want men everywhere to lift up holy hands in prayer, without anger or disputing. Let us be thankful, and so worship God acceptably with reverence and awe.

Who may ascend the hill of the Lord? Who may stand in his holy place? He who has clean hands and a pure heart, who does not lift up his soul to an idol or swear by what is false. He will receive blessing from the Lord and vindication from God his Savior. For this is what the high and lofty One says--he who lives forever, whose name is holy: "I live in a high and holy place, but also with him who is contrite and lowly in spirit, to revive the spirit of the lowly and to revive the heart of the contrite."

One thing I ask of the Lord, this is what I seek: that I may dwell in the house of the Lord all the days of my life, to gaze upon the beauty of the Lord and to seek him in his temple. O God, you are my God, earnestly I seek you; my soul thirsts for you, my body longs for you, in a dry and weary land where there is no water. I have seen you in the sanctuary and beheld your power and your glory.

May the words of my mouth and the meditation of my heart be pleasing in your sight, O Lord, my Rock and my Redeemer.

Psalm 96:7-9. Hebrews 10:25. 1 Timothy 2:8. Hebrews 12:28. Psalm 24:3-5. Isaiah 57:15. Psalm 27:4. Psalm 63:1, 2. Psalm 19:14.

What does the Lord your God ask of you?

Be very careful to keep the commandment and the
law that Moses the servant of the Lord gave you: to
love the Lord your God, to walk in all his ways, to
obey his commands, to hold fast to him and to serve
him with all your heart and all your soul.

To love the Lord your God. Love the Lord, all his
saints! The Lord preserves the faithful but the proud he
pays back in full. Keep yourselves in God's love.

To walk in all his ways. Walk humbly with your
God. Stand at the crossroads and look; ask for the
ancient paths, ask where the good way is, and walk in
it, and you will find rest for your souls.

To obey his commands. Not everyone who says to
me, "Lord, Lord" will enter the kingdom of heaven, but
only he who does the will of my Father who is in heaven.
We must obey God rather than men!

To hold fast to him. Look to the Lord and his
strength; seek his face always. Blessed are they who
keep his statutes and seek him with all their heart.

To serve him with all your heart and all your soul.
Stand firm. Let nothing move you. Always give yourselves fully to the work of the Lord. For we are God's
fellow workers.

---

*Deuteronomy 10:12. Joshua 22:5. Psalm 31:23. Jude 21. Joshua 22:5. Micah
6:8. Jeremiah 6:16. Joshua 22:5. Matthew 7:21. Acts 5:29. Joshua 22:5.
Psalm 105:4. Psalm 119:2. Joshua 22:5. 1 Corinthians 15:58. 1 Corinthians
3:9.*

Turn my eyes away from worthless things

"Meaningless! Meaningless!" says the Teacher. "Utterly meaningless! Everything is meaningless."

A man can do nothing better than to eat and drink and find satisfaction in his work. This too, I see, is from the hand of God, for without him, who can eat or find enjoyment? To the man who pleases him, God gives wisdom, knowledge and happiness. He has also set eternity in the hearts of men.

Your word, O Lord, is eternal; it stands firm in the heavens. Your faithfulness continues through all generations; you established the earth, and it endures. Your laws endure to this day, for all things serve you. If your law had not been my delight, I would have perished in my affliction. I will never forget your precepts, for by them you have preserved my life.

No one is like you, O Lord; you are great, and your name is mighty in power. ... Among all the wise men of the nations and in all their kingdoms, there is no one like you.

God made the earth by his power; he founded the world by his wisdom and stretched out the heavens by his understanding. When he thunders, the waters in the heavens roar; he makes clouds rise from the ends of the earth. He sends lightning with the rain and brings out the wind from his storehouses.

You can do all things; no plan of yours can be thwarted. Teach me, O Lord, to follow your decrees; then I will keep them to the end. Give me understanding, and I will keep your law and obey it with all my heart. Direct me in the path of your commands....

Psalm 119:37. Ecclesiastes 1:2. Ecclesiastes 2:24-26. Ecclesiastes 3:11.
Psalm 119:89-93. Jeremiah 10:6, 7, 12, 13. Job 42:2. Psalm 119:33-35.

O Lord God Almighty, who is like you?

You are mighty, O Lord, and your faithfulness surrounds you. Righteousness and justice are the foundation of your throne; love and faithfulness go before you. Blessed are those who have learned to acclaim you, who walk in the light of your presence, O Lord. They rejoice in your name all day long; they exult in your righteousness. For you are their glory and strength.

Find your joy in the Lord, and I will cause you to ride on the heights of the land and to feast on the inheritance of your father Jacob. Those who are wise will shine like the brightness of the heavens, and those who lead many to righteousness, like the stars for ever and ever. When a man's ways are pleasing to the Lord, he makes even his enemies live at peace with him.

He knows the way that I take; when he has tested me, I will come forth as gold. My feet have closely followed his steps; I have kept to his way without turning aside. I have not departed from the commands of his lips; I have treasured the words of his mouth more than my daily bread.

Yours, O Lord, is the greatness and the power and the glory and the majesty and the splendor, for everything in heaven and earth is yours. Yours, O Lord, is the kingdom; you are exalted as head over all. Wealth and honor come from you; you are the ruler of all things. In your hands are strength and power to exalt and give strength to all. Now, our God, we give you thanks, and praise your glorious name.

Psalm 89:8, 14-17. Isaiah 58:14. Daniel 12:3. Proverbs 16:7. Job 23:10-12. 1 Chronicles 29:11-13.

His great love

"I have seen these people," the Lord said to Moses, "and they are a stiff-necked people." Moses sought the favor of the Lord his God. "O Lord," he said, "why should your anger burn against your people, whom you brought out of Egypt with great power and a mighty hand? Why should the Egyptians say, 'It was with evil intent that he brought them out, to kill them in the mountains and to wipe them off the face of the earth'? Turn from your fierce anger; relent and do not bring disaster on your people." Then the Lord relented and did not bring...the disaster he had threatened.

You are a forgiving God, gracious and compassionate, slow to anger and abounding in love. For great is your love, higher than the heavens; your faithfulness reaches to the skies.

Because of the Lord's great love we are not consumed, for his compassions never fail. They are new every morning; great is your faithfulness.

Rend your heart and not your garments. Return to the Lord your God ... he relents from sending calamity. Who is a God like you, who pardons sin and forgives the transgression of the remnant of his inheritance? You do not stay angry forever but delight to show mercy.

Because of his great love for us, God, who is rich in mercy, made us alive with Christ even when we were dead in transgressions--it is by grace you have been saved. And God raised us up with Christ and seated us with him in the heavenly realms...in order that in coming ages he might show the incomparable riches of his grace, expressed in his kindness to us in Christ Jesus.

Ephesians 2:4. Exodus 32:9, 11, 12, 14. Nehemiah 9:17. Psalm 108:4. Lamentations 3:22, 23. Joel 2:13. Micah 7:18. Ephesians 2:4-7.

The Lord is your life

Come, let us return to the Lord. He has torn us to pieces but he will heal us; he has injured us but he will bind up our wounds. We implore you on Christ's behalf: Be reconciled to God. God made him who had no sin to be sin for us, so that in him we might become the righteousness of God.

If serving the Lord seems undesirable to you, then choose for yourselves this day whom you will serve. But as for me and my household we will serve the Lord. Elijah went before the people and said, "How long will you waver between two opinions? If the Lord is God, follow him."

What I am commanding you today is not too difficult for you or beyond your reach. It is not up in heaven, so that you have to ask, "Who will ascend into heaven to get it and proclaim it to us so we may obey it?" Nor is it beyond the sea, so that you have to ask, "Who will cross the sea to get it and proclaim it to us so we may obey it?" No, the word is very near you; it is in your mouth and in your heart so you may obey it.

See, I set before you today life and prosperity, death and destruction. For I command you today to love the Lord your God, to walk in his ways, and to keep his commands, decrees and laws; then you will live and increase, and the Lord your God will bless you in the land you are entering to possess. Now choose life, so that you and your children may live and that you may love the Lord your God, listen to his voice, and hold fast to him. For the Lord is your life.

Deuteronomy 30:20. Hosea 6:1. 2 Corinthians 5:20, 21. Joshua 24:15.
1 Kings 18:21. Deuteronomy 30:11-16, 19, 20.

We want a king over us

When that day comes, you will cry out for relief from the king you have chosen, and the Lord will not answer you in that day.

The heart is deceitful above all things and beyond cure. Who can understand it? I the Lord search the heart and examine the mind, to reward a man according to his conduct, according to what his deeds deserve.

I know, O Lord, that a man's life is not his own; it is not for man to direct his steps. ... Unless the Lord builds the house, its builders labor in vain. Unless the Lord watches over the city, the watchmen stand guard in vain.

Acknowledge the God of your father, and serve him with wholehearted devotion and with a willing mind, for the Lord searches every heart and understands every motive behind the thoughts. If you seek him, he will be found by you; but if you forsake him, he will reject you forever.

Cursed is the one who trusts in man, who depends on flesh for his strength and whose heart turns away from the Lord. He will be like a bush in the wastelands; he will not see prosperity when it comes. He will dwell in the parched places of the desert, in a salt land where no one lives.

But blessed is the man who trusts in the Lord, whose confidence is in him. He will be like a tree planted by the water that sends out its roots by the stream. It does not fear when heat comes; its leaves are always green. It has no worries in a year of drought and never fails to bear fruit.

---

1 Samuel 8:19, 18. Jeremiah 17:9, 10. Jeremiah 10:23, 24. Psalm 127:1. 1 Chronicles 28:9. Jeremiah 17:58.

A wise man listens to advice

They would not listen or respond to discipline. We must pay more careful attention, therefore, to what we have heard, so that we do not drift away.

Blessed is the man who listens to me, watching daily at my doors, waiting at my doorway. Guard your steps when you go to the house of God. Go near to listen rather than to offer the sacrifice of fools, who do not know that they do wrong.

Everyone who hears these words of mine and puts them into practice is like a wise man who built his house on the rock. The rains came down, the streams rose, and the winds blew and beat against that house; yet it did not fall, because it had its foundation on the rock. But everyone who hears these words of mine and does not put them into practice is like a foolish man who built his house on sand. The rains came down, the streams rose, and the winds blew and beat against that house, and it fell with a great crash.

If you do not obey the Lord, and if you rebel against his commands, his hand will be against you, as it was against your fathers. Fear the Lord and serve him with all faithfulness. Anyone who listens to the word but does not do what it says is like a man who looks at his face in a mirror and, after looking at himself, goes away and immediately forgets what he looks like. But the man who looks intently into the perfect law that gives freedom, and continues to do this, not forgetting what he has heard, but doing it--he will be blessed in what he does.

Proverbs 12:15. Jeremiah 32:33. Hebrews 2:1-4. Proverbs 8:34.Ecclesiastes 5:1. Matthew 7:24-27. 1 Samuel 12:15. Joshua 24:14. James 1:23-25.

Today, if you hear his voice...

do not harden your hearts as you did in the rebellion. Who were they who heard and rebelled? Were they not all those Moses led out of Egypt? And with whom was he angry for forty years? Was it not with those who sinned, whose bodies fell in the desert? And to whom did God swear that they would never enter his rest if not to those who disobeyed? So we see that they were not able to enter, because of their unbelief. Therefore, since the promise of entering his rest still stands, let us be careful that none of you be found to have fallen short of it.

Although the Lord sent prophets to the people to bring them back to him, and though they testified against them, they would not listen. Do not be like your fathers and brothers, who were unfaithful to the Lord, the God of their fathers, so that he made them an object of horror, as you see. Do not be stiff-necked, as your fathers were; submit to the Lord. Come to the sanctuary, which he has consecrated forever. Serve the Lord your God, so that his fierce anger will turn away from you. For the Lord your God is gracious and compassionate. He will not turn his face from you if you return to him.

See to it, brothers, that none of you has a sinful, unbelieving heart that turns away from the living God. But encourage one another daily, as long as it is called Today, so that none of you may be hardened by sin's deceitfulness. We have come to share in Christ if we hold firmly till the end the confidence we had at first.

Hebrews 3:15-19. Hebrews 4:1. 2 Chronicles 24:19. 2 Chronicles 30:7-9. Hebrews 3:12-14.

Come, let us return to the Lord

Let us acknowledge the Lord; let us press on to acknowledge him. As surely as the sun rises, he will appear; he will come to us like the winter rains, like the spring rains that water the earth.

Sow for yourselves righteousness, reap the fruit of unfailing love, and break up your unplowed ground; for it is time to seek the Lord, until he comes and showers righteousness on you. Let my teaching fall like rain and my words descend like dew, like showers on new grass, like abundant rain on tender plants.

I sought the Lord, and he answered me; he delivered me from all my fears. Those who look to him are radiant; their faces are never covered with shame. This poor man called, and the Lord heard him; he saved him out of all his troubles. The angel of the Lord encamps around those who fear him, and he delivers them.

Taste and see that the Lord is good; blessed is the man who takes refuge in him. Fear the Lord, you his saints, for those who fear him lack nothing. The lions may grow weak and hungry, but those who seek the Lord lack no good thing.

The righteous cry out, and the Lord hears them; he delivers them from all their troubles. The Lord is close to the brokenhearted and saves those who are crushed in spirit. A righteous man may have many troubles, but the Lord delivers him from them all. The Lord redeems his servants; no one will be condemned who takes refuge in him.

Hosea 6:1, 3. Hosea 10:12. Deuteronomy 32:2. Psalm 34:4-10. Psalm 34:17-19, 22.

Your will be done on earth as it is in heaven

Do not offer the parts of your body to sin, as instruments of wickedness, but rather offer yourselves to God, as those who have been brought from death to life; Submit yourselves, then, to God. Resist the devil, and he will flee from you.

I desire to do your will, O my God; your law is within my heart. My soul yearns for you in the night; in the morning my spirit longs for you. Whom have I in heaven but you? And earth has nothing I desire besides you. My eyes stay open through the watches of the night, that I may meditate on your promises.

Whatever was to my profit I now consider loss for the sake of Christ. What is more, I consider everything a loss compared to the surpassing greatness of knowing Christ Jesus my Lord, for whose sake I have lost all things. I consider them rubbish, that I may gain Christ and be found in him, not having a righteousness of my own that comes from the law, but that which is through faith in Christ--the righteousness that comes from God and is by faith. I want to know Christ and the power of his resurrection and the fellowship of sharing in his sufferings....

Not that I have already obtained all this, or have already been made perfect, but I press on to take hold of that for which Christ Jesus took hold of me. Brothers, I do not consider myself yet to have taken hold of it. But one thing I do: Forgetting what is behind and straining toward what is ahead, I press on toward the goal to win the prize for which God has called me heavenward in Christ Jesus.

Matthew 6:10. Romans 6:13. James 4:7. Psalm 40:8. Isaiah 26:9. Psalm 73:25. Psalm 119:148. Philippians 3:7-14.

Jesus ... looked toward heaven and prayed

I pray for them. I am not praying for the world, but for those you have given me, for they are yours. All I have is yours, and all you have is mine. And glory has come to me through them. My prayer is not that you take them out of the world but that you protect them from the evil one. My prayer is not for them alone. I pray also for those who will believe in me through their message. Father, I want those you have given me to be with me where I am, and to see my glory, the glory you have given me because you loved me before the creation of the world.

I have prayed for you, Simon, that your faith may not fail.   Jesus said, "Father, forgive them, for they do not know what they are doing." I will ask the Father, and he will give you another Counselor to be with you forever.

Christ Jesus, who died--more than that, who was raised to life--is at the right hand of God and is also interceding for us. He is able to save completely those who come to God through him, because he always lives to intercede for them.

Walk as Jesus did.

John 17:1, 9, 10, 15, 20, 24. Luke 22:32. Luke 23:34. John 14:16. Romans 8:34. Hebrews 7:25. 1 John 2:6.

Pray for each other

Devote yourselves to prayer, being watchful and thankful. Do not be anxious about anything, but in everything, by prayer and petition, with thanksgiving, present your requests to God. Be joyful always; pray continually; give thanks in all circumstances, for this is God's will for you in Christ Jesus.

When you pray, do not be like the hypocrites, for they love to pray standing in the synagogues and on the street corners to be seen by men. I tell you the truth, they have received their reward in full. But when you pray, go into your room, close the door and pray to your Father, who is unseen. Then your Father, who sees what is done in secret, will reward you. And when you pray, do not keep on babbling like pagans, for they think they will be heard because of their many words. Do not be like them, for your Father knows what you need before you ask him.

We do not know what we ought to pray for, but the Spirit himself intercedes for us with groans that words cannot express. And he who searches our hearts knows the mind of the Spirit, because the Spirit intercedes for the saints in accordance with God's will.

James 5:16. Colossians 4:2. Philippians 4:6, 7. 1 Thessalonians 5:16-18. Matthew 6:5-8. Romans 8:26, 27.

Pray for those who persecute you

Jesus said, "Father, forgive them, for they do not know what they are doing."

While they were stoning him, Stephen prayed, "Lord Jesus, receive my spirit." Then he fell on his knees and cried out, "Lord, do not hold this sin against them." When he had said this, he fell asleep.

Do not gloat when your enemy falls; when he stumbles, do not let your heart rejoice. Do not say, "I'll do to him as he has done to me; I'll pay that man back for what he did." If your enemy is hungry, give him food to eat; if he is thirsty, give him water to drink. In doing this, you will heap burning coals on his head, and the Lord will reward you.

You have heard that it was said, "Love your neighbor and hate your enemy." But I tell you: Love your enemies and pray for those who persecute you, that you may be sons of your Father in heaven. He causes his sun to rise on the evil and the good, and sends rain on the righteous and the unrighteous. Bless those who persecute you; bless and do not curse.

"For my thoughts are not your thoughts, neither are your ways my ways," declares the Lord. "As the heavens are higher than the earth, so are my ways higher than your ways and my thoughts than your thoughts."

Matthew 5:44. Luke 23:34. Acts 7:59, 60. Proverbs 24:17, 29. Proverbs 25:21, 22. Matthew 5:43-45. Romans 12:14. Isaiah 55:8, 9.

Pray for the well-being of the king and his sons

I urge, then, first of all, that requests, prayers, intercession and thanksgiving be made for everyone--for kings and all those in authority, that we may live peaceful and quiet lives in all godliness and holiness. This is good, and pleases God our Savior, who wants all men to be saved and to come to a knowledge of the truth. For there is one God and one mediator between God and men, the man Christ Jesus.

At Gibeon the Lord appeared to Solomon during the night in a dream, and God said, "Ask for whatever you want me to give you." Solomon answered, "You have shown great kindness to your servant, my father David, because he was faithful to you and righteous and upright in heart. You have continued this great kindness to him and have given him a son to sit on his throne this very day. Now, O Lord my God, you have made your servant king in place of my father David. But I am only a little child and do not know how to carry out my duties. Your servant is here among the people you have chosen, a great people, too numerous to count or number. So give your servant a discerning heart to govern your people and to distinguish between right and wrong. ?"

If my people, who are called by my name, will humble themselves and pray and seek my face and turn from their wicked ways, then will I hear from heaven and will forgive their sin and will heal their land. Now my eyes will be open and my ears attentive to the prayers offered in this place.

Ezra 6:10. 1 Timothy 2:1-5. 1 Kings 3:5-9. 2 Chronicles 7:14,15.

Always keep on praying for all the saints

Far be it from me that I should sin against the Lord by failing to pray for you.

I keep asking that the God of our Lord Jesus Christ, the glorious Father, may give you the Spirit of wisdom and revelation,so that you may know him better. I pray also that the eyes of your heart may be enlightened in order that you may know the hope to which he has called you, the riches of his glorious inheritance in the sins, and his incomparably great power for us who believe. That power is like the working of his mighty strength, which he exerted in Christ when he raised him from the dead and seated him at his right hand in the heavenly realms.

I kneel before the Father. I pray that out of his glorious riches he may strengthen you with power through his Spirit in your inner being, so that Christ may dwell in your hearts through faith. And I pray that you, being rooted and established in love, may have power, together with all the saints, to grasp how wide and long and high and deep is the love of Christ, and to know this love that surpasses knowledge--that you may be filled to the measure of all the fullness of God.

In all my prayers for all of you, I always pray with joy ... being confident of this, that he who began a good work in you will carry it on to completion until the day of Christ Jesus. And this is my prayer: that your love may abound more and more in knowledge and depth of insight, so that you may be able to discern what is best and may be pure and blameless until the day of Christ.

Ephesians 6:18. 1 Samuel 12:23. Ephesians 1:17-20. Ephesians 3:14-19. Philippians 1:4, 6, 9-11.

August 13

The prayer of a righteous man
is powerful and effective

Elijah was a man just like us. He prayed earnestly that it would not rain, and it did not rain on the land for three and a half years. Again he prayed, and the heavens gave rain, and the earth produced its crops.

If you believe, you will receive whatever you ask for in prayer. If two of you on earth agree about anything you ask for, it will be done for you by my Father in heaven. For where two or three come together in my name, there am I with them.

Dear friends, if our hearts do not condemn us, we have confidence before God and receive from him anything we ask, because we obey his commands and do what pleases him.

Ask and it will be given to you; seek and you will find; knock and the door will be opened to you. For everyone who asks receives; he who seeks finds; and to him who knocks, the door will be opened. You may ask me for anything in my name, and I will do it.

Let us then approach the throne of grace with confidence, so that we may receive mercy and find grace to help us in our time of need.

James 5:16-18. Matthew 21:22. Matthew 18:19, 20. 1 John 3:21, 22. Luke 11:9, 10. John 14:14. Hebrews 4:16.

I always pray with joy

Praise awaits you, O God, in Zion; to you our vows will be fulfilled. O you who hear prayer, to you all men will come.

We give thanks to you, O God, we give thanks, for your Name is near; men tell of your wonderful deeds.

It is good to praise the Lord and make music to your name, O Most High, to proclaim your love in the morning and your faithfulness at night, to the music of the ten-stringed lyre and the melody of the harp. For you make me glad by your deeds, O Lord; I sing for joy at the works of your hands. How great are your works, O Lord, how profound your thoughts!

Shout for joy to the Lord, all the earth. Worship the Lord with gladness; come before him with joyful songs. Know that the Lord is God. It is he who made us, and we are his; we are his people, the sheep of his pasture. Enter his gates with thanksgiving and his courts with praise; give thanks to him and praise his name. For the Lord is good and his love endures forever; his faithfulness continues through all generations.

Philippians 1:4. Psalm 65:1, 2. Psalm 75:1. Psalm 92:1-5. Psalm 100:1-5.

Feed my sheep

My sheep wandered over all the mountains and on every high hill. They were scattered over the whole earth, and no one searched or looked for them.

When he [Jesus] saw the crowds, he had compassion on them, because they were harassed and helpless, like sheep without a shepherd. What do you think? If a man owns a hundred sheep, and one of them wanders away, will he not leave the ninety-nine on the hills and go to look for the one that wandered off? And if he finds it, I tell you the truth, he is happier about that one sheep than about the ninety-nine that did not wander off.

Keep watch over yourselves and all the flock of which the Holy Spirit has made you overseers. Be shepherds of the church of God, which he bought with his own blood. I know that after I leave, savage wolves will come in among you and will not spare the flock. Even from your own number men will arise and distort the truth in order to draw away disciples after them. So be on your guard!

If the watchman sees the sword coming and does not blow the trumpet to warn the people and the sword comes and takes the life of one of them, that man will be taken away because of his sin, but I will hold the watchman accountable for his blood.

Those who are wise will shine like the brightness of the heavens, and those who lead many to righteousness, like the stars for ever and ever.

John 21:17. Ezekiel 34:6. Matthew 9:36. Matthew 18:12, 13. Acts 20:28-31. Ezekiel 33:6. Daniel 12:3.

Prepare God's people for works of service

...So that the body of Christ may be built up until we all reach unity in the faith and in the knowledge of the Son of God and become mature, attaining to the whole measure of the fullness of Christ.

Then we will no longer be infants, tossed back and forth by the waves, and blown here and there by every wind of teaching and by the cunning and craftiness of men in their deceitful scheming. Instead, speaking the truth in love, we will in all things grow up into him who is the Head, that is, Christ. From him the whole body, joined and held together by every supporting ligament, grows and builds itself up in love, as each part does its work.

In the presence of God and of Christ Jesus, who will judge the living and the dead, and in view of his appearing and his kingdom, I give you this charge: Preach the Word; be prepared in season and out of season; correct, rebuke and encourage--with great patience and careful instruction. For the time will come when men will not put up with sound doctrine. Instead, to suit their own desires, they will gather around them a great number of teachers to say what their itching ears want to hear. They will turn their ears away from the truth and turn aside to myths. But you, keep your head in all situations, endure hardship, do the work of an evangelist, discharge all the duties of your ministry.

Ephesians 4:12-16. 2 Timothy 4:1-5.

The fruit of the righteous is a tree of life, and he who wins souls is wise

This is a trustworthy saying that deserves full acceptance (and for this we labor and strive), that we have put our hope in the living God, who is the Savior of all men, and especially of those who believe.

Command and teach these things. Don't let anyone look down on you ... but set an example for the believers in speech, in life, in love, in faith and in purity. ...Devote yourself to the public reading of Scripture, to preaching and to teaching. Be diligent in these matters; give yourself wholly to them, so that everyone may see your progress. Watch your life and doctrine closely. Persevere in them, because if you do, you will save both yourself and your hearers.

Everyone who competes in the games goes into strict training.They do it to get a crown that will not last; but we do it to get a crown that will last forever. Therefore I do not run like a man running aimlessly; I do not fight like a man beating the air. No, I beat my body and make it my slave so that after I have preached to others, I myself will not be disqualified for the prize.

Those who belong to Christ Jesus have crucified the sinful nature with its passions and desires. Since we live by the Spirit, let us keep in step with the Spirit. Let us not become conceited, provoking and envying one another.

Proverbs 11:30. 1 Timothy 4:9-13, 15, 16. 1 Corinthians 9:25-27. Galatians 5:24, 25.

These commandments that I give you today are to be upon your hearts. Impress them on your children

Talk about them when you sit at home and when you walk along the road, when you lie down and when you get up. Tie them as symbols on your hands and bind them on your foreheads. Write them on the door frames of your houses and on your gates.

Fathers, do not exasperate your children; instead, bring them up in the training and instruction of the Lord. He who spares the rod hates his son, but he who loves him is careful to discipline him. Discipline your son, for in that there is hope; do not be a willing party to his death. Train a child in the way he should go, and when he is old he will not turn from it.

The righteous man leads a blameless life; blessed are his children after him. His children will be mighty in the land; each generation of the upright will be blessed.

From everlasting to everlasting the Lord's love is with those who fear him, and his righteousness with their children's children--with those who keep his covenant and remember to obey his precepts.

Deuteronomy 6:6-9. Ephesians 6:4. Proverbs 13:24. Proverbs 19:18. Proverbs 22:6. Proverbs 20:7. Psalm 112:2. Psalm 103:17, 18.

The words of the wise are like goads, their collected sayings like firmly embedded nails

A word aptly spoken is like apples of gold in settings of silver. The Sovereign Lord has given me an instructed tongue, to know the word that sustains the weary. He wakens me morning by morning, wakens my ear to listen like one being taught.

Do not let any unwholesome talk come out of your mouths, but only what is helpful for building others up according to their needs, that it may benefit those who listen. And do not grieve the Holy Spirit of God, with whom you were sealed for the day of redemption. Get rid of all bitterness, rage and anger, brawling and slander, along with every form of malice. Be kind and compassionate to one another, forgiving each other, just as in Christ God forgave you.

For you were once darkness, but now you are light in the Lord. Live as children of light (for the fruit of the light consists in all goodness, righteousness and truth) and find out what pleases the Lord. Have nothing to do with the fruitless deeds of darkness, but rather expose them. For it is shameful even to mention what the disobedient do in secret.

Be very careful, then, how you live--not as unwise but as wise, making the most of every opportunity, because the days are evil. Therefore do not be foolish, but understand what the Lord's will is.

Ecclesiastes 12:11. Proverbs 25:11. Isaiah 50:4. Ephesians 4:29-32. Ephesians 5:8-12, 15-17.

Be shepherds of God's flock that is under your care

...Serving as overseers--not because you must, but because you are willing, as God wants you to be; not greedy for money, but eager to serve; not lording it over those entrusted to you, but being examples to the flock.

You must teach what is in accord with sound doctrine. Teach the older men to be temperate, worthy of respect, self-controlled, and sound in faith, in love and in endurance.

Likewise, teach the older women to be reverent in the way they live, not to be slanderers or addicted to much wine, but to teach what is good. Then they can train the younger women to love their husbands and children, to be self-controlled and pure, to be busy at home, to be kind, and to be subject to their husbands, so that no one will malign the word of God.

Similarly, encourage the young men to be self-controlled. In everything set them an example by doing what is good. In your teaching show integrity, seriousness and soundness of speech that cannot be condemned, so that those who oppose you may be ashamed because they have nothing bad to say about us.

And when the Chief Shepherd appears, you will receive the crown of glory that will never fade away.

---

1 Peter 5:2, 3. Titus 2:1-8. 1 Peter 5:4.

Speak to one another with psalms, hymns and spiritual songs

Sing and make music in your heart to the Lord, always giving thanks to God the Father for everything, in the name of our Lord Jesus Christ.

In your hearts set apart Christ as Lord. Always be prepared to give an answer to everyone who asks you to give the reason for the hope that you have. But do this with gentleness and respect, keeping a clear conscience, so that those who speak maliciously against your good behavior in Christ may be ashamed of their slander. It is better, if it is God's will, to suffer for doing good than for doing evil.

Therefore be clear minded and self-controlled so that you can pray. Above all, love each other deeply, because love covers over a multitude of sins. Offer hospitality to one another without grumbling. Each one should use whatever gift he has received to serve others, faithfully administering God's grace in its various forms. If anyone speaks, he should do it as one speaking the very words of God. If anyone serves, he should do it with the strength God provides, so that in all things God may be praised through Jesus Christ. To him be the glory and the power for ever and ever.

If you spend yourselves in behalf of the hungry and satisfy the needs of the oppressed, then your light will rise in the darkness, and your night will become like the noonday. The Lord will guide you always; he will satisfy your needs in a sun-scorched land and will strengthen your frame. You will be like a well-watered garden, like a spring whose waters never fail.

Ephesians 5:19, 20. 1 Peter 3:15-17. 1 Peter 4:7-11. Isaiah 58:10, 11.

The Lord brings death and makes alive

He brings down to the grave and raises up. The Lord sends poverty and wealth; he humbles and he exalts. He raises the poor from the dust and lifts the needy from the ash heap; he seats them with princes and has them inherit a throne of honor. For the foundations of the earth are the Lord's; upon them he has set the world. He will guard the feet of his saints, but the wicked will be silenced in darkness. It is not by strength that one prevails; those who oppose the Lord will be shattered. He will thunder against them from heaven; the Lord will judge the ends of the earth.

A time to be born and a time to die. No man has power over the wind to contain it; so no one has power over the day of his death.

On that same day the Lord told Moses, "Go up into the Abarim Range to Mount Nebo in Moab, across from Jericho, and view Canaan, the land I am giving the Israelites as their own possession. Thereon the mountain that you have climbed you will die and be gathered to your people." I heard a voice from heaven say, "Write: Blessed are the dead who die in the Lord from now on." "Yes," says the Spirit, "they will rest from their labor, for their deeds will follow them."

You will receive a rich welcome into the eternal kingdom of our Lord and Savior Jesus Christ. As long as it is day, we must do the work of him who sent me. Night is coming, when no one can work.

To live is Christ and to die is gain.

---

1 Samuel 1:6-10. Ecclesiastes 3:2. Ecclesiastes 8:8. Deuteronomy 32:48-50. Deuteronomy 34:5. Revelation 14:13. 2 Peter 1:11. John 9:4. Philippians 1:21.

The plans of the Lord stand firm forever

The Lord reigns, he is robed in majesty; the Lord is robed in majesty and is armed with strength. The world is firmly established; it cannot be moved. Your throne was established long ago; you are from all eternity. The seas have lifted up, O Lord, the seas have lifted up their voice; the seas have lifted up their pounding waves. Mightier than the thunder of the great waters, mightier than the breakers of the sea--the Lord on high is mighty. Your statutes stand firm; holiness adorns your house for endless days, O Lord.

He sits enthroned above the circle of the earth, and its people are like grasshoppers. He stretches out the heavens like a canopy, and spreads them out like a tent to live in. He brings princes to naught and reduces the rulers of this world to nothing. No sooner are they planted, no sooner are they sown, no sooner do they take root in the ground, than he blows on them and they wither, and a whirlwind sweeps them away like chaff.

The king's heart is in the heart of the Lord; he directs it like a watercourse wherever he pleases. He changes times and seasons; he sets up kings and deposes them. He gives wisdom to the wise and knowledge to the discerning. He reveals deep and hidden things; he knows what lies in darkness, and light dwells with him.

He does as he pleases with the powers of heaven and the peoples of the earth. No one can hold back his hand or say to him:"What have you done?" Everything he does is right and all his ways are just. And those who walk in pride he is able to humble.

Psalm 33:11. Psalm 93:1-5. Isaiah 40:22-24. Proverbs 21:1. Daniel 2:21, 22. Daniel 4:35, 37.

From ancient days I am he

Before the mountains were born or you brought forth the earth and the world, from everlasting to everlasting you are God. In the beginning you laid the foundations of the earth, and the heavens are the work of your hands. They will perish, but you remain; they will all wear out like a garment. Like clothing you will change them and they will be discarded. But you remain the same, and your years will never end. The children of your servants will live in your presence; their descendants will be established before you.

Every good and perfect gift is from above, coming down from the Father of the heavenly lights, who does not change like shifting shadows. He provides food for those who fear him; he remembers his covenant forever. The works of his hands are faithful and just; all his precepts are trustworthy. They are steadfast for ever and ever, done in faithfulness and uprightness.He provided redemption for his people; he ordained his covenant forever--holy and awesome is his name.

Your love, O Lord, reaches to the heavens, your faithfulness to the skies. The Lord loves the just and will not forsake his faithful ones. They will be protected forever.

Isaiah 43:13. Psalm 90:2. Psalm 102:25-28. James 1:17. Psalm 111:5, 7-9.
Psalm 36:5. Psalm 37:28.

The eternal God is your refuge

Do not fear, for I am with you; do not be dismayed, for I am your God. I will strengthen you and help you; I will uphold you with my righteous right hand. Even to your old age and gray hairs I am he, I am he who will sustain you. I have made you and I will carry you; I will sustain you and I will rescue you.

Since ancient times no one has heard, no ear has perceived, no eye has seen any God besides you, who acts on behalf of those who wait for him. You come to the help of those who gladly do right, who remember your ways.

Can a mother forget the baby at her breast and have no compassion on the child she has borne? Though she may forget, I will not forget you! See, I have engraved you on the palms of my hands; your walls are ever before me.

I am convinced that neither death nor life, neither angels nor demons, neither the present nor the future, nor any powers, neither height nor depth, nor anything else in all creation, will be able to separate us from the love of God that is in Christ Jesus our Lord. So we say with confidence, "The Lord is my helper; I will not be afraid. What can man do to me?"

The Lord gives wisdom, and from his mouth come knowledge and understanding. He holds victory in store for the upright, he is a shield to those whose walk is blameless, for he guards the course of the just and protects the way of his faithful ones.

Deuteronomy 33:27. Isaiah 41:10. Isaiah 46:4. Isaiah 64:4, 5.Isaiah 49:15, 16. Romans 8:38, 39. Hebrews 13:6. Proverbs 2:6-8.

Your right hand, O Lord, was majestic in power

Ah, Sovereign Lord, you have made the heavens and the earth by your great power and outstretched arm. Nothing is too hard for you. You show love to thousands but bring the punishment for the fathers' sins into the laps of their children after them. O great and powerful God, whose name is the Lord Almighty, great are your purposes and mighty are your deeds. Your eyes are open to all the ways of men; you reward everyone according to his conduct and as his deeds deserve.

His dominion is an eternal dominion; his kingdom endures from generation to generation. All the peoples of the earth are regarded as nothing. He does as he pleases with the powers of heaven and the peoples of the earth. No one can hold back his hand or say to him: "What have you done?" He rescues and he saves; he performs signs and wonders in the heavens and on the earth.

Wealth and honor come from you; you are the ruler of all things. In your hands are strength and power to exalt and give strength to all.

Now to him who is able to do immeasurably more than all we ask or imagine, according to his power that is at work within us, to him be glory in the church and in Christ Jesus throughout all generations, for ever and ever! Amen. For nothing is impossible with God.

Exodus 15:6. Jeremiah 32:17-20. Daniel 4:34, 35. Daniel 6:27.1 Chronicles 29:12. Ephesians 3:20, 21. Luke 1:37.

Lord, you have been our dwelling place throughout all generations

The Lord is a refuge for the oppressed, a stronghold in times of trouble. Those who know your name will trust in you, for you, Lord, have never forsaken those who seek you. Know therefore that the Lord your God is God; he is the faithful God, keeping his covenant of love to a thousand generations of those who love him and keep his commands. Not one word has failed of all the good promises he gave through his servant Moses. He remembers his covenant forever, the word he commanded, for a thousand generations.

Hear my cry, O God; listen to my prayer. From the ends of the earth I call to you, I call as my heart grows faint; lead me to the rock that is higher than I. For you have been my refuge, a strong tower against the foe. I long to dwell in your tent forever and take refuge in the shelter of your wings.

Your word, O Lord, is eternal; it stands firm in the heavens. Your faithfulness continues through all generations; you established the earth, and it endures. Your laws endure to this day, for all things serve you. If your law had not been my delight, I would have perished in my affliction. I will never forget your precepts, for by them you have preserved my life.

Psalm 90:1. Psalm 9:9, 10. Deuteronomy 7:9. 1 Kings 8:56. Psalm 61:1-4. Psalm 119:89-93.

Stand up and praise the Lord your God, who is from everlasting to everlasting

Blessed be your glorious name, and may it be exalted above all blessing and praise. You alone are the Lord. You made the heavens, even the highest heavens, and all their starry host, the earth and all that is on it, the seas and all that is in them. You give life to everything, and the multitudes of heaven worship you.

O Lord, you are my God; I will exalt you and praise your name, for in perfect faithfulness you have done marvelous things, things planned long ago. Sing to the Lord a new song, his praise from the ends of the earth, you who go down to the sea, and all that is in it, you islands, and all who live in them.

They raise their voices, they shout for joy; from the west they acclaim the Lord's majesty. Therefore in the east give glory to the Lord; exalt the name of the Lord, the God of Israel, in the islands of the sea. From the ends of the earth we hear singing: "Glory to the Righteous One."

Praise the Lord. Praise the Lord from the heavens, praise him in the heights above. Praise him, all his angels, praise him, all his heavenly hosts. Praise him, sun and moon, praise him, all you shining stars. Praise him, you highest heavens and you waters above the skies. Let them praise the name of the Lord, for he commanded and they were created. He set them in place for ever and ever; he gave a decree that will never pass away.

Nehemiah 9:5,6. Isaiah 25:1. Isaiah 42:10. Isaiah 24:14-16. Psalm 148:1-6.

Shall we accept good from God, and not trouble?

I know, O Lord, that your laws are righteous, and in faithfulness you have afflicted me. We are the clay, you are the potter; we are all the work of your hand. He is the Lord; let him do what is good in his eyes.

He will sit as a refiner and purifier of silver. No discipline seems pleasant at the time, but painful. Later on, however, it produces a harvest of righteousness and peace for those who have been trained by it.

It is enough for the student to be like his teacher, and the servant like his master. Although he [Jesus] was a son, he learned obedience from what he suffered and, once made perfect, he became the source of eternal salvation for all who obey him.

Rejoice that you participate in the sufferings of Christ, so that you may be overjoyed when his glory is revealed. If you are insulted because of the name of Christ, you are blessed, for the Spirit of glory and of God rests on you. If you suffer, it should not be as a murderer or thief or any other kind of criminal, or even as a meddler. However, if you suffer as a Christian, do not be ashamed, but praise God that you bear that name.

Praise be to the God and Father of our Lord Jesus Christ, the Father of compassion and the God of all comfort, who comforts us in all our troubles, so that we can comfort those in any trouble with the comfort we ourselves have received from God. For just as the sufferings of Christ flow over into our lives, so also through Christ our comfort overflows.

Job 2:10. Psalm 119:75. Isaiah 64:8. 1 Samuel 3:18. Malachi 3:3. Hebrews 12:11. Matthew 10:25. Hebrews 5:8, 9. 1 Peter 4:13-16. 2 Corinthians 1:3-5.

The Lord gave and
the Lord has taken away

Endure hardship with us like a good soldier of Jesus Christ. If we endure, we will also reign with him. You have been given fullness in Christ, who is the head over every power and authority. In whom are hidden all the treasures of wisdom and knowledge. From the fullness of his grace we have all received one blessing after another. For God was pleased to have all his fullness dwell in him.

Set your hearts on things above, where Christ is seated at the right hand of God. Set your minds on things above, not on earthly things. For you died, and your life is now hidden with Christ in God. When Christ, who is your life, appears, then you also will appear with him in glory.

The Lord is my shepherd, I shall not be in want. He makes me lie down in green pastures, he leads me beside quiet waters, he restores my soul. He guides me in paths of righteousness for his name's sake. Even though I walk through the valley of the shadow of death, I will fear no evil, for you are with me; your rod and your staff, they comfort me. You prepare a table before me in the presence of my enemies. You anoint my head with oil; my cup overflows. Surely goodness and love will follow me all the days of my life, and I will dwell in the house of the Lord forever.

Job 1:21. 2 Timothy 2:3, 12. Colossians 2:10, 3. John 1:16. Colossians 1:19. Colossians 3:2-4. Psalm 23:1-6.

The Lord sends poverty and wealth

The brother in humble circumstances ought to take pride in his high position. But the one who is rich should take pride in his low position, because he will pass away like a wild flower. For the sun rises with scorching heat and withers the plant; its blossom falls and its beauty is destroyed. In the same way, the rich man will fade away even while he goes about his business.

One man pretends to be rich, yet has nothing. Rich and poor have this in common: The Lord is the Maker of them all.

I have learned to be content whatever the circumstances. I know what it is to be in need, and I know what it is to have plenty. I have learned the secret of being content in any and every situation, whether well fed or hungry, whether living in plenty or in want. I can do everything through him who gives me strength.

Godliness with contentment is great gain. For we brought nothing into the world, and we can take nothing out of it. Command those who are rich in this present world not to be arrogant nor to put their hope in wealth, which is so uncertain, but to put their hope in God, who richly provides us with everything for our enjoyment. Command them to do good, to be rich in good deeds, and to be generous and willing to share. In this way they will lay up treasure for themselves as a firm foundation for the coming age, so that they may take hold of the life that is truly life.

The blessing of the Lord brings wealth, and he adds no trouble to it.

---

1 Samuel 2:7. James 1:9-11. Proverbs 13:7. Proverbs 22:2. Philippians 4:11-13. 1 Timothy 6:6, 7, 17-19. Proverbs 10:22.

The Lord ... humbles and he exalts

Samuel said to him [Saul], "I will not go back with you. You have rejected the word of the Lord, and the Lord has rejected you as king over Israel!" Tell my servant David, "This is what the Lord Almighty says: I took you from the pasture and from following the flock to be ruler over my people Israel."

It is God who judges: He brings one down, he exalts another. He has brought down rulers from their thrones but has lifted up the humble. The Lord Almighty has a day in store for all the proud and lofty, for all that is exalted (and they will be humbled). The arrogance of man will be brought low and the pride of men humbled; the Lord alone will be exalted in that day.

O Lord, you are my God; I will exalt you and praise your name, for in perfect faithfulness you have done marvelous things, things planned long ago.

"Because he loves me," says the Lord, "I will rescue him; I will protect him, for he acknowledges my name. He will call upon me, and I will answer him; I will be with him in trouble, I will deliver him and honor him. With long life will I satisfy him and show him my salvation."

Then you will find your joy in the Lord, and I will cause you to ride on the heights of the land.

---

1 Samuel 2:7. 1 Samuel 15:26. 2 Samuel 7:8. Psalm 75:7. Luke 1:52. Isaiah 2:12, 17. Isaiah 25:1. Psalm 91:14-16. Isaiah 58:14.

He wounds, but he also binds up; he injures, but his hands also heal

O Lord, do not rebuke me in your anger or discipline me in your wrath. For your arrows have pierced me, and your hand has come down upon me. Because of your wrath there is no health in my body; my bones have no soundness because of my sin. My guilt has overwhelmed me like a burden too heavy to bear.

I say to God my Rock, "Why have you forgotten me? Why must I go about mourning, oppressed by the enemy?" My bones suffer mortal agony as my foes taunt me, saying to me all day long, "Where is your God?" Why are you downcast, O my soul? Why so disturbed within me? Put your hope in God, for I will yet praise him, my Savior and my God.

O afflicted city, lashed by storms and not comforted, I will build you with stones of turquoise, your foundations with sapphires. I will make your battlements of rubies, your gates of sparkling jewels, and all your walls of precious stones.

Know then in your heart that as a man disciplines his son, so the Lord your God disciplines you. He knows the way that I take; when he has tested me, I will come forth as gold. For you, O God, tested us; you refined us like silver. You brought us into prison and laid burdens on our backs. You let men ride over our heads; we went through fire and water, but you brought us to a place of abundance.

Job 5:18. Psalm 38:1-4. Psalm 42:9-11. Isaiah 54:11, 12. Deuteronomy 8:5. Job 23:10. Psalm 66:10-12.

Consider it pure joy ...
whenever you face trials of many kinds

The testing of your faith develops perseverance. Perseverance must finish its work so that you may be mature and complete, not lacking anything. For a little while you may have had to suffer grief in all kinds of trials. These have come so that your faith--of greater worth than gold, which perished even though refined by fire--may be proved genuine and may result in praise, glory and honor when Jesus Christ is revealed.

We also rejoice in our sufferings, because we know that suffering produces perseverance; perseverance, character; and character, hope. He cuts off every branch in me that bears no fruit, while every branch that does bear fruit he prunes so that it will be even more fruitful. Our light and momentary troubles are achieving for us an eternal glory that far outweighs them all.

Endure hardship as discipline; God is treating you as sons. For what son is not disciplined by his father? If you are not disciplined (and everyone undergoes discipline), then you are illegitimate children and not true sons. Moreover, we have all had human fathers who disciplined us and we respected them for it. How much more should we submit to the Father of our spirits and live! Our fathers disciplined us for a little while as they though best; but God disciplines us for our good, that we may share in his holiness.

James 1:2-4. 1 Peter 1:6, 7. Romans 5:3, 4. John 15:2. 2 Corinthians 4:17. Hebrews 12:7-10.

I, even I, am he who comforts you

Because of the Lord's great love we are not consumed, for his compassions never fail. For he does not willingly bring affliction or grief to the children of men. The Lord is full of compassion and mercy.

I will not leave you as orphans; I will come to you. I will ask the Father, and he will give you another Counselor to be with you forever. As a mother comforts her child, so will I comfort you.

Surely he took up our infirmities and carried our sorrows. For we do not have a high priest who is unable to sympathize with our weaknesses, but we have one who has been tempted in every way, just as we are--yet was without sin. Let us then approach the throne of grace with confidence, so that we may receive mercy and find grace to help us in our time of need.

This is what the Lord says--he who created you, O Jacob, he who formed you, O Israel: "Fear not, for I have redeemed you; I have summoned you by name; you are mine. When you pass through the waters, I will be with you; and when you pass through the rivers, they will not sweep over you. When you walk through the fire, you will not be burned; the flames will not set you ablaze.

Though he slay me, yet will I hope in him. My flesh and my heart may fail, but God is the strength of my heart and my portion forever.

Isaiah 51:12. Lamentations 3:22, 23. James 5:11. John 14:18, 16. Isaiah 66:13. Isaiah 53:4. Hebrews 4:15, 16. Isaiah 43:1, 2. Job 13:15. Psalm 73:26.

I groan in anguish of heart

A man was going down from Jerusalem to Jericho, when he fell into the hands of robbers. They stripped him of his clothes, beat him and went away, leaving him half dead. A priest happened to be going down the same road, and when he saw the man, he passed by on the other side. So too, a Levite, when he came to the place and saw him, passed by on the other side.

All my longings lie open before you, O Lord; my sighing is not hidden from you. My heart pounds, my strength fails me; even the light has gone from my eyes. My friends and companions avoid me because of my wounds; my neighbors stay far away. Those who seek my life set their traps, those who would harm me talk of my ruin; all day long they plot deception.

But a Samaritan, as he traveled, came where the man was; and when he saw him, he took pity on him. He went to him and bandaged his wounds, pouring on oil and wine. Then he put the man on his own donkey, took him to an inn and took care of him. The next day he took out two silver coins and gave them to the innkeeper. "Look after him," he said, "and when I return, I will reimburse you for any extra expense you may have."

Whatever you did for one of the least of these brothers of mine, you did for me. Whatever you did not do for one of the least of these, you did not do for me.

Psalm 38:8. Luke 10:30-32. Psalm 38:9-12. Luke 10:33-35. Matthew 25:40, 45.

Be patient and stand firm

As an example of patience in the face of suffering, take the prophets who spoke in the name of the Lord. As you know, we consider blessed those who have persevered. You have heard of Job's perseverance and have seen what the Lord finally brought about. The Lord is full of compassion and mercy.

The Lord blessed the later part of Job's life more than the first.

As he went along, he saw a man blind from birth. His disciples asked him, "Rabbi, who sinned, this man or his parents, that he was born blind?"

"Neither this man nor his parents sinned," said Jesus, "but this happened so that the work of God might be displayed in his life."

The Lord is gracious and compassionate, slow to anger and rich in love. The Lord is good to all; he has compassion on all he has made. All you have made will praise you, O Lord; your saints will extol you. They will tell of the glory of your kingdom and speak of your might, so that all men may know of your mighty acts and the glorious splendor of your kingdom.

He upholds the cause of the oppressed and gives food to the hungry. The Lord sets prisoners free, the Lord gives sight to the blind, the Lord lifts up those who are bowed down, the Lord loves the righteous.

James 5:8, 10, 11. Job 42:12. John 9:1-3. Psalm 145:8-12. Psalm 146:7, 8.

A despairing man should have the devotion of his friends

A friend loves at all times, and a brother is born for adversity. If one falls down, his friend can help him up. But pity the man who falls and has no one to help him up!

We must help the weak, remembering the words the Lord Jesus himself said: "It is more blessed to give than to receive." Carry each other's burdens, and in this way you will fulfill the law of Christ. Clothe yourselves with compassion, kindness, humility, gentleness and patience. And over all these virtues put on love, which binds them all together in perfect unity. All men will know that you are my disciples if you love one another. If you really keep the royal law found in Scripture, "Love your neighbor as yourself," you are doing right.

This is my prayer: that your love may abound more and more in knowledge and depth of insight, so that you may be able to discern what is best and may be pure and blameless until the day of Christ, filled with the fruit of righteousness that comes through Jesus Christ--to the glory and praise of God.

Job 6:14. Proverbs 17:17. Ecclesiastes 4:10. Acts 20:35. Galatians 6:2. Colossians 3:12, 14. John 13:35. James 2:8. Philippians 1:9-11.

Do not forsake your friend

My kinsmen have gone away; my friends have forgotten me. My guests and my maidservants count me a stranger; they look upon me as an alien. I summon my servant, but he does not answer, though I beg him with my own mouth. My breath is offensive to my wife; I am loathsome to my own brothers. Even the little boys scorn me; when I appear, they ridicule me. All my intimate friends detest me; those I love have turned against me. I am nothing but skin and bones; I have escaped with only the skin of my teeth. Have pity on me, my friends, have pity, for the hand of God has struck me. Why do you pursue me as God does? Will you never get enough of my flesh?

My brothers are as undependable as intermittent streams, as the streams that overflow when darkened by thawing ice and swollen with melting snow, but that cease to flow in the dry season, and in the heat vanish from their channels. Even my close friend, whom I trusted, he who shared my bread, has lifted up his heel against me.

If an enemy were insulting me, I could endure it; if a foe were raising himself against me, I could hide from him. But it is you, a man like myself, my companion, my close friend, with whom I once enjoyed sweet fellowship as we walked with the throng at the house of God. The darkness is my closest friend. I lie awake; I have become like a bird alone on a roof. No one came to my support, but everyone deserted me.

Anyone ... who knows the good he ought to do and doesn't do it, sins.

Proverbs 27:10. Job 19:14-22. Job 6:15-17. Psalm 41:9. Psalm 55:12-14. Psalm 88:18. Psalm 102:7. 2 Timothy 4:16. James 4:17.

Two are better than one

Jonathan became one in spirit with David, and he loved him as himself. Jonathan had David reaffirm his oath out of love for him, because he loved him as he loved himself.

Ruth replied, "Don't urge me to leave you or to turn back from you. Where you go I will go, and where you stay I will stay. Your people will be my people and your God my God.

Elisha said, "As surely as the Lord lives and as you live, I will not leave you."

Jesus knew that the time had come for him to leave this world and go to the Father. Many women were there, watching from a distance. They had followed Jesus from Galilee to care for his needs. Among them were Mary Magdalene, Mary the mother of James and Joses, and the mother of Zebedee's sons. Then Thomas (called Didymus) said to the rest of the disciples, "Let us also go, that we may die with him."

Priscilla and Aquila ... risked their lives for me. Not only I but all the churches of the Gentiles are grateful to them.

Onesiphorus ... often refreshed me and was not ashamed of my chains.

He who loves his fellowman has fulfilled the law.

Ecclesiastes 4:9. 1 Samuel 18:1. 1 Samuel 20:17. Ruth 1:16. 2Kings 2:2. John 13:1. Matthew 27:55, 56. John 11:16. Romans 16:3, 4. 2 Timothy 1:16. Romans 13:8.

In humility consider others better than yourselves

Jesus ... got up from the meal, took off his outer clothing, and wrapped a towel around his waist. After that, he poured water into a basin and began to wash his disciples' feet, drying them with the towel that was wrapped around him.

No servant is greater than his master, nor is a messenger greater than the one who sent him. Now that you know these things, you will be blessed if you do them. Be imitators of God, therefore, as dearly loved children and live a life of love, just as Christ loved us and gave himself up for us as a fragrant offering and sacrifice to God.

Your attitude should be the same as that of Christ Jesus: Who, being in very nature God, did not consider equality with God something to be grasped, but made himself nothing, taking the very nature of a servant, being made in human likeness. And being found in appearance as a man, he humbled himself and become obedient to death--even death on a cross!

Greater love has no one than this, that he lay down his life for his friends. Rejoice with those who rejoice; mourn with those who mourn.

Philippians 2:3. John 13:3-5, 16, 17. Ephesians 5:1, 2. Philippians 2:5-8. John 15:13. Romans 12:15.

Serve wholeheartedly, as if you were serving the Lord, not men

The Lord will reward everyone for whatever good he does. God is not unjust; he will not forget your work and the love you have shown him as you have helped his people and continue to help them. Whatever your hand finds to do, do it with all your might.

Just as each of us has one body with many members, and these members do not all have the same function, so in Christ we who are many form one body, and each member belongs to all the others. We have different gifts, according to the grace given us. If a man's gift is prophesying, let him use it in proportion to his faith. If it is serving, let him serve; if it is teaching, let him teach; if it is encouraging, let him encourage; if it is contributing to the needs of others, let him give generously; if it is leadership, let him govern diligently; if it is showing mercy, let him do it cheerfully.

Love must be sincere. Hate what is evil; cling to what is good. Be devoted to one another in brotherly love. Honor one another above yourselves. Never be lacking in zeal, but keep your spiritual fervor, serving the Lord. Be joyful in hope, patient in affliction, faithful in prayer. Share with God's people who are in need. Practice hospitality.

Love your neighbor as yourself. In everything, do to others what you would have them do to you, for this sums up the Law and the Prophets.

Ephesians 6:8. Hebrews 6:10. Ecclesiastes 9:10. Romans 12:4-13. Luke 10:27. Matthew 7:12.

The engulfing waters threatened me, the deep surrounded me

Save me, O God, for the waters have come up to my neck. I sink in the miry depths, where there is no foothold. I have come into the deep waters; the floods engulf me. I am worn out calling for help; my throat is parched. My eyes fail, looking for my God.

I pray to you, O Lord, in the time of your favor; in your great love, O God, answer me with your sure salvation. Rescue me from the mire, do not let me sink; deliver me from those who hate me, from the deep waters. Do not let the floodwaters engulf me or the depths swallow me up or the pit close its mouth over me. Answer me, O Lord, out of the goodness of your love; in your great mercy turn to me.

When I said, "My foot is slipping," your love, O Lord, supported me. When anxiety was great within me, your consolation brought joy to my soul.

Trust in him at all times, O people; pour out your hearts to him, for God is our refuge. I waited patiently for the Lord; he turned to me and heard my cry. He lifted me out of the slimy pit, out of the mud and mire; he set my feet on a rock and gave me a firm place to stand. He put a new song in my mouth, a hymn of praise to our God.

Jonah 2:5. Psalm 69:1-3, 13-16. Psalm 94:18, 19. Psalm 62:8.Psalm 40:1-3.

You toss me about in the storm

Deep calls to deep in the roar of your waterfalls; all your waves and breakers have swept over me. The engulfing waters threatened me, the deep surrounded me; seaweed was wrapped around my head.

Let everyone who is godly pray to you while you may be found; surely when the mighty waters rise, they will not reach him. You are my hiding place; you will protect me from trouble and surround me with songs of deliverance.

Merchants ... mounted up to the heavens and went down to the depths; in their peril their courage melted away. They reeled and staggered like drunken men; they were at their wits' end. Then they cried to the Lord in their trouble, and he brought them out of their distress. He stilled the storm to a whisper; the waves of the sea were hushed. They were glad when it grew calm, and he guided them to their desired haven.

Peter got down out of the boat, walked on the water and came toward Jesus. But when he saw the wind, he was afraid and, beginning to sink, cried out, "Lord, save me!" Immediately Jesus reached out his hand and caught him.

Lord, increase our faith.

Job 30:22. Psalm 42:7. Jonah 2:5. Psalm 32:6, 7. Psalm 107:23, 25-30. Matthew 14:29-31. Luke 17:5.

When I looked for light,
then came darkness

Who among you fears the Lord and obeys the word of his servant? Let him who walks in the dark, who has no light, trust in the name of the Lord and rely on his God.

I will instruct you and teach you in the way you should go; I will counsel you and watch over you. By day the Lord went ahead of them in a pillar of cloud to guide them on their way and by night in a pillar of fire to give them light. Even in darkness light dawns for the upright, for the gracious and compassionate and righteous man. You, O Lord, keep my lamp burning; my God turns my darkness into light. With your help I can advance against a troop; with my God I can scale a wall. Show me your ways, O Lord, teach me your paths; guide me in your truth and teach me, for you are God my Savior, and my hope is in you all day long.

Commit your way to the Lord; trust in him and he will do this: He will make your righteousness shine like the dawn, the justice of your cause like the noonday sun. A chosen people, a royal priesthood, a holy nation, a people belonging to God, that you may declare the praises of him who called you out of darkness into his wonderful light. Once you were not a people, but now you are the people of God; once you had not received mercy, but now you have received mercy.

Job 30:26. Isaiah 50:10. Psalm 32:8. Exodus 13:21. Psalm 112:4. Psalm 25:4, 5. Psalm 18:28, 29. Psalm 37:5, 6. 1 Peter 2:9,10

I cry out to you, O God, but you do not answer

When I felt secure, I said, "I will never be shaken," but when you hid your face, I was dismayed.

A Canaanite woman came to him, crying out,"Lord, Son of David, have mercy on me! My daughter is suffering terribly from demon-possession." Jesus did not answer a word. The woman came and knelt before him. "Lord, help me!" she said. He replied, "It is not right to take the children's bread and toss it to their dogs."

"Yes, Lord," she said, "but even the dogs eat the crumbs that fall from their masters' table." Then Jesus answered, "Woman, you have great faith! Your request is granted." And her daughter was healed.

Suppose one of you has a friend, and he goes to him at midnight and says, "Friend, lend me three loaves of bread, because a friend of mine on a journey has come to me, and I have nothing to set before him." Then the one inside answers, "Don't bother me.The door is already locked and my children are with me in bed. I can't get up and give you anything." I tell you, though he will not get up and give him the bread because he is his friend, yet because of the man's boldness he will get up and give him as much as he needs.

So I say to you: Ask and it will be given to you; seek and you will find; knock and the door will be opened to you. For everyone who asks receives; he who seeks finds; and to him who knocks, the door will be opened.

The testing of your faith develops perseverance. You do not have, because you do not ask God.

Job 30:20. Psalm 30:6, 7. Matthew 15:22, 23, 25-28. Luke 11:5-10. James 1:3. James 4:2.

I have no refuge; no one cares for my life

He has alienated my brothers from me; my acquaintances are completely estranged from me. My kinsmen have gone away; my friends have forgotten me. My guests and my maidservants count me a stranger; they look upon me as an alien. I summon my servant, but he does not answer, though I beg him with my own mouth. My breath is offensive to my wife; I am loathsome to my own brothers. Even the little boys scorn me; when I appear, they ridicule me. All my intimate friends detest me; those I love have turned against me.

You have taken my companions and loved ones from me; the darkness is my closest friend. Everyone deserted him and fled. Could you men not keep watch with me for one hour?

Let us fix our eyes on Jesus, the author and perfector of our faith, who for the joy set before him endured the cross, scorning its shame, and sat down at the right hand of the throne of God. After Job had prayed for his friends, the Lord made him prosperous again and gave him twice as much as he had before.

We share in his sufferings in order that we may also share in his glory.

Psalm 142:4. Job 19:13-19. Psalm 88:18. Mark 14:50. Matthew 26:40. Hebrews 12:2. Job 42:10. Romans 8:17.

Oh, for the days when I was in my prime

The keepers of the house tremble, and the strong men stoop ... the grinders cease because they are few, and those looking through the windows grow dim ... the doors to the street are closed and the sound of grinding fades ... men rise up at the sound of birds, but all their sons grow faint.

I am now eighty years old. Can I tell the difference between what is good and what is not? Can your servant taste what he eats and drinks? Can I still hear the voices of men and women singers? Why should your servant be an added burden to my lord the king? Do not cast me away when I am old; do not forsake me when my strength is gone.

Even to your old age and gray hairs I am he, I am he who will sustain you. I have made you and I will carry you; I will sustain you and I will rescue you. He gives strength to the weary and increases the power of the weak. Those who hope in the Lord will renew their strength. Therefore, strengthen your feeble arms and weak knees. Make level paths for your feet.

Surely goodness and love will follow me all the days of my life, and I will dwell in the house of the Lord forever.

Job 29:4. Ecclesiastes 12:3, 4. 2 Samuel 19:35. Psalm 71:9. Isaiah 46:4. Isaiah 40:29, 31. Hebrews 12:12, 13. Psalm 23:6.

How I long for the months gone by, for the days when God watched over me

Hear my cry, O God; listen to my prayer. From the ends of the earth I call to you, I call as my heart grows faint; lead me to the rock that is higher than I. For you have been my refuge, a strong tower against the foe. I long to dwell in your tent forever, and take refuge in the shelter of your wings.

Blessed are those whose strength is in you, who have set their hearts on pilgrimage. As they pass through the Valley of Baca, they make it a place of springs; the autumn rains also cover it with pools. Be strong, do not fear; your God will come, he will come with vengeance; with divine retribution he will come to save you.

It is better to take refuge in the Lord than to trust in man. It is better to take refuge in the Lord than to trust in princes. Taste and see that the Lord is good; blessed is the man who takes refuge in him. Fear the Lord, you his saints, for those who fear him lack nothing.

He who did not spare his own Son, but gave him up for us all--how will he not also, along with him, graciously give us all things? Oh, the depth of the riches of the wisdom and knowledge of God! How unsearchable his judgments, and his paths beyond tracing out! For from him and through him and to him are all things. To him be the glory forever! Amen.

Job 29:2. Psalm 61:1-4. Psalm 84:5, 6. Isaiah 35:4. Psalm 118:8, 9. Psalm 34:8, 9. Romans 8:32. Romans 11:33, 36.

You can do all things

Our God is in heaven; he does whatever pleases him. For nothing is impossible with God.

There is no one like the God of Jeshurun, who rides on the heavens to help you and on the clouds in his majesty. The eternal God is your refuge, and underneath are the everlasting arms.

By day the Lord directs his love, at night his song is with me--a prayer to the God of my life. For God does speak--now one way, now another--though man may not perceive it. In a dream, in a vision of the night, when deep sleep falls on men as they slumber in their beds, he may speak in their ears and terrify them with warnings, to turn man from wrongdoing and keep him from pride, to preserve his soul from the pit, his life from perishing by the sword. Or a man may be chastened on a bed of pain with constant distress in his bones, so that his very being finds food repulsive and his soul loathes the choicest meal.

When I consider your heavens, the work of your fingers, the moon and the stars, which you have set in place, what is man that you are mindful of him, the son of man that you care for him? You made him a little lower than the heavenly beings and crowned him with glory and honor. You made him ruler over the works of your hands; you put everything under his feet: all flocks and herds, and the beasts of the field, the birds of the air, and the fish of the sea, all that swim the paths of the seas.

O Lord, our Lord, how majestic is your name in all the earth!

Job 42:2. Psalm 115:3. Luke 1:37. Deuteronomy 33:26, 27. Psalm 42:8. Job 33:14-20. Psalm 8:3-9.

No plan of yours can be thwarted.

God's voice thunders in marvelous ways; he does great things beyond our understanding. He says to the snow, "Fall on the earth," and to the rain shower, "Be a mighty downpour." So that all men he has made may know his work, he stops every man from his labor. The animals take cover; they remain in their dens. The tempest comes out from its chamber, the cold from the driving winds. The breath of God produces ice, and the broad waters become frozen. He loads the clouds with moisture; he scatters his lightning through them. At his direction they swirl around over the face of the whole earth to do whatever he commands them. He brings the clouds to punish men, or to water his earth and show his love.

There is no one holy like the Lord; there is no one besides you; there is no Rock like our God. Yes, from ancient days I am he. No one can deliver out of my hand. When I act, who can reverse it?

All the peoples of the earth are regarded as nothing. He does as he pleases with the powers of heaven and the peoples of the earth. No one can hold back his hand or say to him: "What have you done?"

Job 42:2. Job 37:5-13. 1 Samuel 2:2, 3. Isaiah 43:13. Daniel 4:35.

How awesome is the Lord Most High, the great King over all the earth!

He who forms the mountains, creates the wind, and reveals his thoughts to man, he who turns dawn to darkness, and treads the high places of the earth--the Lord Almighty is his name.

The Lord is slow to anger and great in power; the Lord will not leave the guilty unpunished. His way is in the whirlwind and the storm, and clouds are the dust of his feet. He rebukes the sea and dries it up; he makes all the rivers run dry. Bashan and Carmel wither and the blossoms of Lebanon fade. The mountains quake before him and the hills melt away. The earth trembles at his presence, the world and all who live in it. Who can withstand his indignation? Who can endure his fierce anger? His wrath is poured out like fire; the rocks are shattered before him.

The Lord thunders at the head of his army; his forces are beyond number, and mighty are those who obey his command. The day of the Lord is great; it is dreadful. Who can endure it?

I will repay you for the years the locusts have eaten--the great locust and the young locust, the other locusts and the locust swarm--my great army that I sent among you. You will have plenty to eat, until you are full, and you will praise the name of the Lord your God, who has worked wonders for you.

Now to him who is able to do immeasurably more than all we ask or imagine, according to his power that is at work within us.

Psalm 47:2. Amos 4:13. Nahum 1:3-6. Joel 2:11-13, 25, 26. Ephesians 3:20.

Power and might are in your hand, and no one can withstand you

O our God, will you not judge them? For we have no power to face this vast army that is attacking us. We do not know what to do, but our eyes are upon you. This is what the Lord says to you: "Do not be afraid or discouraged because of this vast army. For the battle is not yours, but God's. You will not have to fight this battle. Take up your positions; stand firm and see the deliverance the Lord will give you. ... Do not be afraid; do not be discouraged. Go out to face them tomorrow, and the Lord will be with you."

No one is like you, O Lord; you are great, and your name is mighty in power. Who should not revere you, O King of the nations? This is your due. Among all the wise men of the nations and in all their kingdoms, there is no one like you. I know, O Lord, that a man's life is not his own; it is not for man to direct his steps. Unless the Lord builds the house, its builders labor in vain. Unless the Lord watches over the city, the watchmen stand guard in vain.

A man can receive only what is given him from heaven. Our competence comes from God.

I am the vine; you are the branches. If a man remains in me and I in him, he will bear much fruit; apart from me you can do nothing.

---

2 Chronicles 20:6, 12, 15, 17. Jeremiah 10:6, 7, 23. Psalm 127:1. John 15:5. John 3:27. 2 Corinthians 3:5.

I saw the Lord seated on a throne

"Woe to me!" I cried. "I am ruined! For I am a man of unclean lips, and I live among a people of unclean lips, and my eyes have seen the King, the Lord Almighty.

Job answered the Lord: "I am unworthy--how can I reply to you? My ears had heard of you but now my eyes have seen you. Therefore I despise myself and repent in dust and ashes." When Jacob awoke from his sleep, he thought, "Surely the Lord is in this place, and I was not aware of it." He was afraid and said, "How awesome is this place! This is none other than the house of God; this is the gate of heaven."

Once you were alienated from God and were enemies in your minds because of your evil behavior. But now he has reconciled you by Christ's physical body through death to present you holy in his sight, without blemish and free from accusation--if you continue in your faith, established and firm. The God who made the world and everything in it is the Lord of heaven and earth and does not live in temples built by hands. And he is not served by human hands, as if he needed anything, because he himself gives all men life and breath and everything else. From one man he made every nation of men, that they could inhabit the whole earth; and he determined the times set for them and the exact places where they should live. God did this so that men would seek him and perhaps reach out for him and find him, though he is not far from each one of us. For in him we live and move and have our being.

Isaiah 6:1, 5. Job 40:3, 4. Job 42:5, 6. Genesis 28:16, 17. Colossians 1:21-23. Acts 17:24-28.

Great is the Lord
and most worthy of praise

His greatness no one can fathom. The Lord does whatever pleases him, in the heavens and on the earth, in the seas and all their depths. He makes clouds rise from the ends of the earth; he sends lightning with the rain and brings out the wind from his storehouses.

This is what the Lord says--your Redeemer, who formed you in the womb: I am the Lord, who has made all things, who alone stretched out the heavens, who spread out the earth by myself, who foils the signs of false prophets and makes fools of diviners, who overthrows the learning of the wise and turns it into nonsense.

He sits enthroned above the circle of the earth, and its people are like grasshoppers. He stretches out the heavens like a canopy, and spreads them out like a tent to live in. He brings princes to naught and reduces the rulers of this world to nothing.

He gives strength to the weary and increases the power of the weak. Even youths grow tired and weary, and young men stumble and fall; but those who hope in the Lord will renew their strength. They will soar on wings like eagles; they will run and not grow weary, they will walk and not be faint.

Great are the works of the Lord; they are pondered by all who delight in them. Glorious and majestic are his deeds, and his righteousness endures forever. He has caused his wonders to be remembered; the Lord is gracious and compassionate. He provides food for those who fear him; he remembers his covenant forever.

Psalm 145:3. Psalm 135:6, 7, 13. Isaiah 44:24, 25. Isaiah 40:22-24, 29-31. Psalm 111:2-5.

All nations will come and worship before you

Great and marvelous are your deeds, Lord God Almighty. Just and true are your ways, King of the ages. Who will not fear you, O Lord, and bring glory to your name? For you alone are holy.

Praise the Lord, all you nations; extol him, all you peoples. For great is his love toward us, and the faithfulness of the Lord endures forever. Enter his gates with thanksgiving and his courts with praise; give thanks to him and praise his name.

I heard what sounded like a great multitude, like the roar of rushing waters and like loud peals of thunder, shouting: "Hallelujah! For our Lord God Almighty reigns. Let us rejoice and be glad and give him glory! For the wedding of the Lamb has come, and his bride has made herself ready. Fine linen, bright and clean, was given her to wear."

Behold I am coming soon! My reward is with me, and I will give to everyone according to what he has done. I am the Alpha and the Omega, the First and the Last, the Beginning and the End.

Come! Whoever is thirsty, let him come; and whoever wishes, let him take the free gift of the water of life.

Revelation 15:3, 4. Psalm 117:1, 2. Psalm 100:4. Revelation 19:6-8.
Revelation 22:12, 13, 17.

Sin is a disgrace to any people

The lips of a king speak as an oracle, and his mouth should not betray justice.

I, Daniel, understood from the Scriptures, according to the word of the Lord given to Jeremiah the prophet, that the desolation of Jerusalem would last seventy years. So I turned to the Lord God and pleaded with him in prayer...in fasting, and in sackcloth and ashes.

I prayed to the Lord my God and confessed: "O Lord, the great and awesome God, who keeps his covenant of love with all who love him and obey his commands, we have sinned and done wrong. We have been wicked and have rebelled; we have turned away from your commands and laws. We have not listened to your servants the prophets, who spoke in your name to our kings...our fathers, and to all the people of the land.

"Lord, you are righteous, but this day we are covered with shame--the men of Judah and people of Jerusalem and all Israel, both near and far, in all the countries where you have scattered us because of our unfaithfulness to you. ... The Lord our God is merciful and forgiving, even though we have rebelled against him. The Lord did not hesitate to bring the disaster upon us, for the Lord our God is righteous in everything he does; yet we have not obeyed him.

"Now, our God, hear the prayers and petitions of your servant. For your sake, O Lord, look with favor on your desolate sanctuary. We do not make requests of you because we are righteous, but because of your great mercy. O Lord, listen! O Lord, forgive! O Lord, hear and act!

Proverbs 14:34. Proverbs 16:10. Daniel 9:2-9, 14, 17-19.

It is God who judges

Woe to those ... who acquit the guilty for a bribe, but deny justice to the innocent. How long will you defend the unjust and show partiality to the wicked? It is not for kings, O Lemuel--not for kings to drink wine, not for rulers to crave beer, lest they drink and forget what the law decrees, and deprive all the oppressed of their rights.

In the place of judgment--wickedness was there, in the place of justice--wickedness was there. I thought in my heart, "God will bring to judgment both the righteous and the wicked, for there will be a time for every activity, a time for every deed."

"Woe to the obstinate children," declares the Lord, "to those who carry out plans that are not mine, forming an alliance, but not by my Spirit, heaping sin upon sin; who go down to Egypt without consulting me; who look for help to Pharaoh's protection, to Egypt's shade for refuge."

The nations have fallen into the pit they have dug; their feet are caught in the net they have hidden. The Lord is known by his justice; the wicked are ensnared by the work of their hands. The wicked return to the grave, all the nations that forget God.

Oh, that you would rend the heavens and come down, that the mountains would tremble before you! As when fire sets twigs ablaze and causes water to boil, come down to make your name known to your enemies and cause the nations to quake before you!

Psalm 75:7. Isaiah 5:22, 23. Psalm 82:2. Proverbs 31:4, 5. Ecclesiastes 3:16, 17. Isaiah 30:1, 2. Psalm 9:15-17. Isaiah 64:1, 2.

"If any nation does not listen, I will completely uproot and destroy it," declares the Lord

The Lord said, "The outcry against Sodom and Gomorrah is so great and their sin so grievous that I will go down and see if what they have done is as bad as the outcry that has reached me. If not, I will know."

Abraham approached him and said: "Will you sweep away the righteous with the wicked? What if there are fifty righteous people in the city? Will you really sweep it away and not spare the place for the sake of the fifty righteous people in it? Forty ... thirty ... twenty ... ten?"

He answered, "For the sake of ten, I will not destroy it."

Isaiah cries out concerning Israel: "Though the number of the Israelites be like the sand by the sea, only the remnant will be saved. For the Lord will carry out his sentence on earth with speed and finality."

For if God did not spare angels when they sinned, but sent them to hell, putting them into gloomy dungeons to be held for judgment; if he condemned the cities of Sodom and Gomorrah by burning them to ashes, and made them an example of what is going to happen to the ungodly; and if he rescued Lot, a righteous man, who was distressed by the filthy lives of lawless men (for that righteous man, living among them day after day, was tormented in his righteous soul by the lawless deeds he saw and heard)--if this is so, then the Lord knows how to rescue godly men from trials and to hold the unrighteous for the day of judgment.

Jeremiah 12:17. Genesis 18:20, 23, 24, 29-32. Romans 9:27-29.2 Peter 2:4, 6-9. Job 36:7.

There was no one to intercede

He looked for justice, but saw bloodshed; for righteousness, but heard cries of distress. I looked, but there was no one to help, I was appalled that no one gave support.

I looked for a man among them who would build up the wall and stand before me in the gap on behalf of the land so I would not have to destroy it, but I found none. I look but there is no one--no one among them to give counsel, no one to give answer when I ask them.

Whom shall I send? And who will go for us? You will receive power when the Holy Spirit comes on you; and you will be my witnesses in Jerusalem, and in all Judea and Samaria, and to the ends of the earth.

Be joyful in hope, patient in affliction, faithful in prayer. Be strong in the Lord and in his mighty power. Put on the full armor of God so that you can take your stand against the devil's schemes. For our struggle is not against flesh and blood, but against the rulers, against the authorities, against the powers of this dark world and against the spiritual forces of evil in the heavenly realms.

Pray in the Spirit on all occasions with all kinds of prayers and requests. We do not know what we ought to pray, but the Spirit himself intercedes for us with groans that words cannot express.

Isaiah 59:16. Isaiah 5:7. Isaiah 63:5. Ezekiel 22:30. Isaiah 41:28. Isaiah 6:8. Acts 1:8. Romans 12:12. Ephesians 6:10-12, 18. Romans 8:26.

Righteousness exalts a nation

Through the blessing of the upright a city is exalted. A throne is established through righteousness. Tyranny will be far from you; you will have nothing to fear. Terror will be far removed; it will not come near you.

Love and faithfulness keep a king safe; through love his throne is made secure. By justice a king gives a country stability.

Therefore, you kings, be wise; be warned, you rulers of the earth. Serve the Lord with fear and rejoice with trembling.

Endow the king with your justice, O God, the royal son with your righteousness. He will judge your people in righteousness, your afflicted ones with justice. The mountains will bring prosperity to the people, the hills the fruit of righteousness. He will defend the afflicted among the people and save the children of the needy; he will crush the oppressor.

He will endure as long as the sun, as long as the moon, through all generations. He will be like rain falling on a mown field, like showers watering the earth. In his days the righteous will flourish; prosperity will abound till the moon is no more.

I urge, then, first of all, that requests, prayers, intercession and thanksgiving be made for everyone--for kings and all those in authority, that we may live peaceful and quiet lives in all godliness and holiness. This is good, and pleases God our Savior, who wants all men to be saved and to come to a knowledge of the truth.

Proverbs 14:34. Proverbs 11:11. Proverbs 16:12. Isaiah 54:14. Proverbs 20:28. Proverbs 29:4. Psalm 2:10, 11. Psalm 72:1-7. 1 Timothy 2:1-4.

Righteousness goes before him and prepares the way for his steps

The Lord is exalted over all the nations, his glory above the heavens. Who is like the Lord our God, the One who sits enthroned on high, who stoops down to look on the heavens and the earth? He does as he pleases with the powers of heaven and the peoples of the earth. Your path led through the sea, your way through the mighty waters, though your footprints were not seen.

For the eyes of the Lord range throughout the earth to strengthen those whose hearts are fully committed to him.

Your ways, O God, are holy. What god is so great as our God? You are the God who performs miracles; you display your power among the peoples.

No king is saved by the size of his army; no warrior escapes by his great strength. A horse is a vain hope for deliverance; despite all its great strength it cannot save. But the eyes of the Lord are on those who fear him, on those whose hope is in his unfailing love, to deliver them from death and keep them alive in famine.

We wait in hope for the Lord; he is our help and our shield. In him our hearts rejoice, for we trust in his holy name. May your unfailing love rest upon us, O Lord, even as we put our hope in you.

Psalm 85:13. Psalm 113:4-6. Daniel 4:35. Psalm 77:19. 2 Chronicles 16:9. Psalm 77:13, 14. Psalm 33:16-22.

Show us your unfailing love, O Lord, and grant us your salvation

I will listen to what God the Lord will say; he promises peace to his people, his saints--but let them not return to folly. Surely his salvation is near those who fear him, that his glory may dwell in our land.

Love and faithfulness meet together; righteousness and peace kiss each other. Faithfulness springs forth from the earth, and righteousness looks down from heaven. The Lord will indeed give what is good, and our land will yield its harvest.

Righteousness and justice are the foundation of your throne; love and faithfulness go before you. Blessed are those who have learned to acclaim you, who walk in the light of your presence, O Lord. They rejoice in your name all day long; they exult in your righteousness. For you are their glory and strength, and by your favor you exalt our horn.

The Lord is a refuge for the oppressed, a stronghold in times of trouble. Those who know your name will trust in you, for you, Lord, have never forsaken those who seek you.

He will teach us his ways, so that we may walk in his paths.

Psalm 85:7-12. Psalm 89:14-17. Psalm 9:9, 10. Isaiah 2:3.

Who among the gods is like you, O Lord?

Who is like you--majestic in holiness, awesome in glory, working wonders?

Majestic in holiness. God reigns over the nations; God is seated on his holy throne. Let them praise your great and awesome name--he is holy. The Lord Almighty will be exalted by his justice, and the holy God will show himself holy by his righteousness.

Awesome in glory. How awesome are your deeds! So great is your power that your enemies cringe before you. He rules forever by his power, his eyes watch the nations--let not the rebellious rise up against him. The Lord is robed in majesty and is armed with strength. The God of glory thunders, the Lord thunders over the mighty waters. The voice of the Lord is powerful; the voice of the Lord is majestic.

Working wonders. It was you who split open the sea by your power. It was you who opened up springs and streams; you dried up the ever flowing rivers. You are the God who performs miracles; you display your power among the peoples. Your arm is endued with power; your hand is strong, you right hand exalted.

His incomparably great power. That power is like the working of his mighty strength, which he exerted in Christ when he raised him from the dead and seated him at his right hand in the heavenly realms, far above all rule and authority, power and dominion, and every title that can be given, not only in the present age but also in the one to come.

Exodus 15:11. Psalm 47:8. Psalm 99:3. Isaiah 5:16. Exodus 15:11. Psalm 66:3, 7. Psalm 93:1. Psalm 29:3, 4. Exodus 15:11. Psalm 74:13, 15. Psalm 77:14. Psalm 89:13. Ephesians 1:19-21.

Who can stand in the presence of the Lord, this holy God?

"Do not come any closer," God said. "Take off your sandals, for the place where you are standing is holy ground. Moses hid his face, because he was afraid to look at God.

Joshua fell face down to the ground in reverence.

As he [Saul] neared Damascus on his journey, suddenly a light from heaven flashed around him. He fell to the ground and heard a voice say to him, "Saul, Saul, why do you persecute me?"

"Woe to me!" I [Isaiah] cried. "I am ruined! For I am a man of unclean lips, and I live among a people of unclean lips, and my eyes have seen the King, the Lord Almighty." They bowed low and fell prostrate before the Lord and the king.

Who may ascend the hill of the Lord? Who may stand in his holy place? He who has clean hands and a pure heart, who does not lift up his soul to an idol or swear by what is false. He will receive blessing from the Lord and vindication from God his Savior.

Once you were alienated from God and were enemies in your minds because of your evil behavior. But now he has reconciled you by Christ's physical body through death to present you holy in his sight, without blemish and free from accusation--if you continue in your faith, established and firm, not moved from the hope held out in the gospel.

---

1 Samuel 6:20. Exodus 3:5, 6. Joshua 5:14. Acts 9:3, 4. Isaiah 6:5. 1 Chronicles 29:20. Psalm 24:3-5. Colossians 1:21-23.

The Lord our God is holy

Holy, holy, holy is the Lord Almighty; the whole earth is full of his glory. Holy, holy, holy is the Lord God Almighty, who was, and is, and is to come.

From everlasting to everlasting you are God. The heavens, even the highest heaven, cannot contain you. Oh, the depths of the riches of the wisdom and knowledge of God! How unsearchable his judgments, and his paths beyond tracing out!

Two things have I heard: that you, O God, are strong, and that you, O Lord, are loving. Your faithfulness reaches to the skies. In all that has happened to us, you have been just.

O Lord, you have searched me and you know me. You are familiar with all my ways. Where can I go from your Spirit? Where can I flee from your presence? You are kind and forgiving, O Lord, abounding in love to all who call to you. You are great and do marvelous deeds, you alone are God.

You are worthy, our Lord and God, to receive glory and honor and power. For by him all things were created: things in heaven and on earth, visible and invisible, whether thrones or powers or rulers or authorities; all things were created by him and for him. He is before all things, and in him all things hold together.

Psalm 99:9. Isaiah 6:3. Revelation 4:8. Psalm 90:2. 1 Kings 8:27. Romans 11:33. Psalm 62:11, 12. Psalm 108:4. Nehemiah 9:33. Psalm 139:1, 3, 7. Psalm 86:5, 10. Revelation 4:11. Colossians 1:16, 17.

The whole earth is full of his glory

Is not God in the heights of heaven? And see how lofty are the highest stars! Can his forces be numbered? Upon whom does his light not rise? God's voice thunders in marvelous ways; he does great things beyond our understanding. Out of the north he comes in golden splendor; God comes in awesome majesty.

O Lord, our Lord, how majestic is your name in all the earth! You are resplendent with light, more majestic than mountains rich with game. The heavens declare the glory of God; the skies proclaim the work of his hands.

Declare his glory among the nations, his marvelous deeds among all peoples. For great is the Lord and most worthy of praise; he is to be feared above all gods. Splendor and majesty are before him; strength and glory are in his sanctuary. Ascribe to the Lord, O families of nations, ascribe to the Lord glory and strength.

For from him and through him and to him are all things. To him be the glory forever! Amen.

Isaiah 6:3. Job 22:12. Job 25:3. Job 37:5, 22. Psalm 8:9. Psalm 76:4. Psalm 19:1. Psalm 96:3, 4, 6, 7. Romans 11:36.

Who will not fear you, O Lord, and bring glory to your name?

God, the blessed and only Ruler, the King of kings and Lord of lords, who alone is immortal and who lives in unapproachable light, whom no one has seen or can see. Yours, O Lord, is the greatness and the power and the glory and the majesty and the splendor, for everything in heaven and earth is yours. Yours, O Lord, is the kingdom; you are exalted as head over all. Wealth and honor come from you; you are the ruler of all things. In your hands are strength and power to exalt and give strength to all.

Your statutes stand firm; holiness adorns your house for endless days, O Lord. One thing I ask of the Lord, this is what I seek: that I may dwell in the house of the Lord all the days of my life, to gaze upon the beauty of the Lord and to seek him in his temple. Whom have I in heaven but you? And earth has nothing I desire besides you. My soul yearns for you in the night; in the morning my spirit longs for you.

O Lord, truly I am your servant; I am your servant, the son of your maidservant; you have freed me from my chains. I will sacrifice a thank offering to you and call on the name of the Lord. I will fulfill my vows to the Lord in the presence of all his people.

Revelation 15:4. 1 Timothy 6:15, 16. 1 Chronicles 29:11, 12. Psalm 93:5. Psalm 27:4, 5. Psalm 73:25. Isaiah 26:9. Psalm 116:16-18.

It is God's will that you should be holy

Without holiness no one will see the Lord. Let us purify ourselves from everything that contaminates body and spirit, perfecting holiness out of reverence for God.

You were taught, with regard to your former way of life, to put off your old self, which is being corrupted by its deceitful desires; to be made new in the attitude of your minds; and to put on the new self, created to be like God in true righteousness and holiness.

He chose us in him before the creation of the world to be holy and blameless in his sight. In love he predestined us to be adopted as his sons through Jesus Christ, in accordance with his pleasure and will--to the praise of his glorious grace, which he has freely given us in the One he loves.

Live lives worthy of God, who calls you into his kingdom and glory. This is my prayer: that your love may abound more and more in knowledge and depth of insight, so that you may be able to discern what is best and may be pure and blameless until the day of Christ, filled with the fruit of righteousness that comes through Jesus Christ--to the glory and praise of God.

---

1 Thessalonians 4:3. Hebrews 12:14. 2 Corinthians 7:1. Ephesians 4:22-24. Ephesians 1:4-6. 1 Thessalonians 2:12. Philippians 1:9-11.

Sing to the Lord, you saints of his; praise his holy name

You are a chosen people, a royal priesthood, a holy nation, a people belonging to God, that you may declare the praises of him who called you out of darkness into his wonderful light. Through Jesus, therefore, let us continually offer to God a sacrifice of praise--the fruit of lips that confess his name. Sing praises to the Lord enthroned in Zion; proclaim among the nations what he has done. Praise the Lord with the harp; make music to him on the ten-stringed lyre.

O Lord, open my lips, and my mouth will declare your praise. O Lord, you are my God; I will exalt you and praise your name, for in perfect faithfulness you have done marvelous things, things planned long ago. The path of the righteous is level; O upright One, you make the way of the righteous smooth. Yes, Lord, walking in the way of your laws, we wait for you; your name and renown are the desire of our hearts.

Sing to the Lord a new song, his praise from the ends of the earth, you who go down to the sea, and all that is in it, you islands, and all who live in them. Let the desert and its towns raise their voices; let the settlements where Kedar lives rejoice. Let the people of Sela sing for joy; let them shout from the mountaintops. Let them give glory to the Lord and proclaim his praise in the islands.

Psalm 30:4. 1 Peter 2:9. Hebrews 13:15. Psalm 9:11. Psalm 33:2. Psalm 51:15. Isaiah 25:1. Isaiah 26:7, 8. Isaiah 42:10-12.

The glory of the Lord will be revealed, and all mankind together will see it

Look, he is coming with the clouds, and every eye will see him. This same Jesus, who has been taken from you into heaven, will come back in the same way you have seen him go into heaven.

Christ was sacrificed once to take away the sins of many people; and he will appear a second time, not to bear sin, but to bring salvation to those who are waiting for him. No one knows about that day or hour, not even the angels in heaven, nor the Son, but only the Father.

You ... must be ready, because the Son of Man will come at an hour when you do not expect him. The day of the Lord will come like a thief in the night. Be dressed ready for service and keep your lamps burning, like men waiting for their master to return from a wedding banquet, so that when he comes and knocks they can immediately open the door for him. It will be good for those servants whose master finds them ready, even if he comes in the second or third watch of the night.

Do not forget this one thing, dear friends: With the Lord a day is like a thousand years, and a thousand years are like a day. The Lord is not slow in keeping his promise, as some understand slowness. He is patient with you, not wanting anyone to perish, but everyone to come to repentance.

Isaiah 40:5. Revelation 1:7. Acts 1:11. Hebrews 9:28. Matthew 24:36. Luke 12:40. 1 Thessalonians 5:2. Luke 12:35, 36, 38. 2 Peter 3:8, 9.

The Sovereign Lord comes with power

At that time they will see the Son of Man coming in a cloud with power and great glory. Our citizenship is in heaven. And we eagerly await a Savior from there, the Lord Jesus Christ, who, by the power that enables him to bring everything under his control, will transform our lowly bodies so that they will be like his glorious body. When Christ, who is your life, appears, then you also will appear with him in glory.

The righteous will shine like the sun in the kingdom of their Father. We are heirs--heirs of God and co-heirs with Christ, if indeed we share in his sufferings in order that we may also share in his glory. I consider that our present sufferings are not worth comparing with the glory that will be revealed in us. For our light and momentary troubles are achieving for us an eternal glory that far outweighs them all.

Those who are wise will shine like the brightness of the heavens, and those who lead many to righteousness, like the stars for ever and ever. Whatever you do, work at it with all your heart, as working for the Lord, not for men, since you know that you will receive an inheritance from the Lord as a reward. It is the Lord Christ you are serving.

Isaiah 40:10. Luke 21:27. Philippians 3:20, 21. Colossians 3:4. Matthew 13:43. Romans 8:17, 18. 2 Corinthians 4:17. Daniel 12:3. Colossians 3:23, 24.

His reward is with him

The Son of Man is going to come in his Father's glory with his angels, and then he will reward each person according to what he has done.

I am coming soon. Hold on to what you have, so that no one will take your crown. Everyone who competes in the games goes into strict training. They do it to get a crown that will not last; but we do it to get a crown that will last forever.

The crown of righteousness, which the Lord, the righteous Judge, will reward ... to all who have longed for his appearing. Be faithful, even to the point of death, and I will give you the crown of life. The crown of life ... promised to those who love him. The crown of glory that will never fade away. The Lord will reward everyone for whatever good he does, whether he is slave or free.

Be strong in the Lord and in his mighty power. Put on the full armor of God so that you can take your stand against the devil's schemes. For our struggle is not against flesh and blood, but against the rulers, against the authorities, against the powers of this dark world and against the spiritual forces of evil in the heavenly realms.

When he appears, we shall be like him, for we shall see him as he is.

Isaiah 40:10. Matthew 16:27. Revelation 3:11. 1 Corinthians 9:25. 2 Timothy 4:8. Revelation 2:10. James 1:12. 1 Peter 5:4. Ephesians 6:8, 10-12. 1 John 3:2.

The rough ground shall become level

Every valley shall be raised up, every mountain and hill made low; the rough ground shall become level, the rugged places a plain. The path of the righteous is level; O upright One, you make the way of the righteous smooth. Yes, Lord, walking in the way of your laws, we wait for you; your name and renown are the desire of our hearts.

The Lord Almighty will prepare a feast of rich food for all peoples, a banquet of aged wine--the best of meats and the finest of wines. On this mountain he will destroy the shroud that enfolds all peoples, the sheet that covers all nations; he will swallow up death forever. The Sovereign Lord will wipe away the tears from all faces; he will remove the disgrace of his people from all the earth. The Lord has spoken. In that day they will say, "Surely this is our God; we trusted in him, and he saved us. This is the Lord, we trusted in him; let us rejoice and be glad in his salvation.

He will endure as long as the sun, as long as the moon, through all generations. He will be like rain falling on a mown field, like showers watering the earth. In his days the righteous will flourish; prosperity will abound till the moon is no more.

"No longer will a man teach his neighbor, or a man his brother, saying, 'Know the Lord,' because they will all know me, from the least of them to the greatest," declares the Lord.

Isaiah 40:4. Isaiah 26:7, 8. Isaiah 25:6-9. Psalm 72:5-7. Jeremiah 31:34.

Lift up your voice with a shout

You have come to Mount Zion, to the heavenly Jerusalem, the city of the living God. You have come to thousands upon thousands of angels in joyful assembly, to the church of the firstborn, whose names are written in heaven.

I looked and heard the voice of many angels, numbering thousands upon thousands, and ten thousand times ten thousand. Then I heard what sounded like a great multitude, like the roar of rushing waters and like loud peals of thunder, shouting: "Hallelujah! For our Lord God Almighty reigns. Let us rejoice and be glad and give him glory! For the wedding of the Lamb has come, and his bride has made herself ready. Fine linen, bright and clean, was given her to wear."

I saw the Holy City, the new Jerusalem, coming down out of heaven from God, prepared as a bride beautifully dressed for her husband. And I heard a loud voice from the throne saying, "Now the dwelling of God is with men, and he will live with them. They will be his people, and God himself will be with them and be their God. He will wipe every tear from their eyes. There will be no more death of mourning or crying or pain, for the old order of things has passed away."

No longer will there be any curse. The throne of God and of the Lamb will be in the city, and his servants will serve him. They will see his face, and his name will be on their foreheads. There will be no more night. They will not need the light of a lamp or the light of the sun, for the Lord God will give them light. And they will reign for ever and ever.

Isaiah 40:9. Hebrews 12:22-24. Revelation 5:11. Revelation 19:6-8. Revelation 21:2-5. Revelation 22:3-5.

Behold, I am coming soon!

The end of all things is near. Therefore be clear minded and self-controlled so that you can pray. Above all, love each other deeply, because love covers over a multitude of sins. Offer hospitality to one another without grumbling. Each one should use whatever gift he has received to serve others.

God is love. Whoever lives in love lives in God, and God in him. In this way, love is made complete among us so that we will have confidence on the day of judgment, because in this world we are like him. For in just a very little while, "He who is coming will come."

In my Father's house are many rooms; if it were not so, I would have told you. I am going there to prepare a place for you. And if I go and prepare a place for you, I will come back and take you to be with me that you also may be where I am.

We believe that Jesus died and rose again and so we believe that God will bring with Jesus those who have fallen asleep in him. According to the Lord's own word, we tell you that we who are still alive, who are left till the coming of the Lord, will certainly not precede those who have fallen asleep. For the Lord himself will come down from heaven, with a loud command, with the voice of the archangel and with the trumpet call of God, and the dead in Christ will rise first. After that, we who are still alive and are left will be caught up together with them in the clouds to meet the Lord in the air. And so we will be with the Lord forever. Therefore encourage each other with these words.

Be patient and stand firm. Amen. Come, Lord Jesus.

Revelation 22:7. 1 Peter 4:7-10. 1 John 4:16, 17. Hebrews 10:37. John 14:2, 3. 1 Thessalonians 4:14-18. James 5:8. Revelation 22:20.

Here is your God!

You alone are the Lord. You made the heavens, even the highest heavens, and all their starry host, the earth and all that is on it, the seas and all that is in them. You give life to everything, and the multitudes of heaven worship you.

He will be called Wonderful Counselor, Mighty God, Everlasting Father, Prince of Peace. God exalted him to the highest place and gave him the name that is above every name, that at the name of Jesus every knee should bow, in heaven and on earth and under the earth, and every tongue confess that Jesus Christ is Lord, to the glory of God the Father. Far above all rule and authority, power and dominion, and every title that can be given, not only in the present age but also in the one to come. His dominion is an everlasting dominion that will not pass away, and his kingdom is one that will never be destroyed.

Worthy is the Lamb, who was slain, to receive power and wealth and wisdom and strength and honor and glory and praise! Amen! Praise and glory and wisdom and thanks and honor and power and strength be to our God for ever and ever. Amen!

From the ends of the earth we hear singing: "Glory to the Righteous One." Praise our God, all you his servants, you who fear him, both small and great!

Isaiah 40:9. Nehemiah 9:6. Isaiah 9:6. Philippians 2:9-11. Ephesians 1:21. Daniel 7:14. Revelation 5:12. Revelation 7:12. Isaiah 24:16. Revelation 19:5.

Each of us has turned to his own way

Who can say, "I have kept my heart pure; I am clean and without sin?" There is not a righteous man on earth who does what is right and never sins. For all have sinned and fall short of the glory of God. All of us have become like one who is unclean, and all our righteous acts are like filthy rags; we all shrivel up like a leaf; and like the wind our sins sweep us away.

If we claim to be without sin, we deceive ourselves and the truth is not in us. There is no one righteous, not even one; there is no one who understands, no one who seeks God. All have turned away, they have together become worthless; there is no one who does good, not even one.

For from within, out of men's hearts, come evil thoughts, sexual immorality, theft, murder, adultery, greed, malice, deceit, lewdness, envy, slander, arrogance and folly. All these evils come from inside and make a man "unclean."

If you, O Lord, kept a record of sins, O Lord, who could stand? But with you there is forgiveness; therefore you are feared. With the Lord there is unfailing love and with him is full redemption.

Isaiah 53:6. Proverbs 20:9. Ecclesiastes 7:20. Romans 3:23. Isaiah 64:6. 1 John 1:8. Romans 3:10-12. Mark 7:21-23. Psalm 130:3, 4, 7.

He took up our infirmities and carried our sorrows

He was despised and rejected by men, a man of sorrows, and familiar with suffering. Jesus wept. O Jerusalem, Jerusalem, you who kill the prophets and stone those sent to you, how often I have longed to gather your children together, as a hen gathers her chicks under her wings, but you were not willing. Jesus went through all the towns and villages ... healing every disease and sickness. When he saw the crowds, he had compassion on them, because they were harassed and helpless, like sheep without a shepherd.

This is how we know what love is: Jesus Christ laid down his life for us. Greater love has no one than this, that he lay down his life for his friends. He is patient with you, not wanting anyone to perish, but everyone to come to repentance.

Seek the Lord while he may be found; call on him while he is near. Let the wicked forsake his way and the evil man his thoughts. Let him turn to the Lord, and he will have mercy on him, and to our God, for he will freely pardon. Repent and be baptized, every one of you, in the name of Jesus Christ for the forgiveness of your sins. And you will receive the gift of the Holy Spirit.

Christ suffered for you. When they hurled their insults at him, he did not retaliate; when he suffered, he made no threats. He himself bore our sins in his body on the tree, so that we might die to sins and live for righteousness; by his wounds you have been healed.

Isaiah 53:4, 3. John 11:35. Matthew 23:37. Matthew 9:35, 36. 1 John 3:16. John 15:13. 2 Peter 3:9. Isaiah 55:6, 7. Acts 2:38. 1 Peter 2:21, 23, 24.

He was crushed for our iniquities

Jesus began to explain to his disciples that he must go to Jerusalem and suffer many things at the hands of the elders, chief priests and teachers of the law, and that he must be killed and on the third day be raised to life.

All who see me mock me; they hurl insults, shaking their heads: "He trusts in the Lord; let the Lord rescue him. Let him deliver him, since he delights in him." I am poured out like water, and all my bones are out of joint. My heart has turned to wax; it has melted away within me. My strength is dried up like a potsherd, and my tongue sticks to the roof of my mouth; you lay me in the dust of death. Dogs have surrounded me; a band of evil men has encircled me, they have pierced my hands and my feet. I can count all my bones; people stare and gloat over me.

He was assigned a grave with the wicked, and with the rich in his death, though he had done no violence, nor was any deceit in his mouth.

This is how God showed his love among us: He sent his one and only Son into the world that we might live through him. This is love: not that we loved God, but that he loved us and sent his Son as an atoning sacrifice for our sins.

God made him who had no sin to be sin for us, so that in him we might become the righteousness of God.

Isaiah 53:5. Matthew 16:21. Psalm 22:7, 8, 14-17. Isaiah 53:9. 1 John 4:9, 10. 2 Corinthians 5:21.

Though he was rich, yet for your sakes he became poor

He was with God in the beginning. He is the image of the invisible God, the firstborn over all creation. For by him all things were created: things in heaven and on earth, visible and invisible, whether thrones or powers or rulers or authorities; all things were created by him and for him. He is before all things, and in him all things hold together.

There was no room for them in the inn. He was in the world, and though the world was made through him, the world did not recognize him. He came to that which was his own, but his own did not receive him. They got up, drove him out of the town, and took him to the brow of the hill on which the town was built, in order to throw him down the cliff. They pleaded with him to leave their region. With one voice they cried out, "Away with this man!"

Christ Jesus: Who, being in very nature God, did not consider equality with God something to be grasped, but made himself nothing, taking the very nature of a servant, being made in human likeness. And being found in appearance as a man, he humbled himself and became obedient to death--even death on a cross!

He had to be made like his brothers in every way, in order that he might become a merciful and faithful high priest in service to God, and that he might make atonement for the sins of the people. To all who received him, to those who believed in his name, he gave the right to become children of God.

---

2 Corinthians 8:9. John 1:2. Colossians 1:15-17. Luke 2:7. John 1:10, 11. Luke 4:29. Matthew 8:34. Luke 23:18. Philippians 2:5-8. Hebrews 2:17. John 1:12.

The very nature of a servant

The Son of Man did not come to be served, but to serve, and to give his life as a ransom for many. Your king comes to you, righteous and having salvation, gentle and riding on a donkey, on a colt, the foal of a donkey. He was led like a lamb to the slaughter, and as a sheep before her shearers is silent, so he did not open his mouth.

The rising sun will come to us from heaven to shine on those living in darkness and in the shadow of death, to guide our feet into the path of peace. I have come that they may have life, and have it to the full. I have come into the world as a light, so that no one who believes in me should stay in darkness.

The Spirit of the Sovereign Lord is on me, because the Lord has anointed me to preach good news to the poor. He has sent me to bind up the brokenhearted, to proclaim freedom for the captives and release from darkness for the prisoners, to proclaim the year of the Lord's favor and the day of vengeance of our God, to comfort all who mourn, and provide for those who grieve in Zion--to bestow on them a crown of beauty instead of ashes, the oil of gladness instead of mourning, and a garment of praise instead of a spirit of despair. They will be called oaks of righteousness, a planting of the Lord for the display of his splendor.

Philippians 2:7. Matthew 20:28. Zechariah 9:9. Isaiah 53:7. Luke 1:78, 79. John 10:10. John 12:46. Isaiah 61:1-3.

Obedient to death--even death on a cross!

"I, when I am lifted up from the earth, will draw all men to myself." He said this to show the kind of death he was going to die. Our great God and Savior, Jesus Christ, who gave himself for us to redeem us from all wickedness and to purify for himself a people that are his very own, eager to do what is good. At just the right time, when we were still powerless, Christ died for the ungodly.

"Abba, Father," he said, "everything is possible for you. Take this cup from me. Yet not what I will, but what you will. Shall I not drink the cup the Father has given me?"

He is the atoning sacrifice for our sins, and not only for ours but also for the sins of the whole world. For God so loved the world that he gave his one and only Son, that whoever believes in him shall not perish but have eternal life. For God did not send his Son into the world to condemn the world, but to save the world through him.

Jesus Christ ... the faithful witness, the firstborn from the dead, and the ruler of the kings of the earth. You were slain, and with your blood you purchased men for God from every tribe and language and people and nation. You have made them to be a kingdom and priests to serve our God, and they will reign on the earth.

Philippians 2:8. John 12:32, 33. Titus 2:13, 14. Romans 5:6. Mark 14:36. John 18:11. 1 John 2:2. John 3:16, 17. Revelation 1:5. Revelation 5:9, 10.

Now is the time of God's favor, now is the day of salvation

I pray to you, O Lord, in the time of your favor; in your great love, O God, answer me with your sure salvation. Answer me, O Lord, out of the goodness of your love; in your great mercy turn to me.

This is what the Lord says: In the time of my favor I will answer you, and in the day of salvation I will help you. Here I am! I stand at the door and knock. If anyone hears my voice and opens the door, I will come in and eat with him, and he with me.

To all who received him, to those who believed in his name, he gave the right to become children of God. His sheep follow him because they know his voice. My sheep listen to my voice; I know them, and they follow me. I give them eternal life, and they shall never perish; no one can snatch them out of my hand.

The one who trusts in him will never be put to shame. If God is for us, who can be against us? He who did not spare his own Son, but gave him up for us all-- how will he not also, along with him, graciously give us all things?

Who shall separate us from the love of Christ? Shall trouble or hardship or persecution or famine or nakedness or danger or sword? I am convinced that neither the present nor the future, nor any powers, neither height nor depth, nor anything else in all creation, will be able to separate us from the love of God that is in Christ Jesus our Lord.

---

2 Corinthians 6:2. Psalm 69:13, 16. Isaiah 49:8. Revelation 3:20. John 1:12. John 10:4, 27, 28. Romans 9:33. Romans 8:31, 32, 35, 38, 39.

I will create new heavens and a new earth.

The wolf will live with the lamb, the leopard will lie down with the goat, the calf and the lion and the yearling together; and a little child will lead them. The cow will feed with the bear, their young will lie down together, and the lion will eat straw like the ox. The infant will play near the hole of the cobra, and the young child put his hand into the viper's nest. They will neither harm nor destroy on all my holy mountain, for the earth will be full of the knowledge of the Lord as the waters cover the sea.

The desert and the parched land will be glad; the wilderness will rejoice and blossom. Like the crocus, it will burst into bloom; it will rejoice greatly and shout for joy.

Then will the eyes of the blind be opened and the ears of the deaf unstopped. Then will the lame leap like a deer, and the mute tongue shout for joy. Water will gush forth in the wilderness and streams in the desert. The burning sand will become a pool, the thirsty ground bubbling springs. In the haunts where jackals once lay, grass and reeds and papyrus will grow.

And a highway will be there; it will be called the Way of Holiness. The unclean will not journey on it; it will be for those who walk in that Way; wicked fools will not go about on it. Only the redeemed will walk there.

Isaiah 65:17. Isaiah 11:6-9. Isaiah 35:1, 2, 5-9.

The former things will not be remembered

In the last days the mountain of the Lord's temple will be established as chief among the mountains; it will be raised above the hills, and all nations will stream to it. Many peoples will come and say, "Come, let us go up to the mountain of the Lord, to the house of the God of Jacob. He will teach us his ways, so that we may walk in his paths." The law will go out from Zion, the word of the Lord from Jerusalem. He will judge between the nations and will settle disputes for many peoples. They will beat their swords into plowshares and their spears into pruning hooks. Nations will not take up sword against nation, nor will they train for war anymore. Every warrior's boot used in battle and every garment rolled in blood will be destined for burning, will be fuel for the fire.

A king will reign in righteousness and rulers will rule with justice. Each man will be like a shelter from the wind and a refuge from the storm, like streams of water in the desert and the shadow of a great rock in a thirsty land. Then the eyes of those who see will no longer be closed and the ears of those who hear will listen. The mind of the rash will know and understand, and the stammering tongue will be fluent and clear. No longer will the fool be called noble nor the scoundrel be highly respected.

He must reign until he has put all his enemies under his feet. The last enemy to be destroyed is death. You will go out in joy and be led forth in peace; the mountains and hills will burst into song before you, and all the trees of the field will clap their hands.

Isaiah 65:17. Isaiah 2:2-4. Isaiah 9:5. Isaiah 54:17. Isaiah 32:1-5. 1 Corinthians 15:25, 26. Isaiah 55:12.

A people blessed by the Lord

I am the Lord ... showing love to thousands who love me and keep my commandments.

I am sending an angel ahead of you to guard you along the way and to bring you to the place I have prepared. If you are willing and obedient, you will eat the best from the land. Of the increase of his government and peace there will be no end.

From the ends of the earth we hear singing: "Glory to the Righteous One." In that day the deaf will hear the words of the scroll, and out of gloom and darkness the eyes of the blind will see. Once more the humble will rejoice in the Lord; the needy will rejoice in the Holy One of Israel. The ruthless will vanish, the mockers will disappear, and all who have an eye for evil will be cut down.

Justice will dwell in the desert and righteousness live in the fertile field. The fruit of righteousness will be peace; the effect of righteousness will be quietness and confidence forever. My people will live in peaceful dwelling places, in secure homes, in undisturbed places of rest. Though hail flattens the forest and the city is leveled completely, how blessed you will be, sowing your seed by every stream, and letting your cattle and donkeys range free.

Isaiah 65:23. Exodus 20:2, 6. Exodus 23:20. Isaiah 1:19. Isaiah 9:7. Isaiah 24:16. Isaiah 29:18-20. Isaiah 32:16-20.

The wolf and the lamb will feed together

In that day I will make a covenant for them with the beasts of the field and the birds of the air and the creatures that move along the ground. Bow and sword and battle I will abolish from the land, so that all may lie down in safety. I will betroth you to me forever; I will betroth you in righteousness and justice, in love and compassion. I will betroth you in faithfulness, and you will acknowledge the Lord. Every man will sit under his own vine and under his own fig tree, and no one will make them afraid, for the Lord Almighty has spoken.

He himself is our peace. You are no longer foreigners and aliens, but fellow citizens with God's people and members of God's household, built on the foundation of the apostles and prophets, with Christ Jesus himself as the chief cornerstone. In him the whole building is joined together and rises to become a holy temple in the Lord. And in him you too are being built together to become a dwelling in which God lives by his Spirit.

You will keep in perfect peace him whose mind is steadfast, because he trusts in you. Trust in the Lord forever, for the Lord, the Lord, is the Rock eternal. "Though the mountains be shaken and the hills be removed, yet my unfailing love for you will not be shaken nor my covenant of peace be removed," says the Lord, who has compassion on you.

Isaiah 65:25. Hosea 2:18-20. Micah 4:4. Ephesians 2:14, 19-22. Isaiah 26:3, 4. Isaiah 54:10.

He will wipe every tear from their eyes

There will be no more death or mourning or crying or pain, for the old order of things has passed away. There will be no more gloom for those who were in distress. The moon will shine like the sun, and the sunlight will be seven times brighter, like the light of seven full days, when the Lord binds up the bruises of his people and heals the wounds he inflicted.

Where, O death, are your plagues? Where, O grave, is your destruction? He will swallow up death forever. The Sovereign Lord will wipe away the tears from all faces; he will remove the disgrace of his people from all the earth.

Maidens will dance and be glad, young men and old as well. I will turn their mourning into gladness; I will give them comfort and joy instead of sorrow. Your sun will never set again, and your moon will wane no more; the Lord will be your everlasting light. Arise, shine, for your light has come, and the glory of the Lord rises upon you.

For you who revere my name, the sun of righteousness will rise with healing in its wings. And you will go out and leap like calves released from the stall. "They will be mine," says the Lord Almighty, "in the day when I make up my treasured possession. I will spare them, just as in compassion a man spares his son who serves him. And you will again see the distinction between the righteous and the wicked, between those who serve God and those who do not."

Revelation 21:4. Isaiah 9:1. Isaiah 30:26. Hosea 13:14. Isaiah 25:8. Jeremiah 31:13. Isaiah 60:20, 1. Malachi 4:2. Malachi 3:17, 18.

I am making everything new!

The former things have taken place, and new things I declare; before they spring into being I announce them to you. I am doing anew thing! Now it springs up; do you not perceive it? I am making a way in the desert and streams in the wasteland. The old has gone, the new has come!

I saw a new heaven and a new earth, for the first heaven and the first earth had passed away, and there was no longer any sea. I saw the Holy City, the new Jerusalem, coming down out of heaven from God, prepared as a bride beautifully dressed for her husband. And I heard a loud voice from the throne saying, "Now the dwelling of God is with men, and he will live with them. They will be his people, and God himself will be with them and be their God. The city does not need the sun or the moon to shine on it, for the glory of God gives it light, and the Lamb is its lamp. Nothing impure will ever enter it, nor will anyone who does what is shameful or deceitful, but only those whose names are written in the Lamb's book of life.

The riches of his glorious inheritance. When Christ, who is your life, appears, then you also will appear with him in glory. Live lives worthy of God, who calls you into his kingdom and glory.

You guide me with your counsel, and afterward you will take me into glory. For here we do not have an enduring city, but we are looking for the city that is to come. And you will receive a rich welcome into the eternal kingdom of our Lord and Savior Jesus Christ.

Revelation 21:5. Isaiah 42:9. Isaiah 43:19. 2 Corinthians 5:17. Revelation 21:1-3, 23, 27. Ephesians 1:18. Colossians 3:4. 1 Thessalonians 2:12. Psalm 73:24. Hebrews 13:14. 2 Peter 1:11.

Be glad and rejoice forever

Weeping may remain for a night, but rejoicing comes in the morning. You will fill me with joy in your presence, with eternal pleasures at your right hand. The kingdom of God ... is righteousness, peace and joy in the Holy Spirit. Those who sow in tears will reap with songs of joy.

O Lord, you are my God; I will exalt you and praise your name, for in perfect faithfulness you have done marvelous things, things planned long ago. I delight greatly in the Lord; my soul rejoices in my God. For he has clothed me with garments of salvation and arrayed me in a robe of righteousness, as a bridegroom adorns his head like a priest, and as a bride adorns herself with her jewels. For as the soil makes the sprout come up and a garden causes seeds to grow, so the Sovereign Lord will make righteousness and praise spring up before all nations.

May the peoples praise you, O God; may all the peoples praise you. May the nations be glad and sing for joy, for you rule the peoples justly and guide the nations of the earth. May the peoples praise you, O God; may all the peoples praise you.

Let everything that has breath praise the Lord.

Isaiah 65:18. Psalm 30:5. Psalm 16:11. Romans 14:17. Psalm 126:5. Isaiah 25:11. Isaiah 61:10, 11. Psalm 67:3-5. Psalm 150:6.

Before I formed you in the womb I knew you

You created my inmost being; you knit me together in my mother's womb. My frame was not hidden from you when I was made in the secret place. When I was woven together in the depths of the earth, your eyes saw my unformed body. All the days ordained for me were written in your book before one of them came to be. O Lord, you are our Father. We are the clay, you are the potter; we are all the work of your hand. Many, O Lord my God, are the wonders you have done. The things you planned for us no one can recount to you; were I to speak and tell of them, they would be too many to declare.

"I know the plans I have for you," declares the Lord, "plans to prosper you and not to harm you, plans to give you hope and a future. I will instruct you and teach you in the way you should go; I will counsel you and watch over you."

His way is perfect. The Lord is righteous in all his ways and loving toward all he has made.

Jeremiah 1:5. Psalm 139:13, 15, 16. Isaiah 64:8. Psalm 40:5. Jeremiah 29:11. Psalm 32:8. Psalm 18:30. Psalm 145:17.

Before you were born, I set you apart

You did not choose me, but I chose you and appointed you to go and bear fruit--fruit that will last. He chose us in him before the creation of the world to be holy and blameless in his sight. In love he predestined us to be adopted as his sons through Jesus Christ.

In all things God works for the good of those who love him. What, then, shall we say in response to this? If God is for us, who can be against us? He who did not spare his own Son, but gave him up for us all--how will he not also, along with him, graciously give us all things?

It does not, therefore, depend on man's desire or effort, but on God's mercy. Who works out everything in conformity with the purpose of his will. For you are a people holy to the Lord your God. The Lord your God has chosen you out of all the peoples on the face of the earth to be his people, his treasured possession.

We are God's workmanship, created in Christ Jesus to do good works, which God prepared in advance for us to do. Therefore, as God's chosen people, holy and dearly loved, clothe yourselves with compassion, kindness, humility, gentleness and patience.

Jeremiah 1:5. John 15:16. Ephesians 1:4, 5. Romans 8:28, 31, 32. Romans 9:16. Ephesians 1:11. Deuteronomy 7:6. Ephesians 2:10. Colossians 3:12.

Get yourself ready!

The Lord had said to Abram, "Leave your country, your people and your father's household and go to the land I will show you."

So now, go. I am sending you to Pharaoh to bring my people the Israelites out of Egypt.

The Lord turned to him and said, "Go in the strength you have and save Israel out of Midian's hand. Am I not sending you?"

I heard the voice of the Lord saying, "Whom shall I send? And who will go for us?"

Now get up and stand on your feet. I have appeared to you to appoint you as a servant and as a witness of what you have seen of me and what I will show you.

Not everyone who says to me, "Lord, Lord," will enter the kingdom of heaven, but only he who does the will of my Father who is in heaven. We must obey God rather than men!

Choose for yourselves this day whom you will serve. How long will you waver between two opinions? Jesus looked at him and loved him. "One thing you lack," he said. "Go, sell everything you have and give to the poor, and you will have treasure in heaven. Then, come, follow me."

The task is great. The harvest is plentiful but the workers are few. But those who hope in the Lord will renew their strength. They will soar on wings like eagles; they will run and not grow weary, they will walk and not be faint. Be strong and courageous. Do not be afraid or discouraged, for the Lord God, my God, is with you. He will not fail you or forsake you.

Jeremiah 1:17. Genesis 12:1. Exodus 3:10. Judges 6:14. Isaiah 6:8. Acts 26:16. Matthew 7:21. Acts 5:29. Joshua 24:15. 1 Kings 18:21. Mark 10:21. 1 Chronicles 29:1. Matthew 9:37. Isaiah 40:31. 1 Chronicles 28:20.

I have put my words in your mouth

Open wide your mouth and I will fill it.

The Sovereign Lord has given me an instructed tongue, to know the word that sustains the weary. He wakens me morning by morning,wakens my ear to listen like one being taught. Because the Sovereign Lord helps me, I will not be disgraced. Therefore have I set my face like flint, and I know I will not be put to shame.

Who is going to harm you if you are eager to do good? But even if you should suffer for what is right, you are blessed. Do not fear what they fear, do not be frightened. But in your hearts set apart Christ as Lord. Always be prepared to give an answer to everyone who asks you to give the reason for the hope that you have. But do this with gentleness and respect.

You do not lack any spiritual gift as you eagerly wait for our Lord Jesus Christ to be revealed. He will keep you strong to the end, so that you will be blameless on the day of our Lord Jesus Christ. God, who has called you into fellowship with his Son Jesus Christ our Lord, is faithful.

Think of what you were when you were called. Not many of you were wise by human standards; not many were influential; not many were of noble birth. But God chose the foolish things of the world to shame the wise; God chose the weak things of the world to shame the strong ... so that no one may boast before him.

Jeremiah 1:9. Psalm 81:10. Isaiah 50:4, 5, 7. 1 Peter 3:13-16. 1 Corinthians 1:7-9, 26, 27, 29.

They will fight against you but will not overcome you

He reached down from on high and took hold of me; he drew me out of deep waters. He rescued me from my powerful enemy, from my foes, who were too strong for me. They confronted me in the day of my disaster, but the Lord was my support. He brought me out into a spacious place; he rescued me because he delighted in me.

He trains my hands for battle; my arms can bend a bow of bronze. You give me your shield of victory, and your right hand sustains me; you stoop down to make me great. You broaden the path beneath me, so that my ankles do not turn.

Our struggle is not against flesh and blood, but against the rulers, against the authorities, against the powers of this dark world and against the spiritual forces of evil in the heavenly realms. Be strong in the Lord and in his mighty power. Put on the full armor of God ... the belt of truth ... the breastplate of righteousness ... your feet fitted with the readiness that comes from the gospel of peace ... the shield of faith .... the helmet of salvation ... the sword of the Spirit, which is the word of God. The word of God is living and active. Sharper than any double-edged sword, it penetrates even to dividing soul and spirit, joints and marrow; it judges the thoughts and attitudes of the heart.

The weapons we fight with are not the weapons of the world. On the contrary, they have divine power to demolish strongholds.

Jeremiah 1:9. Psalm 18:16-19, 34-36. Ephesians 6:12, 10, 13-17. Hebrews 4:12. 2 Corinthians 10:4.

Be men of courage; be strong

Do not be terrified by them. Who are you that you fear mortal men, the sons of men, who are but grass. Fear of man will prove to be a snare. Be strong and take heart, all you who hope in the Lord.

This is what the Lord says--he who created you, O Jacob, he who formed you, O Israel: "Fear not, for I have redeemed you; I have summoned you by name; you are mine." I am with you; do not be dismayed, for I am your God. I will strengthen you and help you; I will uphold you with my righteous right hand.

He guards the course of the just and protects the way of his faithful ones. At my first defense, no one came to my support, but everyone deserted me. But the Lord stood at my side and gave me the strength, so that through me the message might be fully proclaimed. The Lord will rescue me from every evil attack and will bring me safely to his heavenly kingdom. To him be glory for ever and ever. Amen.

---

1 Corinthians 16:13. Jeremiah 1:17, 18. Isaiah 51:12. Proverbs 19:25. Psalm 31:24. Isaiah 43:1. Isaiah 41:10. Proverbs 2:8. 2 Timothy 4:16-18.

I am with you ... declares the Lord

You, O Lord, keep my lamp burning, my God turns my darkness into light. With your help I can advance against a troop; with my God I can scale a wall. Your path led through the sea, your way through the mighty waters, though your footprints were not seen.

The message of the cross is foolishness to those who are perishing, but to us who are being saved it is the power of God. For it is written: "I will destroy the wisdom of the wise; the intelligence of the intelligent I will frustrate."

Where is the wise man? Where is the scholar? Where is the philosopher of this age? Has not God made foolish the wisdom of the world? The foolishness of God is wiser than man's wisdom, and the weakness of God is stronger than man's strength.

Do you not know? Have you not heard? The Lord is the everlasting God, the Creator of the ends of the earth. He will not grow tired or weary, and his understanding no one can fathom.

Oh, the depths of the riches of the wisdom and knowledge of God! How unsearchable his judgments, and his paths beyond tracing out!

Jeremiah 1:19. Psalm 18:28, 29. Psalm 77:19. 1 Corinthians 1:18, 20, 25. Isaiah 40:28. Romans 11:33.

Reform your ways and your actions

If you really change your ways and your actions and deal with each other justly, if you do not oppress the alien, the fatherless or the widow and do not shed innocent blood in this place, and if you do not follow other gods...then I will let you live in this place, in the land I gave your forefathers for ever and ever.

Why should you be beaten anymore? Why do you persist in rebellion? Your whole head is injured, your whole heart afflicted. From the sole of your foot to the top of your head there is no soundness--only wounds and welts and open sores, not cleansed or bandaged or soothed with oil.

Wash and make yourselves clean. Take your evil deeds out of my sight! Stop doing wrong, learn to do right! Seek justice, encourage the oppressed. Defend the cause of the fatherless, plead the case of the widow.

"Come now, let us reason together," says the Lord. "Though your sins are like scarlet, they shall be as white as snow; though they are red as crimson, they shall be like wool."

Rid yourselves of all the offenses you have committed, and get a new heart and a new spirit. For the wages of sin is death. God has given us eternal life, and this life is in his Son. Our old self was crucified with him so that the body of sin might be done away with, that we should no longer be slaves to sin--because anyone who has died has been freed from sin.

Now that you have been set free from sin and have become slaves to God, the benefit you reap leads to holiness, and the result is eternal life.

Jeremiah 7:3, 5-7. Isaiah 1:5, 6, 16-18. Ezekiel 18:31. Romans 6:23. 1 John 5:12. Romans 6:6, 7, 22.

"I have been watching!" declares the Lord

"Can anyone hide in secret places so that I cannot see him?" declares the Lord.

If I say, "Surely the darkness will hide me and the light become night around me," even the darkness will not be dark to you; the night will shine like the day, for darkness is as light to you. The eyes of the Lord are everywhere, keeping watch on the wicked and the good. He observes the sons of men; his eyes examine them. He reveals deep and hidden things; he knows what lies in darkness, and light dwells with him.

The Lord searches every heart and understands every motive behind the thoughts. If you seek him, he will be found by you; but if you forsake him, he will reject you forever.

Jesus knew their thoughts and said to them: "Any kingdom divided against itself will be ruined, and a house divided against itself will fall." He did not need man's testimony about man, for he knew what was in a man. His work will be shown for what it is, because the Day will bring it to light. It will be revealed with fire, and the fire will test the quality of each man's work.

Search me, O God, and know my heart; test me and know my anxious thoughts. See if there is any offensive way in me, and lead me in the way everlasting.

Jeremiah 7:11. Jeremiah 23:24. Psalm 139:11, 12. Proverbs 15:3. Psalm 11:4. Daniel 2:22. 1 Chronicles 28:9. Luke 11:17. John 2:25. 1 Corinthians 3:13. Psalm 139:23, 24.

I spoke to you again and again, but you did not listen; I called you, but you did not answer

Am I the one they are provoking? declares the Lord. Are they not rather harming themselves, to their own shame? They refused to pay attention; stubbornly they turned their backs and stopped up their ears. This people's heart has become calloused; they hardly hear with their ears, and they have closed their eyes. Otherwise they might see with their eyes, hear with their ears, understand with their hearts and turn, and I would heal them. Ever hearing but never understanding ... ever seeing but never perceiving.

Why spend money on what is not bread, and your labor on what does not satisfy? Listen, listen to me, and eat what is good, and your soul will delight in the richest of fare.

What good will it be for a man if he gains the whole world, yet forfeits his soul? Or what can a man give in exchange for his soul. For the Son of Man is going to come in his Father's glory with his angels, and then he will reward each person according to what he has done. Come, let us return to the Lord. He has torn us to pieces but he will heal us; he has injured us but he will bind up our wounds.

Be reconciled to God. Who wants all men to be saved and to come to a knowledge of the truth.

Jeremiah 7:13, 19. Zechariah 7:11. Matthew 13:15. Acts 28:26.Isaiah 55:2. Matthew 16:26, 27. Hosea 6:1. 2 Corinthians 5:20. 1 Timothy 2:4.

They went backward and not forward

They did not listen or pay attention; instead, they followed the stubborn inclinations of their evil hearts. A man is a slave to whatever has mastered him. If they have escaped the corruption of the world by knowing our Lord and Savior Jesus Christ and are again entangled in it and overcome, they are worse off at the end than they were at the beginning. It would have been better for them not to have known the way of righteousness, than to have known it and then to turn their backs on the sacred commandment that was passed on to them.

Your silver has become dross, your choice wine is diluted with water. The faithless will be fully repaid for their evil ways. No one who puts his hand to the plow and looks back is fit for service in the kingdom of God. If he shrinks back, I will not be pleased with him.

Holding on to faith and a good conscience. Make every effort to live in peace with all men and to be holy; without holiness no one will see the Lord. See to it that no one misses the grace of God and that no bitter root grows up to cause trouble and defile many.

Jeremiah 7:24. 2 Peter 2:19-21. Proverbs 14:14. Luke 9:62. Hebrews 10:38. 1 Timothy 1:19. Hebrews 12:14, 15.

Do not make light of the Lord's discipline, and do not lose heart when he rebukes you

Blessed is the man who always fears the Lord, but he who hardens his heart falls into trouble. Encourage one another daily, as long as it is called Today, so that none of you may be hardened by sin's deceitfulness. A man who remains stiff-necked after many rebukes will suddenly be destroyed--without remedy.

"For a brief moment I abandoned you, but with deep compassion I will bring you back. In a surge of anger I hid my face from you for a moment, but with everlasting kindness I will have compassion on you. Though the mountains be shaken and the hills be removed, yet my unfailing love for you will not be shaken nor my covenant of peace be removed," says the Lord, who has compassion on you. "O afflicted city, lashed by storms and not comforted, I will build you with stones of turquoise, your foundations with sapphires."

The righteous will hold to their ways, and those with clean hands will grow stronger. The righteous will flourish like a palm tree, they will grow like a cedar of Lebanon. The path of the righteous is like the first gleam of dawn, shining ever brighter till the full light of day.

Where the Spirit of the Lord is, there is freedom. And we, who with unveiled faces all reflect the Lord's glory, are being transformed into his likeness with ever-increasing glory. Be diligent in these matters; give yourself wholly to them, so that everyone may see your progress.

Hebrews 12:5. Proverbs 28:14. Hebrews 3:13. Proverbs 29:1. Isaiah 54:7, 8, 10-12. Job 17:9. Psalm 92:12. Proverbs 4:18. 2 Corinthians 3:17, 18. 1 Timothy 4:15.

Walk in all the ways I command you, that it may go well with you

The Lord gives wisdom, and from his mouth come knowledge and understanding. He holds victory in store for the upright, he is a shield to those whose walk is blameless, for he guards the course of the just and protects the way of his faithful ones. Then you will understand what is right and just and fair--every good path.

I will guide you in the way of wisdom and lead you along straight paths. When you walk, your steps will not be hampered; when you run, you will not stumble. Hold on to instruction, do not let it go; guard it well, for it is your life. Do not set foot on the path of the wicked or walk in the way of evil men.

Direct me in the path of your commands, for there I find delight. Turn my heart toward your statutes and not toward selfish gain. Turn my eyes away from worthless things; preserve my life according to your word. How I long for your precepts! Preserve my life in your righteousness. All the ways of the Lord are loving and faithful for those who keep the demands of his covenant.

The path of the righteous is level; O upright One, you make the way of the righteous smooth. Yes, Lord, walking in the way of your laws, we wait for you; your name and renown are the desire of our hearts. My soul yearns for you in the night; in the morning my spirit longs for you. When your judgments come upon the earth, the people of the world learn righteousness.

Jeremiah 7:23. Proverbs 2:6-11. Proverbs 4:11-14. Psalm 119:36-37, 40. Psalm 25:10. Isaiah 26:7-9.

Obey me, and I will be your God and you will be my people

I will betroth you to me forever; I will betroth you in righteousness and justice, in love and compassion. I will betroth you in faithfulness, and you will acknowledge the Lord. The Lord will call you back as if you were a wife deserted and distressed in spirit. As a bridegroom rejoices over his bride, so will your God rejoice over you. I have summoned you by name; you are mine.

He chose us in him before the creation of the world to be holy and blameless in his sight. To be rich in faith and to inherit the kingdom he promised those who love him.

I delight to sit in his shade, and his fruit is sweet to my taste. Show me your face, let me hear your voice; for your voice is sweet, and your face is lovely. You have heard my vows, O God; you have given me the heritage of those who fear your name. Your statutes are my heritage forever; they are the joy of my heart.

Let us rejoice and be glad and give him glory! For the wedding of the Lamb has come, and his bride has made herself ready.

Jeremiah 7:23. Hosea 2:19, 20. Isaiah 54:6. Isaiah 62:5. Isaiah 43:1. Ephesians 1:4. James 2:5. Song of Solomon 2:3, 14. Psalm 61:5. Psalm 119:111. Revelation 19:7.

Come, follow me

If you want to be perfect, go, sell your possessions and give to the poor, and you will have treasure in heaven. Everyone who has left houses or brothers or sisters or father or mother or children or fields for my sake will receive a hundred times as much.

Peter said to him, "We have left everything to follow you!" Levi got up, left everything and followed him. In the same way, any of you who does not give up everything he has cannot be my disciple.

Whatever was to my profit I now consider loss for the sake of Christ. What is more, I consider everything a loss compared to the surpassing greatness of knowing Christ Jesus my Lord, for whose sake I have lost all things. I consider them rubbish, that I may gain Christ. I want to know Christ and the power of his resurrection and the fellowship of sharing in his sufferings, becoming like him in his death.

A man's pride brings him low. The Lord Almighty has a day in store for all the proud and lofty, for all that is exalted (and they will be humbled). Surely the day is coming; it will burn like a furnace. All the arrogant and every evildoer will be stubble, and that day that is coming will set them on fire, says the Lord Almighty. He has scattered those who are proud in their inmost thoughts.

There will be trouble and distress for every human being who does evil ... but glory, honor and peace for everyone who does good. The Lord will reward everyone for whatever good he does. Many who are first will be last, and many who are last will be first.

Matthew 19:21, 29. Mark 10:28. Luke 5:28. Luke 14:33. Philippians 3:7, 8, 10. Proverbs 29:23. Isaiah 2:12. Malachi 4:1. Luke 1:52. Romans 2:9, 10. Ephesians 6:8. Matthew 19:30.

I will show him how
he must suffer for my name

The apostles left the Sanhedrin, rejoicing because they had been counted worthy of suffering disgrace for the Name. Moses ... chose to be mistreated along with the people of God rather than to enjoy the pleasures of sin for a short time.

I [David] am worn out calling for help; my throat is parched. My eyes fail, looking for my God. Those who hate me without reason outnumber the hairs of my head; many are my enemies without cause, those who seek to destroy me. I am forced to restore what I did not steal.

I [Jeremiah] sat alone because your hand was on me and you had filled me with indignation. Why is my pain unending and my wound grievous and incurable? Will you be to me like a deceptive brook, like a spring that fails?

If you are insulted because of the name of Christ, you are blessed, for the Spirit of glory and of God rests on you. If you suffer, it should not be as a murderer or thief or any other kind of criminal, or even as a meddler. However, if you suffer as a Christian, do not be ashamed, but praise God that you bear that name. So then, those who suffer according to God's will should commit themselves to their faithful Creator and continue to do good.

And the God of all grace, who called you to his eternal glory in Christ, after you have suffered a little while, will himself restore you and make you strong, firm and steadfast.

Acts 9:16. Acts 5:41. Hebrews 11:24, 25. Psalm 69:3, 4. Jeremiah 15:17, 18. 1 Peter 4:14-16, 19. 1 Peter 5:10, 11.

All men will hate you because of me, but he who stands firm to the end will be saved

I am sending you out like sheep among wolves. Therefore be as shrewd as snakes and as innocent as doves.

Be on your guard against men; they will hand you over to the local councils and flog you in their synagogues. On my account you will be brought before governors and kings as witnesses to them and to the Gentiles. But when they arrest you, do not worry about what to say or how to say it. At that time you will be given what to say, for it will not be you speaking, but the Spirit of your Father speaking through you.

They were furious and began to discuss with one another what they might do to Jesus. The Pharisees ... were sneering at Jesus. Many of them said, "He is demon-possessed and raving mad. Why listen to him?" Those who passed by hurled insults at him.

If the world hates you, keep in mind that it hated me first. A student is not above his teacher, nor a servant above his master. It is enough for the student to be like his teacher, and the servant like his master.

Whoever acknowledges me before men, I will also acknowledge him before my Father in heaven. But whoever disowns me before men, I will disown him before my Father in heaven.

Matthew 10:22, 16-20. Luke 6:11. Luke 16:14. John 10:20. Mark 15:29. John 15:18. Matthew 10:24, 25. Matthew 10:32, 33.

Blessed are those who are persecuted because of righteousness for theirs is the kingdom of heaven.

I have become a laughingstock to my friends, though I called upon God and he answered--a mere laughingstock, though righteous and blameless!
O Lord my God, I take refuge in you; save and deliver me from all who pursue me, or they will tear me like a lion and rip me to pieces with no one to rescue me.

Alas, my mother, that you gave me birth, a man with whom the whole land strives and contends! I have neither lent nor borrowed, yet everyone curses me.

Those who pursue us are at our heels; we are weary and find no rest.

Do not be surprised at the painful trial you are suffering, as though something strange were happening to you. But rejoice that you participate in the sufferings of Christ, so that you may be overjoyed when his glory is revealed. Blessed are you when men hate you, when they exclude you and insult you and reject your name as evil, because of the Son of Man. Rejoice in that day and leap for joy, because great is your reward in heaven. If you belonged to the world, it would love you as its own. As it is, you do not belong to the world, but I have chosen you out of the world. That is why the world hates you.

Our light and momentary troubles are achieving for us an eternal glory that far outweighs them all. So we fix our eyes not on what is seen, but on what is unseen. For what is seen is temporary, but what is unseen is eternal.

Matthew 5:10. Job 12:4, 5. Psalm 7:1, 2. Jeremiah 15:10. Lamentations 5:5. 1 Peter 4:12, 13. Luke 6:22, 23. John 15:19-20. 2 Corinthians 4:17, 18.

Fools for Christ

Do not deceive yourselves. If any one of you thinks he is wise by the standards of this age, he should become a "fool" so that he may become wise. Has not God chosen those who are poor in the eyes of the world to be rich in faith and to inherit the kingdom he promised those who love him?

To this very hour we go hungry and thirsty, we are in rags, we are brutally treated, we are homeless. We work hard with our own hands. When we are cursed, we bless; when we are persecuted, we endure it; when we are slandered, we answer kindly. Up to this moment we have become the scum of the earth, the refuse of the world. I am not writing this to shame you, but to warn you.

As servants of God we commend ourselves in every way: in great endurance; in troubles, hardships and distresses; in beatings, imprisonments and riots; in hard work, sleepless nights and hunger; in purity, understanding, patience and kindness; in the Holy Spirit and in sincere love; in truthful speech and in the power of God; with weapons of righteousness in the right hand and in the left; through glory and dishonor, bad report and good report; genuine, yet regarded as impostors; known, yet regarded as unknown; dying, and yet we live on; beaten, and yet not killed; sorrowful, yet always rejoicing; poor, yet making many rich; having nothing, and yet possessing everything.

Treasures in heaven, where moth and rust do not destroy, and where thieves do not break in and steal.

---

1 Corinthians 4:10. 1 Corinthians 3:18. James 2:5. 1 Corinthians 4:11-14. 2 Corinthians 6:4-10. Matthew 6:20.

Whoever loses his life for my sake will find it

He chose the lowly things of this world and the despised things--and the things that are not--to nullify the things that are, so that no one may boast before him. I tell you the truth, unless a kernel of wheat falls to the ground and dies, it remains only a single seed. But if it dies, it produces many seeds. The man who loves his life will lose it, while the man who hates his life in the world will keep it for eternal life.

I am the true vine, and my Father is the gardener. He cuts off every branch in me that bears no fruit, while every branch that does bear fruit he prunes so that it will be even more fruitful.

So, my brothers, you also died to the law through the body of Christ, that you might belong to another, to him who was raised from the dead, in order that we might bear fruit for God.

You say, "I am rich; I have acquired wealth and do not need a thing." But you do not realize that you are wretched, pitiful, poor, blind and naked. I counsel you to buy from me gold refined in the fire, so you can become rich; and white clothes to wear, so you can cover your shameful nakedness; and salve to put on your eyes, so you can see.

To him who overcomes, I will give the right to sit with me on my throne.

I consider everything a loss compared to the surpassing greatness of knowing Christ Jesus my Lord, for whose sake I have lost all things. I consider them rubbish, that I may gain Christ.

Matthew 10:39. 1 Corinthians 1:28, 29. John 12:24, 25. John 15:2. Romans 7:4. Revelation 13:17-21. Philippians 3:8.

To live is Christ and to die is gain

To live is Christ. I tell you the truth, whoever hears my word and believes him who sent me has eternal life and will not be condemned; he has crossed over from death to life. I will give you a new heart and put a new spirit in you; I will remove from you your heart of stone and give you a heart of flesh. If anyone is in Christ, he is a new creation; the old has gone, the new has come!

He is like a tree planted by streams of water, which yields its fruit in season and whose leaf does not wither. Whatever he does prospers. They will still bear fruit in old age, they will stay fresh and green. Christ in you, the hope of glory.

To die is gain. Even though I walk through the valley of the shadow of death, I will fear no evil, for you are with me; your rod and your staff, they comfort me. Precious in the sight of the Lord is the death of his saints. Even in death the righteous have a refuge. If we die, we die to the Lord. Then the righteous will shine like the sun in the kingdom of their Father.

So whether we live or die, we belong to the Lord.

Philippians 1:21. John 5:24. Ezekiel 36:26. 2 Corinthians 5:17. Psalm 1:3.
Psalm 92:14. Colossians 1:27. Philippians 1:21. Psalm 23:4. Psalm 116:15.
Proverbs 14:32. Romans 14:8. Matthew 13:43. Romans 14:8.

A new covenant

I will put my laws in their minds and write them on their hearts. I will be their God, and they will be my people. By calling this covenant "new," he has made the first one obsolete; and what is obsolete and aging will soon disappear.

The former regulation is set aside because it was weak and useless (for the law made nothing perfect), and a better hope is introduced, by which we draw near to God. The law is only a shadow of the good things that are coming--not the realities themselves. For this reason it can never, by the same sacrifices repeated endlessly year after year, make perfect those who draw near to worship.

Jesus the mediator of a new covenant. The ministry Jesus has received is as superior to theirs as the covenant of which he is mediator is superior to the old one, and it is founded on better promises. Now he has appeared once for all at the end of the ages to do away with sin by the sacrifice of himself. Just as man is destined to die once, and after that to face judgment, so Christ was sacrificed once to take away the sins of many people; and he will appear a second time, not to bear sin, but to bring salvation to those who are waiting for him.

After he had provided purification for sins, he sat down at the right hand of the Majesty in heaven.

Jeremiah 31:31. Hebrews 8:10, 13. Hebrews 7:18, 19. Hebrews 10:1. Hebrews 12:24. Hebrews 8:6. Hebrews 9:26-28. Hebrews 1:3.

I will watch over them to build and to plant

From heaven the Lord looks down and sees all mankind; from his dwelling place he watches all who live on earth--he who forms the hearts of all, who considers everything they do. The eyes of the Lord are on the righteous and his ears are attentive to their cry.

"Can anyone hide in secret places so that I cannot see him?" declares the Lord. "Do not I fill heaven and earth?" declares the Lord. "I the Lord search the heart and examine the mind, to reward a man according to his conduct, according to what his deeds deserve. Like clay in the hand of the potter, so are you in my hand."

Reform your ways and your actions. Rid yourselves of all the offenses you have committed, and get a new heart and a new spirit.Repent, then, and turn to God, so that your sins may be wiped out, that times of refreshing may come from the Lord.

For we are the temple of the living God. As God has said: "I will live with them and walk among them, and I will be their God, and they will be my people. Touch no unclean thing, and I will receive you. I will be a Father to you, and you will be my sons and daughters." Since we have these promises, dear friends, let us purify ourselves from everything that contaminates body and spirit, perfecting holiness out of reverence for God.

Jeremiah 31:28. Psalm 33:13-15. Psalm 34:15. Jeremiah 23:24. Jeremiah 17:10. Jeremiah 18:6, 11. Ezekiel 18:31. Acts 3:19. 2 Corinthians 6:16-18. 2 Corinthians 7:1.

I will put my law in their minds and write it on their hearts

It is God who makes both us and you stand firm in Christ. He anointed us, set his seal of ownership on us, and put his Spirit in our hearts as a deposit, guaranteeing what is to come.

"Though the mountains be shaken and the hills be removed, yet my unfailing love for you will not be shaken nor my covenant of peace be removed," says the Lord, who has compassion on you.

Give ear and come to me; hear me, that your soul may live. He is the Lord our God; his judgments are in all the earth. He remembers his covenant forever, the word he commanded, for a thousand generations.

Who can proclaim the mighty acts of the Lord or fully declare his praise? Blessed are they who maintain justice, who constantly do what is right. Remember me, O Lord, when you show favor to your people, come to my aid when you save them, that I may enjoy the prosperity of your chosen ones, that I may share in the joy of your nation and join your inheritance in giving praise.

For no matter how many promises God has made, they are "Yes" in Christ. Not one word has failed of all the good promises he gave through his servant Moses.

Thanks be to God, who always leads us in triumphal procession in Christ and through us spreads everywhere the fragrance of the knowledge of him.

Jeremiah 31:33. 2 Corinthians 1:21, 22. Isaiah 54:10. Isaiah 55:3. Psalm 105:7, 8. Psalm 106:2-5. 2 Corinthians 1:20. 1 Kings 8:56. 2 Corinthians 2:14.

I will be their God,
and they will be my people

I will give them singleness of heart and action, so that they will always fear me for their own good and the good of their children after them. I will make an everlasting covenant with them: I will never stop doing good to them, and I will inspire them to fear me, so that they will never turn away from me. I will rejoice in doing them good and will assuredly plant them in this land with all my heart and soul.

For you are a people holy to the Lord your God. Out of all the peoples on the face of the earth, the Lord has chosen you to be his treasured possession.

This is what the Lord says ... "Fear not, for I have redeemed you; I have summoned you by name; you are mine. I will be a Father to you, and you will be my sons and daughters."

You are all sons of God through faith in Christ Jesus, for all of you who were baptized into Christ have clothed yourselves with Christ. There is neither Jew nor Greek, slave nor free, male nor female, for you are all one in Christ Jesus.

Because you are sons, God sent the Spirit of his Son into our hearts, the Spirit who calls out, "Abba, Father." So you are no longer a slave, but a son; and since you are a son, God has made you also an heir.

Jeremiah 31:33. Jeremiah 32:39-41. Deuteronomy 14:2. Isaiah 43:1. 2 Corinthians 6:18. Galatians 3:26-28. Galatians 4:6, 7.

They will all know me, from the least of them to the greatest, declares the Lord

God does not show favoritism but accepts men from every nation who fear him and do what is right. For there is no difference between Jew and Gentile--the same Lord is Lord of all and richly blesses all who call on him, for, "Everyone who calls on the name of the Lord will be saved." The Lord ... is patient with you, not wanting anyone to perish, but everyone to come to repentance.

Whoever drinks the water I give him will never thirst. Indeed, the water I give him will become in him a spring of water welling up to eternal life. Whoever is thirsty, let him come; and whoever wishes, let him take the free gift of the water of life.

Everyone who believes in him receives forgiveness of sins through his name. All the ends of the earth will remember and turn to the Lord, and all the families of the nations will bow down before him, for dominion belongs to the Lord and he rules over the nations. The earth will be full of the knowledge of the Lord as the waters cover the sea.

May the nations be glad and sing for joy, for you rule the peoples justly and guide the nations of the earth. May the peoples praise you, O God; may all the peoples praise you.

Jeremiah 31:34. Acts 10:34, 35. Romans 10:12, 13. 2 Peter 3:9. John 4:14. Revelation 22:17. Acts 10:43. Psalm 22:27, 28. Isaiah 11:9. Psalm 67:4, 5.

I will remember their sins no more

I, even I, am he who blots out your transgressions, for my own sake, and remembers your sins no more. I have swept away your offenses like a cloud, your sins like the morning mist.

The law requires that nearly everything be cleansed with blood, and without the shedding of blood there is no forgiveness. Jesus ... took the cup, gave thanks and offered it to them, saying, "Drink from it, all of you. This is my blood of the covenant, which is poured out for many for the forgiveness of sins." It was not with perishable things such as silver or gold that you were redeemed from the empty way of life handed down to you from your forefathers, but with the precious blood of Christ, a lamb without blemish or defect. Through Jesus the forgiveness of sins is proclaimed to you.

Who is a God like you, who pardons sin and forgives the transgression of the remnant of his inheritance? You do not stay angry forever but delight to show mercy. He does not treat us as our sins deserve or repay us according to our iniquities. For as high as the heavens are above the earth, so great is his love for those who fear him; as far as the east is from the west, so far has he removed our transgressions from us.

Blessed is he whose transgressions are forgiven, whose sins are covered. Blessed is the man whose sin the Lord does not count against him and in whose spirit is no deceit.

Jeremiah 31:34. Isaiah 43:25. Isaiah 44:22. Hebrews 9:22. Matthew 26:26-28. 1 Peter 1:18, 19. Acts 13:38. Micah 7:18. Psalm 103:10-12. Psalm 32:1, 2.

Let us acknowledge the Lord

Let him who boasts boast about this: that he understands and knows me, that I am the Lord, who exercises kindness, justice and righteousness on the earth, for in these I delight, declares the Lord.

You will know the truth, and the truth will set you free.

This is eternal life: that they may know you, the only true God, and Jesus Christ, whom you have sent.

We know that this man really is the Savior of the world.

We know that we have passed from death to life, because we love our brothers.

We know that in all things God works for the good of those who love him, who have been called according to his purpose.

We know that if the earthly tent we live in is destroyed, we have a building from God, an eternal house in heaven, not built by human hands.

I know whom I have believed, and am convinced that he is able to guard what I have entrusted to him for that day.

I know that my Redeemer lives, and that in the end he will stand upon the earth.

We know that when he appears, we shall be like him, for we shall see him as he is.

Hosea 6:3. Jeremiah 9:24. John 8:32. John 17:3. John 4:42. 1 John 3:14. Romans 8:28. 2 Corinthians 5:1. 2 Timothy 1:12. Job 19:25. 1 John 3:2.

Your prayer has been heard

The people grumbled against Moses, saying, "What are we to drink?" Then Moses cried out to the Lord, and the Lord showed him a piece of wood. He threw it into the water, and the water became sweet.

Gideon said to God, "Do not be angry with me. Let me make just one more request. Allow me one more test with the fleece. This time make the fleece dry and the ground covered with dew." That night God did so. Only the fleece was dry; all the ground was covered with dew.

I [Hannah] prayed for this child, and the Lord has granted me what I asked of him.

While Samuel was sacrificing the burnt offering, the Philistines drew near to engage Israel in battle. But that day the Lord thundered with loud thunder against the Philistines and threw them into such a panic that they were routed before the Israelites.

The Lord said to him [Solomon]; "I have heard the prayer and plea you have made before me; I have consecrated this temple, which you have built, by putting my Name there forever. My eyes and my heart will always be there."

Answer me [prayed Elijah], O Lord, answer me, so these people will know that you, O Lord, are God, and that you are turning their hearts back again. Then the fire of the Lord fell and burned up the sacrifice, the wood, the stones and the soil, and also licked up the water in the trench.

So I say to you: Ask and it will be given to you; seek and you will find; knock and the door will be opened....

Luke 1:13. Exodus 15:24, 25. Judges 6:39, 40. 1 Samuel 1:27. 1 Samuel 7:10. 1 Kings 9:3. 1 Kings 18:37, 38. Luke 11:9.

Tell the righteous it will be well with them, for they will enjoy the fruit of their deeds

Fear the Lord, you his saints, for those who fear him lack nothing. The lions may grow weak and hungry, but those who seek the Lord lack no good thing.

The righteous cry out, and the Lord hears them; he delivers them from all their troubles. The Lord is close to the brokenhearted and saves those who are crushed in spirit. A righteous man may have many troubles, but the Lord delivers him from them all.

If the Lord delights in a man's way, he makes his steps firm; though he stumble, he will not fall, for the Lord upholds him with his hand. I was young and now I am old, yet I have never seen the righteous forsaken or their children begging bread. They are always generous and lend freely; their children will be blessed.

He who dwells in the shelter of the Most High will rest in the shadow of the Almighty. I will say of the Lord, "He is my refuge and my fortress, my God, in whom I trust." Surely he will save you from the fowler's snare and from the deadly pestilence. He will cover you with his feathers, and under his wings you will find refuge; his faithfulness will be your shield and rampart. For he will command his angels concerning you to guard you in all your ways; they will lift you up in their hands, so that you will not strike your foot against a stone.

Isaiah 3:10. Psalm 34:9, 10, 17-19. Psalm 37:23-26. Psalm 91:1-4, 11.

Teach me your way, O Lord;
lead me in a straight path

This is what the Lord says--your Redeemer, the Holy One of Israel: "I am the Lord your God, who teaches you what is best for you, who directs you in the way you should go."

He guides the humble in what is right and teaches them his way. When he, the Spirit of truth, comes, he will guide you into all truth.

He makes me lie down in green pastures, he leads me beside quiet waters. Whether you turn to the right or to the left, your ears will hear a voice behind you, saying, "This is the way; walk in it."

You will guide me with your counsel, and afterward you will take me into glory. For this God is our God for ever and ever; he will be our guide even to the end.

Light is shed upon the righteous and joy on the upright in heart. Even in darkness light dawns for the upright, for the gracious and compassionate and righteous man.

The path of the righteous is like the first gleam of dawn, shining ever brighter till the full light of day. For the Lord God is a sun and shield; the Lord bestows favor and honor; no good thing does he withhold from those whose walk is blameless.

Psalm 27:11. Isaiah 48:17. Psalm 25:9. John 16:13. Psalm 23:2. Isaiah 30:21. Psalm 73:24. Psalm 48:14. Psalm 97:11. Psalm 112:4. Proverbs 4:18. Psalm 84:11.

God is exalted in his power. Who is a teacher like him?

Who endowed the heart with wisdom or gave understanding to the mind? Who has the wisdom to count the clouds? Who can tip over the water jars of the heavens when the dust becomes hard and the clods of earth stick together?

Wisdom is supreme; therefore get wisdom. Though it cost all you have, get understanding. But the wisdom that comes from heaven is first of all pure; then peace loving, considerate, submissive, full of mercy and good fruit, impartial and sincere. It cannot be bought with the gold of Ophir, with precious onyx or sapphires. She is more profitable than silver and yields better returns than gold. Wisdom is more precious than rubies, and nothing you desire can compare with her. Wisdom makes one wise man more powerful than ten rulers in a city.

If any of you lacks wisdom, he should ask God, who gives generously to all without finding fault, and it will be given to him. For I will give you words and wisdom that none of your adversaries will be able to resist or contradict.

The Lord gives wisdom, and from his mouth come knowledge and understanding. He holds victory in store for the upright, he is a shield to those whose walk is blameless, for he guards the course of the just and protects the way of his faithful ones.

Job 36:22. Job 38:36-38. Proverbs 4:7. James 3:17. Job 28:16. Proverbs 3:14. Proverbs 8:11. Ecclesiastes 7:19. Proverbs 2:6- 8.

Those who hope in the Lord will renew their strength

They will soar on wings like eagles; they will run and not grow weary, they will walk and not be faint.

So do not fear, for I am with you; do not be dismayed, for I am your God. I will strengthen you and help you; I will uphold you with my righteous right hand.

He will be ... a source of strength to those who turn back the battle at the gate. God chose the foolish things of the world to shame the wise; God chose the weak things of the world to shame the strong. He said to me, "My grace is sufficient for you, for my power is made perfect in weakness."

Blessed are those whose strength is in you, who have set their hearts on pilgrimage. As they pass through the Valley of Baca, they make it a place of springs.

What more shall I say? I do not have time to tell about Gideon, Barak, Samson, Jephthah, David, Samuel and the prophets, who through faith conquered kingdoms, administered justice, and gained what was promised; who shut the mouths of lions, quenched the fury of the flames, and escaped the edge of the sword; whose weakness was turned to strength; and who became powerful in battle and routed foreign armies.

The Lord is the strength of his people. My flesh and my heart may fail, but God is the strength of my heart and my portion forever.

Sing for joy to God our strength.

Isaiah 40:31. Isaiah 41:10. Isaiah 28:6. 1 Corinthians 1:27. 2 Corinthians 12:9, 10. Psalm 84:5, 6. Hebrews 11:32-34. Psalm 28:8. Psalm 73:26. Psalm 81:1.

Not one word has failed

For no matter how many promises God has made, they are "Yes" in Christ. And so through him the "Amen" is spoken by us to the glory of God.

He has given us his very great and precious promises, so that through them you may participate in the divine nature and escape the corruption in the world caused by evil desires. Weeping may remain for a night, but rejoicing comes in the morning.

A righteous man may have many troubles, but the Lord delivers him from them all. When you pass through the waters, I will be with you; and when you pass through the rivers, they will not sweep over you. When you walk through the fire, you will not be burned; the flames will not set you ablaze.

In all things God works for the good of those who love him, who have been called according to his purpose. For our light and momentary troubles are achieving for us an eternal glory that far outweighs them all. Dear friends, do not be surprised at the painful trial you are suffering as though something strange were happening to you. But rejoice that you participate in the sufferings of Christ, so that you may be overjoyed when his glory is revealed.

Do not let your hearts be troubled. Trust in God; trust also in me. In my Father's house are many rooms; if it were not so, I would have told you. I am going there to prepare a place for you. There will be no more death or mourning or crying or pain, for the old order of things has passed away.

---

1 Kings 8:56. 2 Corinthians 1:20. 2 Peter 1:4. Psalm 30:5. Psalm 34:19. Isaiah 43:2. Romans 8:28. 2 Corinthians 4:17. 1 Peter 4:12, 13. John 14:1, 2. Revelation 21:4.

In keeping with his promise we are looking forward to a new heaven and a new earth, the home of righteousness

The heavens and the earth were completed in all their vast array./I saw a new heaven and a new earth, for the first heaven and the first earth had passed away.

God made two great lights--the greater light to govern the day and the lesser light to govern the night./The city does not need the sun or the moon to shine on it, for the glory of God gives it light, and the Lamb is its lamp.

The Lord God had planted a garden in the east, in Eden./I saw the Holy City, the new Jerusalem, coming down out of heaven from God. The nations will walk by its light, and the kings of the earth will bring their splendor into it.

"You will not surely die," the serpent said to the woman. "For God knows that when you eat of it your eyes will be opened, and you will be like God, knowing good and evil."/The devil, who deceived them, was thrown into the lake of burning sulfur, where the beast and the false prophet had been thrown. They will be tormented day and night for ever and ever.

To the woman he said, "I will greatly increase your pains in childbearing; with pain you will give birth to children." To Adam he said ... "Cursed is the ground because of you; through painful toil you will eat of it all the days of your life."/No longer will there be any curse.

---

2 Peter 3:13. Genesis 2:1. Revelation 21:1. Genesis 1:16. Revelation 21:23. Genesis 2:8. Revelation 21:2, 24. Genesis 3:4, 5. Revelation 20:10. Genesis 3:16, 17. Revelation 22:3. Genesis 3:22.

The virgin will be with child

The Lord himself will give you a sign: The virgin will be with child and will give birth to a son, and will call him Immanuel.

God sent the angel Gabriel to Nazareth, a town in Galilee, to a virgin pledged to be married to a man named Joseph, a descendant of David. The virgin's name was Mary. The angel went to her and said, "Greetings, you who are highly favored! The Lord is with you. The Holy Spirit will come upon you, and the power of the Most High will overshadow you. So the holy one to be born will be called the Son of God."

This is how the birth of Jesus Christ came about: His mother Mary was pledged to be married to Joseph, but before they came together, she was found to be with child through the Holy Spirit. Without father or mother, without genealogy, without beginning of days or end of life.

You, Bethlehem Ephrathah, though you are small among the clans of Judah, out of you will come for me one who will be ruler over Israel, whose origins are from old, from ancient times. In the beginning was the Word, and the Word was with God, and the Word was God. He was with God in the beginning.

Alpha and Omega, the First and the Last, the Beginning and the End.

Isaiah 7:14. Luke 1:26-28. Luke 1:35. Matthew 1:18. Hebrews 7:3. Micah 5:2. John 1:1, 2. Revelation 22:13.

Mary said: "My soul glorifies the Lord...

"...And my spirit rejoices in God my Savior, for he has been mindful of the humble state of his servant. From now on all generations will call me blessed, for the Mighty One has done great things for me--holy is his name."

Who among the gods is like you, O Lord? Who is like you-- majestic in holiness, awesome in glory, working wonders? Among the gods there is none like you, O Lord; no deeds can compare with yours. All the nations you have made will come and worship before you, O Lord; they will bring glory to your name. For you are great and do marvelous deeds; you alone are God.

Your ways, O God, are holy. What God is so great as our God? You are the God who performs miracles; you display your power among the peoples. For nothing is impossible with God.

Now to him who is able to do immeasurably more than all we ask or imagine, according to his power that is at work within us, to him be glory in the church and in Christ Jesus throughout all generations, for ever and ever! Amen.

Luke 1:46-49. Exodus 15:11. Psalm 86:8-10. Psalm 77:13, 14. Luke 1:37. Ephesians 3:20, 21.

The holy one to be born will be called the Son of God

When the time had fully come, God sent his Son, born of a woman, born under law, to redeem those under law, that we might receive the full rights of sons. God so loved the world that he gave his one and only Son, that whoever believes in him shall not perish but have eternal life. For what the law was powerless to do in that it was weakened by the sinful nature, God did by sending his own Son in the likeness of sinful man to be a sin offering.

This is my Son, whom I love; with him I am well pleased. Here is my servant whom I have chosen, the one I love, in whom I delight; I will put my Spirit on him, and he will proclaim justice to the nations. He will not quarrel or cry out; no one will hear his voice in the streets. A bruised reed he will not break, and a smoldering wick he will not snuff out, till he leads justice to victory. In his name the nations will put their hope.

Jesus said ... "I am the good shepherd; I know my sheep and my sheep know me--just as the Father knows me and I know the Father--and I lay down my life for the sheep. I have other sheep that are not of this sheep pen. I must bring them also. They too will listen to my voice, and there shall be one flock and one shepherd. The reason my Father loves me is that I lay down my down my life--only to take it up again. No one takes it from me, but I lay it down of my own accord. I have authority to lay it down and authority to take it up again. This command I received from my Father."

Luke 1:35. Galatians 4:4, 5. John 3:16. Romans 8:3. Matthew 3:17. Matthew 12:18-21. John 9:41. John 10:14-18.

You are to give him the name Jesus

You are to give him the name Jesus, because he will save his people from their sins.

Christ Jesus: Who, being in very nature God, did not consider equality with God something to be grasped, but made himself nothing, taking the very nature of a servant, being made in human likeness. And being found in appearance as a man, he humbled himself and became obedient to death--even death on a cross! Therefore God exalted him to the highest place and gave him the name that is above every name, that at the name of Jesus every knee should bow, in heaven and on earth and under the earth, and every tongue confess that Jesus Christ is Lord, to the glory of God the Father.

The Son is the radiance of God's glory and the exact representation of his being, sustaining all things by his powerful word. After he had provided purification for sins, he sat down at the right hand of the Majesty in heaven. So he became as much superior to the angels as the name he has inherited is superior to theirs.

There is one God and one mediator between God and men, the man Christ Jesus. He has a name written on him that no one knows but he himself. King of kings and Lord of lords.

Luke 1:31. Matthew 1:21. Philippians 2:5-11. Hebrews 1:3, 4. 1 Timothy 2:5. Revelation 19:12, 16.

He will be great

Who is this coming from Edom, from Bozrah, with his garments stained crimson? Who is this, robed in splendor, striding forward in the greatness of his strength? "It is I, speaking in righteousness, mighty to save."

I will give him a portion among the great, and he will divide the spoils with the strong, because he poured out his life unto death, and was numbered with the transgressors. For he bore the sin of many, and made intercession for the transgressors.

The scepter will not depart from Judah, nor the ruler's staff from between his feet, until he comes to whom it belongs and the obedience of the nations is his. A star will come out of Jacob; a scepter will rise out of Israel. Those who oppose the Lord will be shattered. He will thunder against them from heaven; the Lord will judge the ends of the earth.

Who is this King of glory? The Lord strong and mighty, the Lord mighty in battle. Gird your sword upon your side, O mighty one; clothe yourself with splendor and majesty. In your majesty ride forth victoriously in behalf of truth, humility and righteousness; let your right hand display awesome deeds. Your throne, O God, will last for ever and ever.

He will rule from sea to sea and from the River to the ends of the earth. The desert tribes will bow before him and his enemies will lick the dust. The kings of Tarshish and of distant shores will bring tribute to him; the kings of Sheba and Seba will present him gifts. All kings will bow down to him and all nations will serve him.

Luke 1:32. Isaiah 63:1. Isaiah 53:12. Genesis 49:10. Numbers 24:17. 1 Samuel 2:10. Psalm 24:8. Psalm 45:3-6. Psalm 72:8-11.

His kingdom will never end

He is before all things, and in him all things hold together. He was chosen before the creation of the world, but was revealed in these last times for your sake.

To us a child is born, to us a son is given, and the government will be on his shoulders. And he will be called Wonderful Counselor, Mighty God, Everlasting Father, Prince of Peace. Of the increase of his government and peace there will be no end.

He is the living God and he endures forever; his kingdom will not be destroyed, his dominion will never end. He rescues and he saves; he performs signs and wonders in the heavens and on the earth. He was given authority, glory and sovereign power; all peoples, nations and men of every language worshiped him. His dominion is an everlasting dominion that will not pass away and his kingdom is one that will never be destroyed.

He will proclaim peace to the nations. His rule will extend from sea to sea and from the River to the ends of the earth. May his name endure forever; may it continue as long as the sun. All nations will be blessed through him, and they will call him blessed. Praise be to his glorious name forever; may the whole earth be filled with his glory. Amen and Amen.

Luke 1:33. Colossians 1:17. 1 Peter 1:20. Isaiah 9:6, 7. Daniel 6:26, 27. Daniel 7:14. Zechariah 9:10. Psalm 72:17, 19.

Who is he, this King of glory?

The Sovereign Lord comes with power, and his arm rules for him. See his reward is with him, and his recompense accompanies him. The virgin will be with child and will give birth to a son, and they will call him Immanuel--which means, "God with us."

Prepare the way for the Lord, make straight paths for him. Lift up your voice with a shout, lift it up, do not be afraid; say to the towns of Judah, "Here is your God!"

When Christ came into the world, he said: "Sacrifice and offering you did not desire, but a body you prepared for me; with burnt offerings and sin offerings you were not pleased."

Then he said, "Here I am, I have come to do your will." He sets aside the first to establish the second. And by that will, we have been made holy through the sacrifice of the body of Jesus Christ once for all.

Therefore, since we have been justified through faith, we have peace with God through our Lord Jesus Christ. You see, at just the right time, when we were still powerless, Christ died for the ungodly.

The gift of God is eternal life in Christ Jesus our Lord. The gift is not like the trespass. The gift of God is not like the result of the one man's sin: The judgment followed one sin and brought condemnation, but the gift followed many trespasses and brought justification.

Thanks be to God for his indescribable gift!

Psalm 24:10. Isaiah 40:9, 10. Matthew 1:23. Matthew 3:3. Hebrews 10:5, 6, 9. Romans 5:1, 6. Romans 6:23. Romans 5:15, 16. 2 Corinthians 9:15.

She gave birth to her firstborn, a son

She wrapped him in cloths and placed him in a manger, because there was no room for them in the inn.

Before I was born the Lord called me; from my birth he has made mention of my name. The true light that gives light to every man was coming into the world. He was in the world, and though the world was made through him, the world did not recognize him. He came to that which was his own, but his own did not receive him. The Son of Man has no place to lay his head.

Though he was rich, yet for your sakes he became poor, so that you through his poverty might become rich. The Lamb of God, who takes away the sin of the world! A lamb without blemish or defect.

He was oppressed and afflicted, yet he did not open his mouth; he was led like a lamb to the slaughter, and as a sheep before her shearers is silent, so he did not open his mouth.

Greater love has no one than this, that he lay down his life for his friends. Be imitators of God, therefore, as dearly loved children and live a life of love, just as Christ loved us and gave himself up for us as a fragrant offering and sacrifice to God.

Luke 2:7. Isaiah 49:1. John 1:9-11. Matthew 8:20. 2 Corinthians 8:9. John 1:29. 1 Peter 1:19. Isaiah 53:7. John 15:13. Ephesians 5:2.

An angel of the Lord appeared

There were shepherds living out in the fields nearby, keeping watch over their flocks at night. An angel of the Lord appeared to them, and the glory of the Lord shone around them, and they were terrified. But the angels said to them, "Do not be afraid. I bring you good news of great joy that will be for all the people. Today in the town of David a Savior has been born to you; he is Christ the Lord. This will be a sign to you: You will find a baby wrapped in cloths and lying in a manger."

When the time had fully come, God sent his Son, born of a woman, born under law, to redeem those under law, that we might receive the full rights of sons. The kindness and love of God our Savior appeared.

This is how God showed his love among us: He sent his one and only Son into the world that we might live through him. This is love: not that we loved God, but that he loved us and sent his Son as an atoning sacrifice for our sins.

The Word became flesh and made his dwelling among us. We have seen his glory, the glory of the One and Only, who came from the Father, full of grace and truth.

Luke 2:9, 8-12. Galatians 4:4, 5. Titus 3:4. 1 John 4:9, 10. John 1:14.

Let all God's angels worship him

Suddenly a great company of the heavenly host appeared with the angels, praising God and saying, "Glory to God in the highest, and on earth peace to men on whom his favor rests."

Praise the Lord, you his angels, you mighty ones who do his bidding, who obey his word. Praise the Lord, all his heavenly hosts, you his servants who do his will. Praise the Lord, all his works everywhere in his dominion. Praise the Lord, O my soul.

Praise the Lord from the heavens, praise him in the heights above. Praise him, all his angels, praise him, all his heavenly hosts. Praise him, sun and moon, praise him, all you shining stars. Praise him, you highest heavens and you waters above the skies. Let them praise the name of the Lord, for he commanded and they were created. He set them in place for ever and ever; he gave a decree that will never pass away.

You alone are the Lord. You made the heavens, even the highest heavens, and all their starry hosts, the earth and all that is on it, the seas and all that is in them. You give life to everything, and the multitudes of heaven worship you.

Hebrews 1:6. Luke 2:13, 14. Psalm 103:20-22. Psalm 148:1-6. Nehemiah 9:6.

The shepherds said to one another, "Let's go to Bethlehem"

They hurried off and found Mary and Joseph, and the baby, who was lying in the manger. When they had seen him, they spread the word concerning what had been told them about this child, and all who heard it were amazed at what the shepherds said to them.

"You are my witnesses," declares the Lord, "and my servant whom I have chosen, so that you may know and believe me and understand that I am he." You did not choose me, but I chose you.

Brothers, think of what you were when you were called. Not many of you were wise by human standards; not many were influential; not many were of noble birth. But God chose the foolish things of the world to shame the wise; God chose the weak things of the world to shame the strong. Do not be ashamed to testify about our Lord.

Whoever acknowledges me before men, I will also acknowledge him before my Father in heaven. The shepherds returned, glorifying and praising God for all the things they had heard and seen, which were just as they had been told.

Enter his gates with thanksgiving and his courts with praise; give thanks to him and praise his name.

Luke 2:15-18. Isaiah 43:10. John 15:16. 1 Corinthians 1:26, 27. 2 Timothy 1:8. Matthew 10:32. Luke 2:20. Psalm 100:4.

They hurried off and found Mary and Joseph, and the baby, who was lying in the manger

Come, let us bow down in worship, let us kneel before the Lord our Maker; for he is our God and we are the people of his pasture, the flock under his care.

All the earth bows down to you; they sing praise to you, they sing praise to your name. Kings will see you and raise up, princes will see and bow down. All the ends of the earth will remember and turn to the Lord, and all the families of the nations will bow down before him.

He will be great and will be called the Son of the Most High. To give his people the knowledge of salvation through the forgiveness of their sins, because of the tender mercy of our God, by which the rising sun will come to us from heaven to shine on those living in darkness and in the shadow of death, to guide our feet into the path of peace. The Spirit of the Lord will rest on him--the Spirit of wisdom and of understanding, the Spirit of counsel and of power, the Spirit of knowledge and of the fear of the Lord.

Luke 2:16. Psalm 95:6, 7. Psalm 66:4. Isaiah 49:7. Psalm 22:27. Luke 1:32, 77-79. Isaiah 11:2.

Sing joyfully to the Lord, you righteous; it is fitting for the upright to praise him

Praise the Lord with the harp, make music to him on the ten-stringed lyre. Sing to him a new song; play skillfully, and shout for joy.

We wait in hope for the Lord; he is our help and our shield. In him our hearts rejoice, for we trust in his holy name. May your unfailing love rest upon us, O Lord, even as we put our hope in you.

Shout for joy to the Lord, all the earth, burst into jubilant song with music; make music to the Lord with the harp, with the harp and the sound of singing, with trumpets and the blast of the ram's horn--shout for joy before the Lord, the King.

Let the sea resound, and everything in it, the world, and all who live in it. Let the rivers clap their hands, let the mountains sing together for joy; let them sing before the Lord, for he comes to judge the earth. He will judge the world in righteousness and the peoples with equity.

Praise the Lord. Kings of the earth and all nations, you princes and all rulers on earth, young men and maidens, old men and children. Let them praise the name of the Lord, for his name alone is exalted; his splendor is above the earth and the heavens.

Psalm 33:1-3, 20-22. Psalm 98:4-9. Psalm 148:1, 11-13.

I will sing to the Lord all my life;
I will sing praise to my God as long as I live

My tongue will speak of your righteousness and of your praises all day long.

I will exalt you, my God the King; I will praise your name for ever and ever. Every day I will praise you and extol your name for ever and ever.

I will praise the Lord all my life; I will sing praise to my God as long as I live. He upholds the cause of the oppressed and gives food to the hungry. The Lord sets prisoners free, the Lord gives sight to the blind, the Lord lifts up those who are bowed down, the Lord loves the righteous. The Lord watches over the alien and sustains the fatherless and the widow.

O Lord, you are my God; I will exalt you and praise your name, for in perfect faithfulness you have done marvelous things, things planned long ago.

I will bow down toward your holy temple and will praise your name for your love and your faithfulness, for you have exalted above all things your name and your word. How good it is to sing praises to our God, how pleasant and fitting to praise him!

Psalm 104:33. Psalm 35:28. Psalm 145:1, 2. Psalm 146:2, 7-9. Isaiah 25:1. Psalm 138:2. Psalm 147:1.

Simeon ... righteous and devout

He was waiting for the consolation of Israel, and the Holy Spirit was upon him. It had been revealed to him by the Holy Spirit that he would not die before he had seen the Lord's Christ.

Yes, Lord, walking in the way of your laws, we wait for you; your name and renown are the desire of our hearts. This is our God; we trusted in him, and he saved us. This is the Lord, we trusted in him; let us rejoice and be glad in his salvation.

O Lord, be gracious to us; we long for you. Be our strength every morning, our salvation in time of distress. The Lord is good to those whose hope is in him, to the one who seeks him; it is good to wait quietly for the salvation of the Lord. The salvation of the righteous comes from the Lord; he is their stronghold in time of trouble.

Surely God is my salvation; I will trust and not be afraid. The Lord, the Lord, is my strength and my song; he has become my salvation. The Lord your God is with you, he is mighty to save. He will take great delight in you, he will quiet you with his love, he will rejoice over you with singing.

Sovereign Lord, as you have promised, you now dismiss your servant in peace. For my eyes have seen your salvation, which you have prepared in the sight of all people.

Luke 2:25, 26. Isaiah 26:8. Isaiah 25:9. Isaiah 33:2. Lamentations 3:25, 26. Psalm 37:39. Isaiah 12:2. Zephaniah 3:17. Luke 2:29-31.

Anna ... worshiped night and day, fasting and praying

She was very old; she had lived with her husband seven years after her marriage, and then was a widow until she was eighty- four. She never left the temple. She gave thanks to God and spoke about the child to all who were looking forward to the redemption of Jerusalem.

Everything that was written in the past was written to teach us, so that through endurance and the encouragement of the Scriptures we might have hope. Praise the Lord, all you servants of the Lord who minister by night in the house of the Lord.

In the morning, O Lord, you hear my voice; in the morning I lay my requests before you and wait in expectation. I rise before dawn and cry for help; I have put my hope in your word. By day the Lord directs his love, at night his song is with me--a prayer to the God of my life.

Even to your old age and gray hairs I am he, I am he who will sustain you. I have made you and I will carry you; I will sustain you and I will rescue you. The righteous will flourish like a palm tree. They will still bear fruit in old age, they will stay fresh and green. With long life will I satisfy him and show him my salvation. Through me your days will be many, and years will be added to your life.

The fear of the Lord adds length to life. Whoever would love life and see good days must keep his tongue from evil and his lips from deceitful speech.

Luke 2:36, 37, 38. Romans 15:4. Psalm 134:1. Psalm 5:3. Psalm 119:147. Psalm 42:8. Isaiah 46:4. Psalm 92:12, 14. Psalm 91:16. Proverbs 9:11. Proverbs 10:27. 1 Peter 3:10.

When the fullness of time was come, God sent his Son

Bethlehem Ephrathah, though you are small among the clans of Judah, out of you will come for me one who will be ruler over Israel, whose origins are from of old, from ancient times. Today in the town of David a Savior has been born to you; he is Christ the Lord.

The Son of Man came to seek and to save what was lost. For God did not send his Son into the world to condemn the world, but to save the world through him. God exalted him to his own right hand as Prince and Savior that he might give repentance and forgiveness of sins to Israel. Therefore he is able to save completely those who come to God through him, because he always lives to intercede for them.

We have seen and testify that the Father has sent his Son to be the Savior of the world. If anyone acknowledges that Jesus is the Son of God, God lives in him and he in God. And so we know and rely on the love God has for us. I in them and you in me.

If Christ is in you, your body is dead because of sin, yet your spirit is alive because of righteousness. I have been crucified with Christ and I no longer live, but Christ lives in me. The life I live in the body, I live by faith in the Son of God, who loved me and gave himself for me.

I pray that you, being rooted and established in love, may have power, together with all the saints, to grasp how wide and long and high and deep is the love of Christ, and to know this love that surpasses knowledge.

Galatians 4:4. Micah 5:2. Luke 2:11. Luke 19:10. John 3:17. Acts 5:31. Hebrews 7:25. 1 John 4:14-16. John 17:23. Romans 8:10. Galatians 2:20. Ephesians 3:17-19.

Christ Jesus came into the world to save sinners

At just the right time, when we will still powerless, Christ died for the ungodly. Very rarely will anyone die for a righteous man, though for a good man someone might possibly dare to die. But God demonstrates his own love for us in this: While we were still sinners, Christ died for us.

For what the law was powerless to do in that it was weakened by the sinful nature, God did by sending his own Son in the likeness of sinful man to be a sin offering. And so he condemned sin in sinful man, in order that the righteous requirements of the law might be fully met in us, who do not live according to the sinful nature but according to the Spirit. Christ is the end of the law so that there may be righteousness for everyone who believes.

This righteousness from God comes through faith in Jesus Christ to all who believe. There is no difference, for all have sinned and fall short of the glory of God, and are justified freely by his grace through the redemption that came by Christ Jesus. Once you were alienated from God and were enemies in your minds because of your evil behavior. But now he has reconciled you by Christ's physical body through death to present you holy in his sight, without blemish and free from accusation--if you continue in your faith, established and firm, not moved from the hope held out in the gospel. He is the atoning sacrifice for our sins, and not only for ours but also for the sins of the whole world.

---

1 Timothy 1:15. Romans 5:6-8. Romans 8:3, 4. Romans 10:4. Romans 3:22-24. Colossians 1:21-23. 1 John 2:2.

My eyes have seen your salvation

Yes, Lord, walking in the way of your laws, we wait for you; your name and renown are the desire of our hearts.

All mankind will see God's salvation. Everyone who calls on the name of the Lord will be saved. For the grace of God that brings salvation has appeared to all men.

The Lord ... is patient with you, not wanting anyone to perish, but everyone to come to repentance. For God so loved the world that he gave his one and only Son, that whoever believes in him shall not perish but have eternal life.

For the wages of sin is death, but the gift of God is eternal life in Christ Jesus our Lord. He who did not spare his own Son, but gave him up for us all--how will he not also, along with him, graciously give us all things?

Seek the Lord while he may be found; call on him while he is near. Let the wicked forsake his way and the evil man his thoughts. Let him turn to the Lord, and he will have mercy on him, and to our God, for he will freely pardon. Who is a God like you, who pardons sin and forgives the transgression of the remnant of his inheritance? You do not stay angry forever but delight to show mercy. You will again have compassion on us; you will tread our sins underfoot and hurl all our iniquities into the depths of the sea.

Luke 2:30. Isaiah 26:8. Luke 3:6. Romans 10:13. Titus 2:11. 2 Peter 3:9. John 3:16. Romans 6:23. Romans 8:32. Isaiah 55:6, 7. Micah 7:18, 19.

Thanks be to God for his unspeakable gift!

It is by grace you have been saved, through faith--and this not from yourselves, it is the gift of God. Having been justified by his grace, we ... become heirs having the hope of eternal life.

He who did not spare his own Son, but gave him up for us all--how will he not also, along with him, graciously give us all things? To us a child is born, to us a son is given, and the government will be on his shoulders. And he will be called Wonderful Counselor, Mighty God, Everlasting Father, Prince of Peace. Of the increase of his government and peace there will be no end. He will reign on David's throne and over his kingdom, establishing and upholding it with justice and righteousness from that time on and forever.

Sing praises to the Lord, enthroned in Zion; proclaim among the nations what he has done. Praise the Lord with the harp; make music to him on the ten-stringed lyre. May the peoples praise you, O God; may all the peoples praise you. Let them give glory to the Lord and proclaim his praise in the islands.

You are a chosen people, a royal priesthood, a holy nation, a people belonging to God, that you may declare the praises of him who called you out of darkness into his wonderful light.

---

2 Corinthians 9:15. Ephesians 2:8. Titus 3:7. Isaiah 9:6, 7. Psalm 9:11. Psalm 33:2. Psalm 67:3. Isaiah 42:12. 1 Peter 2:9.

From the fullness of his grace we have all received one blessing after another

God placed all things under his feet and appointed him to be head over everything for the church, which is his body, the fullness of him who fills everything in every way. For in Christ all the fullness of the Deity lives in bodily form. Love that surpasses knowledge-- that you may be filled to the measure of all the fullness of God.

You have been given fullness in Christ, who is the head over every power and authority. When you were dead in your sins and in the uncircumcision of your sinful nature, God made you alive with Christ. Having canceled the written code, with its regulations, that was against us and that stood opposed to us; he took it away, nailing it to his cross.

You anoint my head with oil; my cup overflows. Taste and see that the Lord is good; blessed is the man who takes refuge in him. The Lord loves righteousness and justice; the earth is full of his unfailing love.

Praise the Lord. Young men and maidens, old men and children. Let them praise the name of the Lord, for his name alone is exalted; his splendor is above the earth and the heavens.

John 1:16. Ephesians 1:22-24. Colossians 2:9. Ephesians 3:19. Colossians 2:10, 13, 14. Psalm 23:5. Psalm 34:8. Psalm 33:5. Psalm 148:1, 12, 13.

He has anointed me to preach good news to the poor

Blessed are the poor in spirit, for theirs is the kingdom of heaven. Humility and the fear of the Lord bring wealth and honor and life. A man's pride brings him low, but a man of lowly spirit brings honor.

For this is what the high and lofty One says--he who lives forever, whose name is holy: "I live in a high and holy place, but also with him who is contrite and lowly in spirit, to revive the spirit of the lowly and to revive the heart of the contrite."

When someone invites you to a wedding feast, do not take the place of honor, for a person more distinguished than you may have been invited. But when you are invited, take the lowest place, so that when your host comes, he will say to you, "Friend, move up to a better place." Then you will be honored in the presence of all your fellow guests. Do not think of yourself more highly than you ought.

He has showed you, O man, what is good. And what does the Lord require of you? To act justly and to love mercy and to walk humbly with your God. Whoever humbles himself ... is the greatest in the kingdom of heaven. Humble yourselves before the Lord, and he will lift you up.

Luke 4:18. Matthew 5:3. Proverbs 22:4. Proverbs 29:23. Isaiah 57:15. Luke 14:8, 10, 11. Romans 12:3. Micah 6:8. Matthew 18:4. James 4:10.

He has sent me to proclaim freedom to the prisoners

I tell you the truth, everyone who sins is a slave to sin. The evil deeds of a wicked man ensnare him; the cords of his sin hold him fast. Don't you know that when you offer yourselves to someone to obey him as slaves, you are slaves to the one whom you obey-- whether you are slaves to sin, which leads to death, or to obedience, which leads to righteousness?

I find this law at work: When I want to do good, evil is right there with me. For in my inner being I delight in God's law; but I see another law at work in the members of my body, waging war against the law of my mind and making me a prisoner of the law of sin at work within my members. What a wretched man I am! Who will rescue me from this body of death?

There is now no condemnation for those who are in Christ Jesus, because through Christ Jesus the law of the Spirit of life set me free from the law of sin and death. For what the law was powerless to do in that it was weakened by the sinful nature, God did by sending his own Son in the likeness of sinful man to be a sin offering. And so he condemned sin in sinful man, in order that the righteous requirements of the law might be fully met in us, who do not live according to the sinful nature but according to the Spirit. Liberated from its bondage to decay and brought into the glorious freedom of the children of God.

The Lord is the Spirit, and where the Spirit of the Lord is, there is freedom.

Luke 4:18. John 8:34. Proverbs 5:22. Romans 6:16. Romans 7:21-25. Romans 8:1-4, 21. 2 Corinthians 3:17, 18.

He has sent me to proclaim ...
recovery of sight for the blind

The eye is the lamp of the body. If your eyes are good, your whole body will be full of light. But if your eyes are bad, your whole body will be full of darkness.

Like the blind we grope along the wall, feeling our way like men without eyes. At midday we stumble as if it were twilight; among the strong, we are like the dead. The god of this age has blinded the minds of unbelievers, so that they cannot see the light of the gospel of the glory of Christ, who is the image of God. They are darkened in their understanding and separated from the life of God because of the ignorance that is in them due to the hardening of their hearts. Whoever hates his brother is in the darkness and walks around in the darkness; he does not know where he is going, because the darkness has blinded him.

This is the verdict: Light has come into the world, but men loved darkness instead of light because their deeds were evil. The night is nearly over; the day is almost here. So let us put aside the deeds of darkness and put on the armor of light.

You will surely forget your trouble. Life will be brighter than noonday, and darkness will become like morning. You will be secure, because there is hope; you will look about you and take your rest in safety.

Jesus spoke ... "I am the light of the world. Whoever follows me will never walk in darkness, but will have the light of life." Light is shed upon the righteous and joy on the upright in heart.

Luke 4:18. Matthew 6:22, 23. Isaiah 59:10. 2 Corinthians 4:4. Ephesians 4:18. 1 John 2:11. John 3:19. Romans 13:12. Job 11:16- 18. John 8:12. Psalm 97:11.

He has sent me ... to release the oppressed

I offered my back to those who beat me, my cheeks to those who pulled out my beard; I did not hide my face from mocking and spitting. He was pierced for our transgressions, he was crushed for our iniquities; the punishment that brought us peace was upon him, and by his wounds we are healed.

We are heirs--heirs of God and co-heirs with Christ, if indeed we share in his sufferings in order that we may also share in his glory. Blessed are you when people insult you, persecute you and falsely say all kinds of evil against you because of me. Rejoice and be glad, because great is your reward in heaven, for in the same way they persecuted the prophets who were before you. The apostles left the Sanhedrin, rejoicing because they had been counted worthy of suffering disgrace for the Name.

Store up for yourselves treasures in heaven. I commit you to God and to the word of his grace, which can build you up and give you an inheritance among all those who are sanctified. Giving thanks to the Father, who has qualified you to share in the inheritance of the saints in the kingdom of light. You will receive an inheritance from the Lord as a reward. An inheritance that can never perish, spoil or fade--kept in heaven for you, who through faith are shielded by God's power until the coming of the salvation that is ready to be revealed in the last time.

Luke 4:18. Isaiah 50:6. Isaiah 53:5. Romans 8:17. Matthew 5:10-12. Acts 5:41. Matthew 6:20. Acts 20:32. Colossians 1:2. Colossians 3:24. 1 Peter 1:4, 5.

He has sent me
... to comfort all who mourn

Blessed are those who mourn, for they will be comforted. As a mother comforts her child, so will I comfort you. God, who comforts the downcast. The Father of compassion and the God of all comfort.

The Lord saw her, his heart went out to her and he said, "Don't cry." Do not let your hearts be troubled. Trust in God; trust also in me. I will not leave you as orphans; I will come to you. You will grieve, but your grief will turn to joy.

Weeping may remain for a night, but rejoicing comes in the morning. He who goes out weeping, carrying seed to sow, will return with songs of joy, carrying sheaves with him. With joy you will draw water from the wells of salvation.

I delight greatly in the Lord; my soul rejoices in my God. For he has clothed me with garments of salvation and arrayed me in a robe of righteousness, as a bridegroom adorns his head like a priest, and as a bride adorns herself with her jewels. When your words came, I ate them; they were my joy and my heart's delight, for I bear your name, O Lord God Almighty.

You believe in him and are filled with an inexpressible and glorious joy.

Isaiah 61:2. Matthew 5:4. Isaiah 66:13. 2 Corinthians 7:6. 2 Corinthians 1:3. Luke 7:13. John 14:1, 18. John 16:20. Psalm 30:5. Psalm 126:5. Isaiah 12:3. Isaiah 61:10. Jeremiah 15:16. 1 Peter 1:8.

He has sent me ... to proclaim the year of the Lord's favor

In the time of my favor I heard you, and in the day of salvation I helped you. For the Lord God is a sun and shield; the Lord bestows favor and honor; no good thing does he withhold from those whose walk is blameless.

The Lord is with you when you are with him. If you seek him, he will be found by you, but if you forsake him, he will forsake you. The Lord confides in those who fear him; he makes his covenant known to them. You will pray to him, and he will hear you, and you will fulfill your vows.

From the Lord comes deliverance. I pray to you, O Lord, in the time of your favor; in your great love, O God, answer me with your sure salvation. Rescue me from the mire, do not let me sink; deliver me from those who hate me, from the deep waters. Do not let the floodwaters engulf me or the depths swallow me up or the pit close its mouth over me. Answer me, O Lord, out of the goodness of your love; in your great mercy turn to me. For surely, O Lord, you bless the righteous.

The Lord was my support. He brought me out into a spacious place; he rescued me because he delighted in me. The Lord will rescue me from every evil attack and will bring me safely to his heavenly kingdom. To him be glory for ever and ever. Amen.

To him who sits on the throne and to the Lamb be praise and honor and glory and power, for ever and ever!

Luke 4:18, 19. 2 Corinthians 6:2. Psalm 84:11. 2 Chronicles 15:2. Psalm 25:14. Job 22:27. Psalm 3:8. Psalm 69:13-16. Psalm 5:12. Psalm 18:18, 19. 2 Timothy 4:18. Revelation 5:13.